The Librarian's
Copyright Companion

The Librarian's Copyright Companion

by
James S. Heller

William S. Hein & Co., Inc.
Buffalo, New York
2004

Library of Congress Cataloging-in-Publication Data

Heller, James S.
    The librarian's copyright companion / James S. Heller.
        p. cm.
    Includes bibliographical references and index.
    ISBN: 0-8377-3300-6 (cloth : acid-free paper)
        1. Copyright—United States. 2. Librarians—United
    States—Handbooks, manuals, etc. I. Title.

KF2995.H45 2003
346.7304'82—dc21   2003056624

Printed in the United States of America

This volume is printed on acid-free paper
by William S. Hein & Co., Inc.

DEDICATION

ℰℭ

The Librarian's Copyright Companion is dedicated to my wife, Janet Crowther, and to our sons, Ben and Seth.

TABLE OF CONTENTS

ഌരു

PREFACE

ℬↃↄℬ

American copyright law is not easy to understand. Examining the Copyright Act of 1976, its amendments, and court decisions that interpret the Act recalls the days of black-and-white television: a little black, a little white, and a lot of gray. This grayness may leave librarians uncertain about what we may or may not do in our workplace.

The Librarian's Copyright Companion is designed to provide a framework that will help you analyze copyright issues in your library, whether you work in a for-profit or non-profit environment. It cannot provide "yes" or "no" answers to every copyright question you may have, nor address every possible scenario. This book is based on workshops I present to librarians and educators, during which we are able to discuss questions and the nuances of copyright law. Although we do not have that luxury here, I hope you find this book somewhat illuminating, and at times, even entertaining.

Several thanks: To Joe Wrkich, a law student at the William & Mary Law School who provided superb research and editing support. To Fred Dingledy, reference librarian at William & Mary, and Professors Peter Alces and Trotter Hardy, also of William & Mary, for their comments and advice. And to our Law Library's administrative assistant, Betta Labanish, for her overall help on this project and excellent work preparing the manuscript.

James S. Heller
Director of the Law Library and Professor of Law
The College of William & Mary, Williamsburg, Va.
November 2003

Chapter One
GENERAL PRINCIPLES

৪০৫৪

Copyright Defined

1.1. Copyright

- ৪০ Exclusive right to use
- ৪০ Original work
- ৪০ Specified time

First things first. The Copyright Act begins with definitions of about fifty words and phrases, but not the word "copyright."[1] American copyright law traces its origins to the British Statute of Anne in the early eighteenth century,[2] so how about the *Oxford English Dictionary* (OED)? The OED defines copyright as "[t]he exclusive right given by law for a certain term of years to an author, composer, designer, etc. (or his assignee) to print, publish, and sell copies of his original work."[3]

American copyright law has evolved quite a bit from its English origins, however. *Random Houses* defines copyright as: "The exclusive

---

1. 17 U.S.C. § 101 (2000).
2. An Act for the Encouragement of Learning, by Vesting the Copies of Printed Books in the Authors or Purchasers of such Copies, during the Times therein mentioned. 8 Anne c. 19 (1710).
3. OXFORD ENGLISH DICTIONARY (2d ed. 1991).

right to make copies, license, or otherwise exploit a literary, musical, or artistic work, whether printed, audio, video, etc."[4] Better, but I prefer a definition that combines the two: Subject to specific limitations, a copyright is the exclusive ownership of and right to make use of an original literary, musical, or artistic work for a specified period of time.

The Copyright Act

1.2. U.S. Constitution, Article I, Section 8, Clause 8

Congress may "promote the progress of science and the useful arts by securing for a limited time to authors and inventors the exclusive right to their writings and discoveries."

Copyright protection does not just "happen." The U.S. Constitution authorizes Congress to pass copyright legislation,[5] and Congress has enacted legislation pursuant to that authorization. The Copyright Revision Act of 1976[6]—the legislation now in force in the United States—was the first complete revision of our federal copyright statute since 1909.

Congress recognized as early as the 1950s that the 1909 Act was outdated. But Congress, as we know, usually moves more at the speed of the tortoise than the hare. The 1976 Act, which took more than twenty years to pass, was only the third major revision of our federal copyright statute since the first such Act was passed in 1790,[7] the others occurring in 1831[8] and 1870.[9]

In drafting the 1976 Act, Congress tried to balance the often competing interests of copyright owners on the one hand, and of those who use copyrighted works on the other. Input from creators, publishers, educators, librarians, and other interested parties resulted in

---

4. RANDOM HOUSE UNABRIDGED DICTIONARY (2d ed. 1993).
5. U.S. CONST. art. I, § 8, cl. 8.
6. Pub. L. No. 94-553, 90 Stat. 2541 (1976).
7. 1 Stat. 124 (1790).
8. 4 Stat. 436 (1831).
9. 16 Stat. 198 (1870).

an Act one commentator called "a body of detailed rules reminiscent of the Internal Revenue Code."[10]

But we are not given "detailed rules" for everything. Occasionally Congress gave us guidelines, such as those for classroom copying and off-air taping, rather than legislation. Although not part of the Act, some guidelines were included in its legislative history and have been cited by courts attempting to interpret Congressional intent. Additionally, some provisions of the Act were intentionally left ambiguous to allow for later interpretation by the courts.

Congress recognized the needs of educators, scholars, and librarians in the 1976 Act, although not always to their satisfaction. Teaching, scholarship, and research are specifically mentioned in section 107, the fair use provision. Library copying is addressed in section 108. Certain public performances for instructional purposes are permitted under section 110. Each of those sections is discussed in greater detail later in this book.

The 1976 Act also created a single structure of copyright, one which is governed exclusively by federal law. There is no state copyright law. This means that if you research a copyright question, you need only use federal sources of law such as the United States Code and decisions from federal courts. Do not look for copyright law in a state code or state court decisions, except perhaps for a state statute that disclaims copyright protection in works by the state.

Copyright does *not* place an author's work in a lockbox. The primary purpose of copyright is *not* to compensate creators. The U.S. Supreme Court has stated, many times, that copyright is a means to a greater societal end: the dissemination and promotion of knowledge.[11] With this in mind, when there is a close call whether a certain

---

10. 1 MELVILLE NIMMER, NIMMER ON COPYRIGHT, Preface to the 1978 Comprehensive Treatise Revision.

11. "The primary purpose of copyright is not to reward the author, but is rather to secure 'the general benefits derived by the public from the labors of authors.'" New York Times Corp. v. Tasini, 533 U.S. 483, 519 (2001) (quoting 1 M. NIMMER & D. NIMMER, NIMMER ON COPYRIGHT § 1.03[A] (2001), quoting Fox Film Corp. v. Doyal, 286 U.S. 123, 127 (1932)). "But the ultimate aim is, by this incentive, to stimulate artistic creativity for the general public good." Twentieth Century Music Corp. v. Aiken, 422 U.S. 151, 156 (1975). *See also* United States v. Paramount Pictures, 334 U.S. 131 (1948); Feist Publ'ns v. Rural Tel. Ser., 499 U.S. 340 (1991). Congress has made similar statements. Working on the Berne Convention Implementation Act of 1988, the House Judiciary Committee wrote "The primary objective of our copyright laws is not to reward the author, but rather to secure for the public the benefits from the creations of authors." H.R. REP. NO. 100-609, at 22 (1988).

use is or is not allowed, I resolve the answer in favor of the user, rather than the copyright owner.

Organizations that represent publishers and other copyright owners, such as the Copyright Clearance Center (CCC) and the Association of American Publishers (AAP), take a more restrictive view of user rights. For example, the AAP wrote that "[t]he purpose of the copyright law is to ensure authors and publishers the economic wherewithal to devote their energies, talents and funds to the creation and effective packaging and distribution of intellectual works."[12] When you read statements from organizations representing publishers and copyright owners about permissible uses of copyrighted works, remember whence they came.

International Issues

1.3. Treaties

  ಊ Universal Copyright Convention
  ಊ Berne Convention
  ಊ Home country agrees to protect:

    • Author from a UCC or Berne country
    • Work first published in a UCC or Berne country
    • Work published by U.N. or O.A.S.

the same as it protects works published in its country or by its authors.

Intellectual property knows no geographic boundaries. Governing law may include national law (in our case, U.S. law), foreign law, and international treaties. Notwithstanding international agreements, a nation's copyright laws are unique; each country creates its own laws.

Many of the recent changes in United States law were enacted to align our laws more closely to the international arena, especially Europe. Examples include eliminating the requirement of a formal

---

12. ASSOCIATION OF AMERICAN PUBLISHERS, STATEMENT OF THE AAP ON DOCUMENT DELIVERY (Apr. 13, 1994), *available at* <http://www.publishers.org>.

"notice of copyright" for a work to be copyrighted,[13] and extending the length of time a work is protected.[14]

The United States is a party to two international copyright conventions. The United States ratified the Universal Copyright Convention (UCC),[15] which is administered by United Nations Educational, Scientific and Cultural Organization (UNESCO), in 1954. In 1988 the U.S. joined the Berne Convention,[16] which is administered by the World Intellectual Property Organization (WIPO).

The core of these treaties is "national treatment." A country that belongs to a treaty agrees to protect works prepared in other countries that signed the treaty, as well as works created by authors from those countries, at the same level it protects works created by its own authors.[17] In a nutshell, this means that a work created by a foreign author who is a national of a country that signed the Berne or UCC treaties is protected under U.S. law to the same extent as are works prepared in the United States.[18] The same is true for works published in those countries. Furthermore, works published by the United Nations and by the Organization of American States also are protected.[19]

The Berne and UCC treaties do not provide an international forum to resolve disputes between litigants, and the treaties have no enforcement mechanism. Consequently, disputes must be resolved in

---

13. Voluntary use of notice still is recommended so as to make it more difficult for someone to claim they were an "innocent infringer."

14. The Sonny Bono Copyright Term Extension Act of 1998, Pub. L. No. 105-298, 112 Stat. 2827 (1998).

15. Universal Copyright Convention as revised at Paris on 24 July 1971, *available at* <http://www.unesco.org>.

16. Berne Convention for the Protection of Literary and Artistic Works (Paris Act of July 24, 1971), *available at* WIPO website <http://www.wipo.org>.

17. Occasionally this produces somewhat strange results. For example, U.S. law provides that works of our federal government may not be copyrighted. However, Canadian law provides that works of the Canadian government *are* subject to copyright protection. Because a country must protect foreign works as it protects its own works, this means that works of the U.S. government are protected in Canada, though not in the United States.

18. U.S. COPYRIGHT OFFICE, CIRCULAR 38A: INTERNATIONAL COPYRIGHT RELATIONS OF THE UNITED STATES (May 1999); CIRCULAR 93: HIGHLIGHTS OF U. S. ADHERENCE TO THE BERNE CONVENTION (1999). Many Copyright Office circulars can be found on the Copyright Office homepage *at* <http://www.loc.gov/copyright>.

19. The Berne Treaty also provides for so-called "moral rights." These include the rights of attribution (the author has the right to claim authorship of his or her work) and integrity (the right of the author to object to any distortion, mutilation, other modification, or derogatory action in relation to the work that prejudices his reputation). Under the Berne Treaty, moral rights are inalienable; they cannot be transferred or derogated.

a nation's courts. For example, a British author who claims that an American infringed her copyright will litigate her claim in a British or American court, under British or American law.

Copyrightable Works

1.4. Section 102
Copyrightable Works

80 Literary works
80 Musical works
80 Dramatic works
80 Pantomimes and choreographic works
80 Pictorial, graphic, and sculptural works
80 Motion pictures and other AV works
80 Sound recordings
80 Architectural works

If the work is original, and fixed in any tangible medium of expression

But not ideas, procedures, processes, systems, concepts . . .

Copyright protection is very broad. The Copyright Act provides that a wide array of works may be copyrighted, as long as they are "original" and "fixed in a tangible medium of expression."[20] By "original" is meant that the work must evidence some level of creativity.[21] The U.S. Copyright Office lists several categories of works generally *not* eligible for federal copyright protection:

80 Titles, names, short phrases, and slogans; familiar symbols or designs; mere variations of typographic ornamentation, lettering, or coloring; mere listings of ingredients or contents;

80 Ideas, procedures, methods, systems, processes, concepts, principles, discoveries, or devices, as distinguished from a description, explanation, or illustration; and

80 Works consisting entirely of information that is common property and containing no original authorship (for example: standard calendars, height and weight charts, tape measures and rulers, and

---

20. 17 U.S.C. § 102(a) (2000).
21. Feist Publ'ns v. Rural Tel. Serv., 499 U.S. 340, 340 (1991).

lists or tables taken from public documents or other common sources).[22]

Although the works mentioned above are not copyrightable, they may be subject to other types of legal protection, such as patent, trademark, trade secret, or unfair competition law.

There must also be an *expression* for copyright to attach. This is often called the idea/expression dichotomy: Only the expression of an idea is protected by copyright, not the idea by itself.[23] For example, you cannot copyright the idea of a romance between a northern gunrunner and a southern belle in the post–Civil War South, but Margaret Mitchell could copyright the *expression* of that idea in her novel *Gone With The Wind*.

Because procedures or methods of operation are not subject to copyright protection, something like a simple recipe cannot be copyrighted. A Julia Child cookbook that includes recipes, descriptive text, and illustrations (and presumably many calories), however, is copyrightable. If you had any doubt whether a computer program is an unprotected method of operation or instead protected expression, remove the doubt: Computer programs *may* be protected by copyright.[24]

Copyright is available only for works "fixed in a tangible medium of expression."[25] Fixation occurs when the embodiment of the work "is sufficiently permanent or stable to permit it to be perceived, reproduced, or otherwise communicated for a period of more than transitory duration."[26] Fixation is easily accomplished. The legislative history to the 1976 Act notes the breadth of Congress's intent:

> Under the bill it makes no difference what the form, manner, or medium of fixation may be—whether it is in words, numbers, notes, sounds, pictures, or any other graphic or symbolic indicia, whether embodied in a physical object in written, printed, photographic, sculptural, punched, magnetic, or any other stable form, and whether it is capable of perception directly or by means of any machine or device 'now known or later developed.'[27]

---

22. U.S. COPYRIGHT OFFICE, CIRCULAR 1: COPYRIGHT BASICS (revised June 2002).

23. SunTrust Bank v. Houghton Mifflin Co., 268 F.3d 1257, 1263–64 (11th Cir. 2001).

24. Computer Mgmt. Assistance Co. v. Robert F. DeCastro, Inc., 220 F.3d 396, 400 (5th Cir. 2000); Atari Games Corp. v. Nintendo of Am., Inc., 975 F. 2d 832, 838 (Fed. Cir. 1992).

25. 17 U.S.C. § 102(a) (2000).

26. *Id.* § 101.

27. H.R. REP. NO. 94-1476, at 52 (1976). The House Report is reprinted in the 1976 *United States Code Congressional & Administrative News* (U.S.C.C.A.N.) at 5659.

In other words, text, images, and graphics—essentially anything we can see in print, on a television screen or computer monitor, or in some other medium —are sufficiently "fixed" to be copyrighted.

The Bottom Line: If you can see, hear, or touch a work, then you should assume it is protected by copyright (tasting or smelling are not enough).

Copyright Notice

A copyright notice is not required for a work to be copyrighted. Copyright attaches automatically when an original work is created. A work is created "when it is fixed in a copy or phonorecord for the first time."[28]

There *are* advantages to including a copyright notice. First, the notice identifies the copyright owner and indicates the date the work was published. Second, it informs the public that the work is protected. Third, the notice makes it difficult for a defendant in an infringement suit to claim that he or she was an innocent infringer—someone who was not aware and had no reason to believe that his or her acts were infringing (This is important for copyright owners, for a court may reduce statutory damages if the infringer was an "innocent" infringer).[29]

The Copyright Act specifies the form and position of the copyright notice for "visually perceptible copies," which are those that can be seen or read. The notice must be "affixed to the copies in such a man-

---

28. The U.S. Copyright Office writes:

> "Copies" are material objects from which a work can be read or visually perceived either directly or with the aid of a machine or device, such as books, manuscripts, sheet music, film, videotape, or microfilm. "Phonorecords" are material objects embodying fixations of sounds (excluding, by statutory definition, motion picture soundtracks), such as cassette tapes, CDs, or LPs. Thus, for example, a song (the "work") can be fixed in sheet music ("copies") or in phonograph disks ("phonorecords"), or both.

U.S. COPYRIGHT OFFICE, CIRCULAR 1: COPYRIGHT BASICS (revised June 2002).

29. 17 U.S.C. § 504 (c)(2) (2000).

ner and location as to give reasonable notice of the claim of copyright,"[30] and should include the following elements.

- ഔ the symbol © or the word "Copyright," or the abbreviation "Copr.";
- ഔ the year of first publication of the work; and
- ഔ the name of the copyright owner.[31]

Although copyright notices provide important information, watch out for notices that try to tell you what you cannot do. For example, what do you think about the following notice that appears on the verso of the title page of Haynes Johnson's *The Best of Times: America in the Clinton Years*?

> All rights reserved. No part of this publication may be reproduced or transmitted in any form or by any means, electronic or mechanical including photocopy, recording, or any information storage and retrieval system, without permission in writing from the publisher.

This notice suggests that you cannot copy anything from this book. That is simply not true. A simple copyright notice cannot dilute your rights. You did not agree to be bound by the copyright notice in *The Best of Times* when you bought that book. You *will* honor binding contracts (most common for digital products) to which you have agreed. But just because a copyright notice says "you cannot do this" does not mean that you can't.

Here is another notice that appears in many publications of the Bureau of National Affairs (BNA): "Copyright policy: Authorization to photocopy selected pages for internal or personal use is granted provided that appropriate fees are paid to Copyright Clearance Center." BNA's website, which explains its copyright policies more fully, includes the following statement:

> The charge for lawful reproduction made through CCC or directly to BNA is currently $1.00 per page per copy for nonacademic use or for those who do not have one of CCC's annual licenses. Copies of portions of a publication, but not the entire issue or section, may be made for personal or internal use, or for the personal or internal use of specific clients, upon payment of the fee. Automatic payment to CCC negates the need for seeking permission from the publisher.[32]

BNA writes that you can copy portions from its publications, but only if you pay the royalty fee. Guess what? If your copying from a

---

30. *Id.* § 401(c).
31. *Id.* § 401(b).
32. For more information on BNA's copyright policies, see <http://www.bna.com>.

BNA publication is permitted under the Copyright Act (as a fair use or under the section 108 library exemption, for example), you do not have to receive BNA's permission, nor must you pay the $1.00 per page charge. BNA's notice of copyright does not create a contract between you and BNA.

On the other hand, some journals spell out what users may do with the articles. Most scholarly journals published by U.S. law schools have a notice similar to the one you find in the *William and Mary Law Review*:

> Copyright © 2003 by the *William and Mary Law Review*. Except as otherwise provided, the author of each article in this issue has granted permission for copies of that article to be made available for classroom use, provided that (1) the copies are distributed at or below cost, (2) the author and the *William and Mary Law Review* are identified, (3) proper notice of copyright is affixed to each copy and (4) the *William and Mary Law Review* is notified of the use.

Broader and better yet is the notice in *The Journal of Economic Literature* and the publications of the American Economic Association:

> Permission to make digital or hard copies of part or all of American Economic Association publications for personal or classroom use is granted without fee provided that copies are not distributed for profit or direct commercial advantage and that copies show this notice on the first page or initial screen of a display along with the full citation, including the name of the author. Copyrights for components of this work owned by others than AEA must be honored. Abstracting with credit is permitted. To copy otherwise, to republish, to post on servers, to redistribute to lists, or to use any component of this work in other works, requires prior specific permission and/or a fee.

The Bottom Line: First, if you agree by contract not to use a work in a particular way, you will abide by the contract. Second, some copyright notices are better than others. Do not be swayed by a copyright notice that purports to tell you what you may not do. Third, assume that a work is protected by copyright—even if it does not include a copyright notice—unless it happens to be in the public domain.

Works in the Public Domain

1.5. Works in the Public Domain

- ❧ Materials never were copyrighted
- ❧ Copyright has expired
- ❧ Works of the U.S. government

Works in the public domain are not protected by copyright. When a work is not protected by copyright because it is in the public domain—or if the work *is* protected by copyright but the use is allowed under the Copyright Act—you do not have to receive permission, or pay royalties, to use it. Works in the public domain include those that never were copyrighted, works in which copyright has expired, and works of the United States government.

Under the Act, works of the U.S. government—any work prepared by an officer or employee of the federal government as part of his or her official duties—may not be copyrighted.[33] Although this appears straightforward, there are some possible twists, such as works prepared for the government under contract, and copyrighted works included in government publications.

Whether a work prepared by an independent contractor under a federal contract or grant is copyrightable generally depends on the terms of the contract between the government and the contractor. The status also may be governed by legislation or agency regulations.[34] Therefore, even though a work prepared by the Rand Corporation under a government contract may have been funded with taxpayer dollars (which one might think should place it in the public domain), it may be protected by copyright if the contract or a federal statute or regulation so provides.

A copyrighted work does not lose its copyright status just because it is included in a work of the U.S. government. For example, Senator Blowhard wants to include in the *Congressional Record* a copyrighted poem written by one of his constituents. As a work of the federal government, the *Record* is not protected by copyright. However, the poem does not lose its copyright protection because it is reprinted in the *Record*.

---

33. 17 U.S.C. § 105 (2000).
34. H.R. Rep. No. 94-1476, at 59.

Conversely, a non-copyrightable governmental work that is reprinted by a private publisher, or a portion of a governmental work included in a privately created work, does not lose its public domain status.[35] For example:

- A private publisher who reprints all of the federal statutes dealing with public education cannot claim copyright in the text of those non-copyrightable laws.
- A private publisher who reprints a public domain report prepared by the Surgeon General of the United States cannot claim copyright in the text of the report.
- A private publisher who includes in its newsletter proposed and enacted federal regulations from the *Federal Register* and the *Code of Federal Regulations* cannot claim copyright in the text of the regulations.

Materials published by state or local governments—unlike works of the federal government—may be copyrighted.[36] This means that a report published by a state Department of Transportation *may* be protected. As more and more states place more and more information on their websites, states are publicizing their perceived intellectual property rights. For example, here is what the state of Florida writes about its "MyFlorida" website:

> MyFlorida.com is owned and operated by THE STATE OF FLORIDA, STATE TECHNOLOGY OFFICE (referred to as "STO" herein). No material from MyFlorida.com or any Web site owned, operated, licensed or controlled by THE STATE OF FLORIDA or STO may be copied, reproduced, republished, uploaded, posted, transmitted, or distributed in any way. Materials may be downloaded on any single computer [for] personal, non-commercial use only providing all copyright and other proprietary notices are kept intact. Modification of the materials or use of the materials for any other purpose is a violation of THE STATE OF FLORIDA and STO's copyright and other proprietary rights. For purposes of this Agreement, the use of any

---

35. *See* Building Officials & Code Adm'rs, Inc. v. Code Tech., Inc., 628 F.2d. 730 (1st Cir. 1980).

36. Although most states do not expressly claim copyright in all state publications, there are exceptions. Pennsylvania, for example, gives its Department of General Services the power and the duty "to copyright, in the name of the Commonwealth, all publications of the Commonwealth, or of any department, board, or commission or officer thereof, including the State Reports. . . ." PA. STAT. ANN. tit. 71, § 636(i) (West Supp. 2003). Other states expressly provide that certain state publications are not protected. For example, Illinois provides its state code is in the public domain (25 ILL. COMP. STAT. ANN. 135/5.04 (West 2001), while Kentucky says that the decisions of its Supreme Court may not be copyrighted (KY. REV. STAT. ANN. § 21A.070 (Michie 1999)).

such material on any other Web site or networked computer environment is prohibited. All trademarks, service marks, and trade names are proprietary to THE STATE OF FLORIDA and STO.[37]

Who are these cocoanuts? The State of Florida claims copyright not only in its website as a compilation (discussed below), but in *all* of the materials in the website. That is wrong. State or local governmental works such as court decisions, statutes, regulations, ordinances, and attorney general opinions—in other words, the law—may *not* be copyrighted.[38]

Some words of caution: Although judicial decisions are not protected by copyright, two federal appeals courts had differing conclusions as to whether a publisher may claim copyright in a *compilation* of court decisions that are published as court reporters. In 1986, the U.S. Court of Appeals for the Eighth Circuit held that the West Publishing Company's arrangements of judicial decisions in its reporters were original works of authorship entitled to copyright protection.[39] But a decade later the Second Circuit came to the opposite conclusion when it held that West Publishing could *not* claim copyright in its reporters because they lacked the creativity necessary for copyright protection.[40]

The situation for legislation is somewhat similar. Statutes and ordinances that emanate from state or local governments are not copyrightable. It is unclear, however, whether a privately published, subject-arranged compilation of state statutes or local ordinances—in other words, a "code"—is in the public domain.[41] Furthermore, it remains an open question whether statutes or administrative codes prepared by private entities (such as a building code) that are subsequently adopted by a state or local government enter the public domain when they are adopted into law.[42]

---

37. MYFLORIDA.COM COPYRIGHT STATEMENT: CONDITIONS OF USE, *available at* <http://www.myflorida.com/myflorida/copyright.html>.
38. Georgia v. Harrison Co., 548 F. Supp. 110 (N.D. Ga. 1982), *order vacated*, 559 F. Supp. 37 (N.D. Ga. 1983); Banks v. Manchester, 128 U.S. 244 (1888); Wheaton v. Peters, 33 U.S. 591 (1834).
39. West Publ'g Co. v. Mead Data Cent., Inc., 799 F.2d 1219 (8th Cir. 1986), *cert. denied* 479 U.S. 1070 (1987).
40. Matthew Bender & Co., Inc. v. West Publ'g Co., 158 F.3d 674 (2d Cir. 1998).
41. Texas v. West Publ'g Co., 882 F.2d 171 (5th Cir. 1989).
42. In Building Officials & Code Adm'rs, Inc. v. Code Tech., Inc., 628 F.2d 730 (1st Cir. 1980), a federal appeals court was doubtful that a privately prepared model building code would retain its copyright after enactment by a state. More recently, the Fifth Circuit held that after a model building code was adopted into law by two municipalities, the creator could not prevent a non-profit organization from posting the codes on its website. Veeck v. Southern

The Bottom Line: You may copy sections from a federal, state, or local code. It does not matter if you are a student, a teacher, or an attorney who charges $250 an hour. You also may copy sections from a privately prepared code, for the law is not protected by copyright. But do not copy or scan an entire volume of a privately prepared code for any purpose—even an educational one—without permission. Remember that codes produced by private sector publishers (in the United States this generally is LexisNexis and the West Group) include copyrightable information such as references, research aides, notes, and case summaries, which are protectible.

A few final words on government information. It seems clear that court records—the oral or written transcript of the trial proceedings—are in the public domain.[43] It appears that briefs submitted by attorneys to federal or state courts also may be freely copied; several courts have held that court briefs enter the public domain when they become part of the judicial record.[44] In fact, briefs are commonly copied into microformat, and often are digitized and made freely available on many websites.

Compilations and Collective Works

Copyright in compilations and collective works is a bit different from copyright in an individual work such as an article or a novel. Under the Copyright Act, a collective work is "a work, such as a periodical issue, anthology, or encyclopedia, in which a number of contributions, constituting separate and independent works in themselves, are assembled into a collective whole."[45] A compilation is "a work formed by the collection and assembling of preexisting materials or of data that are selected, coordinated, or arranged in such a way that the resulting work as a whole constitutes an original work of authorship."[46]

Bldg. Code Cong. Int'l, Inc., 293 F.3d 791 (5th Cir. 2002) (en banc).

43. Lipman v. Massachusetts, 475 F.2d 565 (1st Cir. 1973).
44. In a case in which the court was deciding whether audiotapes played in court and introduced into evidence were in the public domain, the U.S. Court of Appeals for the District of Columbia wrote that "until destroyed or placed under seal, tapes played in open court and admitted into evidence—no less than the court reporter's transcript, the parties' briefs, and the judge's orders and opinions—remain a part of the public domain." Cottone v. Reno, 193 F. 3d 550, 554 (D.C. Cir. 1999). *See also* Krynicki v. Falk II, 983 F.2d 74, 77 (7th Cir. 1992).
45. 17 U.S.C. § 101 (2000).
46. *Id.*

1.6. Section 103 Compilations and Derivative Works

- ❧ Protection for original material contributed by the author
- ❧ Independent of and does not affect copyright status of pre-existing material

There are two possible levels of protection for collective works. Take, for example, a compilation of twentieth-century poetry. The underlying materials—each individual poem—would be subject to copyright protection. Furthermore, the entire work also may be protected as a copyrightable compilation if the editor exhibited sufficient skill and judgment selecting, organizing and arranging the poems. Here, copyright will extend only to the original material contributed by the editor: the selection and arrangement of the underlying content. Under the Act

> The copyright in a compilation or derivative work extends only to the material contributed by the author of such work, as distinguished from the preexisting material employed in the work, and does not imply any exclusive right in the preexisting material. The copyright in such work is independent of, and does not affect or enlarge the scope, duration, ownership, or subsistence of, any copyright protection in the preexisting material.[47]

This means that if you want to copy one of the poems from the anthology, then you will need permission from the person who holds copyright in the poem, *unless* the use is otherwise permitted under the Copyright Act as, say, a fair use. If the anthology is also protected as a compilation, someone who wants to use a significant number of poems from *The 100 Best Poems of the 20th Century* also must get permission from whomever has copyright in it as a compilation, generally the editor or the publisher.

If the compilation consists of underlying material that is in the public domain, such as facts, the facts are not protected. Here copyright protection exists, if at all, in the particular selection or arrangement, not in the underlying content. For example, both *Guinness World Records* and *The Times Almanac with Information Please* may record that Mt. Everest, at 29,035 feet, is the highest place on

---

47. 17 U.S.C. § 103(b) (2000). The Copyright Act treats similarly protection for collective and derivative works. The copyright owner's right to prepare derivative works is addressed in the next chapter.

earth. The copyright owners of these two compilations can neither protect this information, nor any other facts in their almanacs. They may, however, copyright their works as compilations, where protection extends to the selection and arrangement of the facts in their respective publications.

Not all compilations may be copyrighted, however. Take, for example, the common white pages telephone directory. In *Feist Publications, Inc. v. Rural Telephone Service*,[48] the U.S. Supreme Court ruled that a garden-variety white pages telephone directory contained so little creativity in selecting, arranging or coordinating the unprotected underlying facts that it could not be copyrighted as a compilation. The *Feist* decision discredited what is called the "sweat of the brow" doctrine: effort alone will not make a work copyrightable. The Court made it clear that compilations require a certain level of creativity to be afforded copyright protection: the creator must exercise some skill and discretion in selecting and arranging the underlying information.[49]

Efforts designed to effectively overturn the *Feist* decision have centered on database protection legislation. In the United States, such legislation has been introduced in Congress several times since the mid 1990s, but has not yet been passed into law.[50] On the international front, although database protection legislation has not been enacted under the Berne Convention, a European Union directive creates sui generis protection of databases if there was a "substantial investment in either the obtaining, verification or presentation of the contents to prevent extraction and/or re-utilization of the whole or of a substantial part."[51]

---

48. 499 U.S. 340 (1991).
49. "Thus, even a directory that contains absolutely no protectible written expression, only facts, meets the constitutional minimum for copyright protection if it features an original selection or arrangement." 499 U.S. at 348.
50. H.R. 3531, 104th Cong. (1996), H.R. 2652, 105th Cong. (1998), S. 2291, 105th Cong. (1998). More recently, Congress has considered two different approaches. During the 106th Congress, H.R. 1858 used an unfair competition theory to protect creators, but at the same time attempted to preserve access to facts and information by excerpting news gathering to use for scientific, educational, or research purposes. The bill would have given the Federal Trade Commission authority to bring actions for database theft. By contrast, H.R. 354, also introduced during the 106th Congress, would have amended copyright law to provide private relief for misappropriation and harmful use of a database. It included no exception for educational or research purposes.
51. Directive 96/9/EC of the European Parliament and of the Council of 11 March 1996 on the Legal Protection of Databases, O.J. (L 077) 27/03/1996, 0020–0028.

The Bottom Line: You may use the height of Mt. Everest and other facts from Guinness and the almanac as much as you want. However, if you scan *Guinness World Records*, rename it *My Big Fat Book of Facts* and sell it at a discount, you violate Guinness World Records, Ltd.'s compilation copyright.

Duration of Copyright Protection

Section 302 of the Act prescribes the term of copyright protection. As noted earlier, the Sonny Bono Copyright Extension Act of 1998 brought the United States in line with the European Union's 1993 directive extending the term of protection.[52]

Copyright protection lasts much longer today than it did under our original 1790 Copyright Act, which prescribed a term of fourteen years with a possible fourteen-year renewal.[53] Up until the 1976 Act, copyrights were issued for twenty-eight years, with an option to renew and extend the copyright for an additional twenty-eight-year term.[54]

Following are the current terms of protection for the most common types of work.

ↄ For a work by a single author, protection lasts for the author's life plus another seventy years.

ↄ When a work is authored by two or more individuals (called joint authorship), copyright lasts for seventy years after the death of last surviving author.

ↄ Copyright in anonymous works, works by corporate authors, and works made for hire, last for ninety-five years from the year of first publication or 120 years from its creation, whichever expires first.

The length of copyright protection gets more complicated than this, particularly with regard to works created before January 1, 1978, the effective date of the 1976 Act. Here are some other terms.

ↄ A work published from 1923 to 1963 and that has a copyright notice is protected for twenty-eight years, with the possibility of an additional sixty-seven years if the renewal option is exercised; if not, the work enters the public domain.

---

52. Council Directive 93/98/EEC of 29 October 1993 Harmonizing the Term of Protection of Copyright and Certain Related Rights. O.J. (L 290) 24/11/1993, 0009–0013.
53. Act of May 31, 1790, ch. 15, § 1, 1 Stat. 124.
54. 17 U.S.C. § 24 (1970).

Ø A work published between 1964 and 1977 is protected, if it had a copyright notice, for ninety-five years from the date of publication.

Ø A work created before 1978 but *not* published is protected for the author's life plus seventy years—or thru 2002—whichever is greater.

Ø A work created before 1978 that was published before 2003 is protected for the author's life plus seventy years or through 2047, whichever is greater.

Dazed and confused? You're not alone!

The Bottom Line: Copyright, like the Gary White tune (made famous by Linda Ronstadt), lasts a long, long time. To see things a little more clearly, take a look at the following chart.[55]

1.7. Section 302
Term of Copyright

Works created in 1978 or later

Personal author	Life of the author plus 70 years
Joint authors	Life plus 70 years after last surviving author's death
Anonymous or corporate authors or works made for hire	95 years after date of first publication, or 120 years after date of creation, whichever expires first
Published 1964–1977	95 years after date of first publication with © notice
Published 1923–63	28 years after date of first publication with © notice, plus 67 years if renewed
Published before 1923	In public domain
Created before 1978 but not published or registered on 1/1/78	Life plus 70 (or 95/120 term) or thru 2002, whichever is greater

---

55. Adapted from *When Works Pass Into the Public Domain*, by Professor Laura Gasaway, University of North Carolina School of Law.

Chapter Two
THE COPYRIGHT OWNER'S RIGHTS

&)(&

2.1. Section 106
Copyright Owner's Rights

- ∞ Reproduction
- ∞ Derivative works
- ∞ Public distribution
- ∞ Public performance
- ∞ Public display
- ∞ Digital audio transmission of sound recordings

For works of visual art (106a)

- ∞ Attribution
- ∞ Integrity

The Copyright Act gives a copyright owner the exclusive right, and the right to authorize others, to reproduce the protected work; to prepare derivative works based upon the copyrighted work; to distribute, perform or display the work publicly; and in the case of sound recordings, to perform the work publicly by means of a digital audio transmission.[1] But this does not end the discussion. A copyright owner's rights are subject to sections 107 to 122 of the Act, which expressly

---

1. 17 U.S.C. § 106 (2000).

permit certain uses. Users' rights are addressed later. For now, we will stay with *owners'* rights. Let's address each, in turn.

The Reproduction Right (Section 106(1))

The reproduction right is the right to copy a copyrighted work—period. Copies may be made in all sorts of different formats, such as paper, microform, or digital.

Derivative Works (Section 106(2))

A copyright owner has the right to prepare derivative works from his or her copyrighted work.[2] According to the U.S. Copyright Office, a derivative work is "a work based on one or more preexisting works."[3] A derivative work may be created when someone recasts, reformats, or adapts an earlier work. Simple examples include translations and adaptations.

Elmore Leonard has the exclusive right to translate his novel *Get Shorty* to another language, and also to authorize a screenplay or film from the novel. If Mr. Leonard refuses to give permission to translate his novel, or to prepare a screenplay or film from it, someone who does so could be liable for infringement. Like collective works, the copyright status of a derivative work is distinct from that of the original work from which it was derived.[4] This means that the screenplay for *Get Shorty* will be copyrighted independently of the novel, so long as it meets the requirements for protection: an original work of authorship fixed in a tangible medium of expression.

What about abridgments or abstracts? Whether a small portion or summary of a copyrighted work is a derivative work—and therefore requires permission from the original work's copyright owner—depends most on the extent to which the summary substitutes for the

---

2. 17 U.S.C. § 106(2) (2000).
3. UNITED STATES COPYRIGHT OFFICE, FORM VA: BASIC INFORMATION (rev'd June 2002). Various forms are available at the Copyright Office's website at <http://www.loc.gov/copyright>.
4. 17 U.S.C. § 103(b) (2000).

original. The more a person would be able to use the abstract *instead of* the original work, the more likely the abstract would be deemed a protected derivative work. The longer and more comprehensive the abstract is, the greater the chance it will be considered a derivative work. But even a short abstract that distills the essence of the original work—one which can substitute quite well for the original work—may also be considered a derivative work.

The Bottom Line: You *may* create a summary or abstract of a copyrighted work without permission if it is not a derivative work that can substitute for the original. A librarian may summarize individual journal articles, and also create annotated bibliographies from numerous articles on the same topic. However, a one-page abstract that distills the essence of a five-page article, and that can really serve as a substitute for the original, is probably a derivative work. Keep your abstracts brief. Whet the reader's appetite, but do not fill his or her stomach.

The Distribution Right and the First Sale Doctrine (Sections 106(3) and 109)

2.2. Section 109
First Sale Doctrine

Owner may sell or otherwise dispose of a lawful copy:

- ∞ but may not lease or lend sound recordings or computer programs for direct or indirect commercial advantage

- ∞ but library/school lending exemption

Section 106(3) of the Copyright Act gives a copyright owner the right to distribute his or her work to the public by sale or other transfer of ownership, including rental, lease, or lending. But the distribution right is not absolute; it is subject to section 109 of the Act—the "first sale doctrine." The first sale doctrine permits the owner of a lawfully made copy of a copyrighted work to lease, rent, sell or otherwise dispose of possession of the copy without permission. Libraries distribute their works publicly when they lend them out, but they have the right to do so because of the first sale doctrine.[5]

You only have to drive as far as your nearest strip mall to find a video rental store. Although you can find plenty of films, you cannot rent sound recordings ("records" or "CDs," depending on your generation) or software.[6] The big store, Blockbuster, does not rent sound recordings or software because Congress amended section 109 in 1984 and 1990.

The Record Rental Amendment Act of 1984[7] and the Computer Software Rental Amendment Act of 1990[8] prohibit owners of sound recordings or computer programs, for a purpose of direct or indirect commercial advantage, to rent, lease, or lend those items. But there are exceptions in both amendments that permit non-profit libraries and non-profit educational institutions to lend sound recordings and computer programs. Here is the language from the Act:

> Nothing in the preceding sentence [which prohibits the transfer of computer programs and sound recordings] . . . shall apply to the rental lease, or lending of a phonorecord for nonprofit purposes by a nonprofit library or nonprofit educational institution. The transfer of possession of a lawfully made copy of a computer program by a nonprofit educational institution to another nonprofit educational institution or to faculty, staff, and students does not constitute rental, lease, or lending for direct or indirect commercial purposes under this subsection.[9]

It is not always easy to figure out what Congress intended to do. This section indicates that nonprofit libraries and nonprofit educational institutions may lend phonorecords (CDs, tapes, etc.) to anyone. As for computer programs, it seems that the exemption applies

---

5. In *Hotaling v. Church of Jesus Christ of Latter-Day Saints*, 118 F.3d 199 (4th Cir. 1997), violation of the distribution right was invoked against a library. In *Hotaling,* copyrighted genealogical materials were published in microfiche and commercially marketed. The Church acquired a legitimate copy of the fiche, and added it to its main library's collection in Salt Lake City. Sometime later, several microfiche copies were made for branch libraries without permission. The appeals court wrote that "a library distributes a published work within the meaning of the Copyright Act . . . when it places an unauthorized copy of the work in its collection, includes the copy in its catalog or index system, and makes a copy available to the public." 118 F.3d at 201.
6. Congress considered, but did not include, a prohibition against lending computer game cartridges. This is why you can rent Nintendo and PlayStation games from video rental stores. *See* S. REP. NO. 101-265 (1990).
7. Pub. L. No. 98-450, 98 Stat. 1727 (1984) (as amended).
8. Pub. L. No. 101-650, 104 Stat. 5134 (1990) (as amended).
9. 17 U.S.C. § 109(b)(1)(A) (2000).

only to non-profit educational institutions, which would include their libraries. They may lend software to other educational institutions, and to faculty, students and staff, because such lending is not "for direct or indirect commercial purposes." But read on, for later in section 109, we see this:

> Nothing in this subsection shall apply to the lending of a computer program for nonprofit purposes by a nonprofit library if each copy of a computer program which is lent by such library has affixed to the packaging containing the program a warning of copyright in accordance with requirements that the Register of Copyrights shall prescribe by regulation.[10]

Here, Congress writes that *any* type of non-profit library may lend a computer program so long as it does so for non-profit purposes, and if it includes on the package the following warning:

> Computer Program Warning Label
> Notice: Warning of Copyright Restrictions
>
> The copyright law of the United States (Title 17, United States Code) governs the reproduction, distribution, adaptation, public performance, and public display of copyrighted material.
>
> Under certain conditions specified in law, nonprofit libraries are authorized to lend, lease, or rent copies of computer programs to patrons on a nonprofit basis for nonprofit purposes. Any person who makes an unauthorized copy or adaptation of the computer program, or redistributes the loan copy, or publicly performs or displays the computer program, except as permitted by Title 17 of the United States Code, may be liable for copyright infringement.
>
> This institution reserves the right to refuse to fill a loan request if, in its judgment, fulfillment of the request would lead to violation of the copyright law.

Note that you do not need to affix a warning label to sound recordings, as Congress did not include such a requirement in the 1990 Record Rental Amendment Act.

The exemption for lending software and sound recordings, then, applies both to non-profit libraries and non-profit educational institutions, if done for non-profit purposes. What about libraries in for-profit organizations such as law firms and corporations? May they lend sound recordings and software to their employees? In passing

---

10. 17 U.S.C. § 109(b)(2)(A) (2000). The label prescribed by the Register of Copyrights can be found at 37 C.F.R. § 201.24 (2002).

the 1984 Record Rental Amendment Act, the House Judiciary Committee wrote

> The direct link between the commercial rental of a phonorecord and the making of a copy of a record without permission of or compensation to the copyright owner is the economic and policy concern behind this legislation. The Subcommittee has found that the nexus of commercial record rental and duplication may directly and adversely affect the ability of copyright holders to exercise their reproduction and distribution rights under the Copyright Act.[11]

The Judiciary Committee clearly wanted to keep stores like Blockbuster from renting sound recordings; it did not discuss the lending of sound recordings within an organization.

As for software, here is what the Senate Committee on the Judiciary wrote when it was working on the Software Rental Amendments Act: "The committee received testimony that in some parts of the country businesses have appeared, offering daily rental of popular application software for a fraction of the purchase price."[12] In a similar vein, the House Judiciary Committee wrote

> In 1984, Congress was presented with evidence demonstrating that the nascent record rental business posed a genuine threat to the record industry. Copies of phonorecords were being rented at a fraction of their cost, in conjunction with advertisements exhorting customers to 'never buy another record.' Congress responded by prohibiting the rental of phonorecords for purposes of direct or indirect commercial advantage.
>
> Congress has now been presented with similar evidence by the computer software industry. Indeed, in some respects, the evidence is even more compelling in the case of software. . . . Short term rental of software is, under most circumstances, inconsistent with the purposes for which software is intended.[13]

It seems clear that Congress wanted to nip in the bud the software rental business, but both the House and the Senate wanted to carve out an exception for non-profit libraries. The House Judiciary Committee wrote, "[t]he Committee does not wish, however, to prohibit nonprofit lending by nonprofit libraries and nonprofit educational institutions."[14]

You should notice the huge gap—everything between the Blockbusters on one hand, and non-profit libraries and educational

---

11. H.R. REP. NO. 98-987, at 2 (1984).
12. S. REP. NO. 101-265, at 3 (1990).
13. H.R. REP. NO. 101-735, at 8 (1990).
14. *Id.*

institutions on the other. What about for-profit businesses and corporations that are *not* Blockbuster—those whose business is *not* renting copyrighted works for a profit?

Recall that the prohibition in section 109(b) applies to the renting, leasing, or lending sound recordings and computer programs "for the purpose of direct or indirect commercial advantage." Congress did not write that for-profit companies such as architectural firms, law firms, or pharmaceutical companies could not circulate sound recordings or computer programs within their organizations. This interpretation is supported by a statement by Representative Kastenmeier, one of the bill's sponsors:

> Certain for-profit companies have inquired whether this language implies that the common practices of employees of a company carrying portable computers and associated software to other worksites, and of transferring employee-owned software among employees at the same location would be considered to constitute direct or indirect commercial advantage.
>
> The bill is not intended to prohibit these common practices. The sole purpose of the quoted language is to highlight legitimate activities that occur in a nonprofit educational setting. The committee did not intend the provision to imply that similar activities, if carried out by for-profit entities, would be infringing. The transfer of copies within a single entity, whether nonprofit or for-profit, is exempt.[15]

The Bottom Line: Non-profit libraries and educational institutions may lend sound recordings and software. Software must include a warning label. Although the language of the 1984 and 1990 amendments is less than perfectly clear, they seem not to prohibit the lending of computer software or sound recordings within a for-profit organization. This includes free-standing software, and also diskettes or CD-ROMs that today accompany many printed books.

---

15. CONG. REC. H13314–13315 (daily ed. Oct. 27, 1990) (statement of Rep. Kastenmeier). Furthermore, one of the foremost authorities on copyright law writes "The fact that Congress expressly exempted certain transfers by nonprofit educational institutions does not mean that transfers within for-profit institutions, such as from one employee to another at the same work site, are necessarily barred. PAUL GOLDSTEIN, COPYRIGHT § 5.6.1.c (2d ed. 1996–2003).

The Public Display and Public Performance Rights (Sections 106(4) and 106(5))

A copyright owner has the right to display and perform the copyrighted work publicly. The public performance right applies to literary, musical, dramatic, choreographic, pantomimes, motion pictures, and other audiovisual works.[16] The public display right applies to those same works, and also to graphic and sculptural works.[17]

The performance right is a bit different from the display right, especially with regard to audiovisual works, such as films. The *performance* of an audiovisual work means to show the images in sequence.[18] The *display* of an audiovisual work involves showing individual images non-sequentially.[19] Showing the Marx Brothers' film *Duck Soup* would be a performance, while showing selected images of Groucho as Rufus T. Firefly, the President of Freedonia, would be a display.

Not all performances or displays are protected by copyright, but only those which are "public." Under the Act,

> To perform or display a work "publicly" means—
>
> (1) to perform or display it at a place open to the public or at any place where a substantial number of persons outside of a normal circle of family and its social acquaintances is gathered; or
> (2) to transmit or otherwise communicate a performance or display of the work to a place specified by clause (1) or to the public by means of any device or process, whether the members of the public are capable of receiving the performance or display receive it in the same place or in separate places and at the same time or at different times.[20]

What about images or text on a computer monitor? The Act provides that the owner of a lawful copy, or anyone authorized by the owner, may display the copy publicly "either directly or by the projection of no more than one image at a time, to viewers present at the place where the copy is located."[21] You may not send digital images on

---

16. 17 U.S.C. § 106(4) (2000).
17. *Id.* § 106(5).
18. *Id.* § 101.
19. *Id.*
20. *Id.*
21. *Id.* § 109(c).

a monitor to the world at large, but you *may* display the images on public access terminals in a library. You also may display images on a projection device to a group, such as students in a classroom.

Rather than beat this horse further right now, public performances and displays are addressed in more detail in Chapter Eight.

The Digital Sound Recording Transmission Right (Section 106(6))

The Digital Performance Right in Sound Recordings Act of 1995 gave an owner of copyright in a sound recording the right to perform his or her work publicly by means of certain digital audio transmissions.[22] The right was qualified by various (and pretty complicated) exceptions, which are spelled out in section 114 of the Act.

The digital audio transmission right, and the section 114 exemptions, affect most directly libraries with collections of sound recordings. To be frank, this part of the Copyright Act remains somewhat of a mystery to me. A better source of information is the Music Library Association.[23] Indeed, the MLA published a *Statement on the Digital Transmission of Electronic Reserves,* which supports providing aural access to musical works to students in the classroom and through course reserve, and also the dubbing and digital copying of musical works for course reserve. The MLA Statement, which includes guidelines on creating and transmitting digital audio file copies of musical works for course reserve, is included in the appendices.

Works of Visual Art: Rights of Attribution and Integrity (Section 106a)

When Congress passed the Visual Artists Rights Act of 1990,[24] for the first time by legislation it protected what are called moral rights—the rights of attribution and integrity—but only for visual arts. Works of visual art include a single copy of a painting, drawing, print, photo-

---

22. 17 U.S.C. § 106(6) (2000).
23. <http://www.musiclibraryassoc.org>.
24. Pub. L. No. 101-650, Title VI, 104 Stat. 5128 (1990).

graph, or sculptural work, or if they are produced in multiple copies, to a limited edition of fewer than 200 numbered copies.[25] They do *not* include posters, maps, charts, technical drawings, motion pictures or other audiovisual works, electronic publications, or advertisements. And they do not include works made for hire.[26]

Here is what the U.S. Copyright Office writes about the rights of attribution and integrity:

> The right of attribution ensures that artists are correctly identified with the works of art they create and that they are not identified with works created by others. The right of integrity allows artists to protect their works against modifications and destructions that are prejudicial to the artists' honor or reputation. These rights may not be transferred by the author, but they may be waived in a written instrument. Transfer of the physical copy of a work of visual art or of the copyright does not affect the moral rights accorded to the author.[27]

Generally, the Copyright Act gives an author of a work of visual art the right (1) to claim authorship of the work; (2) to prevent the use of his or her name as the author of a work he or she did not create; (3) to prevent the use of the author's name on a work that was distorted, mutilated, or otherwise modified if those changes prejudiced the author's honor or reputation; (4) to prevent the intentional distortion, mutilation, or other modification of the work that prejudices the author's honor or reputation; and (5) to prevent the destruction of certain works.[28] The artist's rights are subject to certain exemptions, which are spelled out in section 113.

Although an artist's attribution and integrity rights may not appear to impact many libraries significantly, there is a bottom line: Whenever you "use" someone else's work—even if that use is permitted under fair use or another provision of the Copyright Act—you should credit the authors. If you modify the original work, you should provide credit, and also note the changes that were made from the original work.

---

25. 17 U.S.C. § 101 (2000).
26. *Id.*
27. UNITED STATES COPYRIGHT OFFICE, CIRCULAR 40: COPYRIGHT REGISTRATION FOR WORKS OF THE VISUAL ARTS (rev'd June 2002).
28. 17 U.S.C. § 106(A) (2000).

Chapter Three
LIABILITY FOR INFRINGEMENT

ಐ೦ಬಟ

Remedies and Damages (Section 504)

3.1. Section 504 Damages

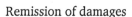

ಐ೦ Actual damages and profits, or
ಐ೦ Statutory damages
  $750 to $30,000 per infringement;
  $150,000 for willful infringement;
  $200 for innocent infringer

Remission of damages

ಐ೦ Employee or agent of a nonprofit educational
  institution, library, or archives
ಐ೦ Acting within scope of employment
ಐ೦ Reasonable belief the use was fair

Remedies and damages for infringement are governed by section 504 of the Act. In a nutshell, a copyright owner may seek actual or statutory damages, and also may enjoin (i.e., prohibit) the infringing activity.

Actual damages are measured by what was lost as a result of the infringing activity. Statutory damages can range from $750 to $30,000 per infringing event, and usually will exceed actual damages. If the infringement was willful—if the defendant engaged in the infringing activity knowing that his or her conduct was infringing, or recklessly disregarded the copyright owner's rights—statutory damages can be as much as $150,000 per infringing act.

But do not start sweating as if you were spending a night in Casablanca in July. Even if a court finds that there was an infringement, statutory damages may be reduced significantly if the defendant was an "innocent infringer," someone who was not aware of and had no reason to believe that his or her acts were infringing. When this is the case, a court has discretion to reduce statutory damages to as little as $200.[1]

Furthermore, a court may not assess *any* damages if the infringer is an employee of a non-profit educational institution, library, or archives who, acting under the scope of his or her employment, actually and reasonably believed that the use was fair under section 107.[2] Although section 504 does not expressly say so, one might reason that no damages will be assessed against a library employee who believed that the use was permitted under the section 108 library exemption, and in all likelihood, other uses permitted under any of the statutory exemptions in the Act.

This does not, of course, give you a license to copy. The damage remission provision does not apply if the employee knew or should have known that his or her actions were infringing. What if, for example, a library has an internal policy against photocopying at any one time more than two articles from a journal issue for a faculty member? If that copying was infringing (and I do not suggest that it is), an employee who disregards the policy will not be protected by the reduced damages provisions for two reasons. First, because the library had a policy prohibiting that level of copying, the employee probably had no reason to believe that her copying was fair or otherwise permitted under the Act. Second, because the employee disregarded library policy, arguably she did not act within the scope of her employment.

Plaintiffs in an infringement lawsuit are not interested in getting damages from the person who runs the photocopier, of course. They want a judgment against the organization, which, if it has not declared bankruptcy due to misconduct by its officers or accountants, has the "deep pockets." This brings us to the issue of the liability of an employer for the acts of its employees.

---

1. 17 U.S.C. § 504(c)(2) (2000).
2. *Id.*

Institutional Responsibility: Vicarious Liability and Contributory Infringement

3.2. Institutional Liability

Vicarious Liability
- ᔕ Right to supervise
- ᔕ Financial benefit

Contributory Infringement
- ᔕ Knowledge of infringing activity
- ᔕ Induce, cause, or materially contribute

Whether a library or its parent institution may be responsible for an employee's infringement depends on the library's involvement in the infringing activity, or its relationship to the infringer. The institution may be liable under either of two legal theories: vicarious liability (sometimes called respondeat superior) or as a contributory infringer.

Vicarious liability generally means that an employer will be liable for harmful acts done by employees who acted within the scope of their employment. A library may be liable for the acts of its employees if it had the right and ability to supervise the employee, and also derived a financial benefit from exploiting the copyrighted work.[3] Knowledge of the infringing activity is not necessary. The financial benefit is found if the institution is getting something for free that it should have paid for, or even when there is an indirect benefit.[4]

A library that provides guidance as to which activities are and are not permitted is less likely to be responsible for the acts of its employees. But it will not do the library any good if administrators and staff disregard the policy. The library, or any organization for that matter, cannot enforce its policy with a wink and a nod. This is what happened to the Kinko's Corporation when it was found liable for employees who photocopied copyrighted articles and book chapters to create coursepacks for students.[5] Kinko's had a policy, but

---

3. A&M Records, Inc. v. Napster Inc., 239 F.3d 1004, 1022 (9th Cir. 2001).

4. In the *Napster* case, the court found that Napster reaped a financial benefit when the availability of infringing materials acted as a draw for customers. 239 F.3d at 1023.

5. Basic Books, Inc. v. Kinko's Graphics, 758 F. Supp. 1522 (S.D.N.Y. 1991).

failed to enforce it. The court found that Kinko's used the policy only to "cover" itself.[6]

Contributory infringement is a little different. A library or its parent institution may be liable as a contributory infringer if, with knowledge of the infringing activity, it induces, causes, or renders substantial assistance to, or materially contributes to the activity.[7] Actual knowledge is not necessary; it is enough if the library *should have known* that an infringement was taking place. We can use the lending of audio cassettes as an example. A college library may lend its audio cassettes to students and faculty to play on library equipment. But the library would be well-advised not to lend equipment that enables someone to make tape-to-tape copies of the cassettes. (It would be even more egregious if the library lent taping equipment, provided instructions on how to make copies, and sold blank cassettes for $2.00 a pop.)

A final word on equipment, for now (equipment issues are discussed in greater detail in Chapter Five). A library is not liable for infringing activities that take place on unsupervised photocopying equipment if the equipment has the following warning label.[8]

> **WARNING: THE MAKING OF A COPY MAY BE SUBJECT TO THE UNITED STATES COPYRIGHT LAW (TITLE 17 UNITED STATES CODE)**

---

6. Kinko's instructions to its workers possessed little of the nuance of the copyright law. They provided no hypothetical situations nor any factual summary of the state of the law presently. There was no mention of the facts of the Sony case, the Salinger case, the Harper & Row case or others which may illustrate some of the complexities of this doctrine. This can hardly be considered a "good faith" effort on Kinko's part to educate their employees. To the contrary, it appears more to be a way to "cover" themselves while Kinko's remained willfully blind to the consequences of their activity.

   Id. at 1545.

7. A&M Records, Inc. v. Napster Inc., 239 F.3d at 1019 (9th Cir. 2001); Cable/Home Communications Corp. v. Network Prods., Inc., 902 F.2d 829, 845 (11th Cir. 1990).

8. 17 U.S.C. § 108(f)(1) (2000).

It may be prudent to include a similar label on audio listening and video viewing equipment that the library makes available to patrons, such as

WARNING: THE MAKING OF A COPY AND PUBLIC DISTRIBUTION, PERFORMANCES OR DISPLAYS MAY BE SUBJECT TO THE UNITED STATES COPYRIGHT LAW (TITLE 17 UNITED STATES CODE).

The Bottom Line: A library should give its staff guidance on what they may or may not do. Create a written policy, make sure that the staff is aware of it, and enforce it. Put a warning label on equipment. Do not provide equipment or assistance that facilitates copyright infringement.

Government Immunity

What if the library is part of a federal, state, or local government, such as a city or county public library, a state-funded university library, or a federal agency library? Can the government be liable for acts of its employees? The answer is "maybe." In some circumstances a government has what is called sovereign immunity, meaning that you cannot recover damages from it.

Congress has passed legislation waiving the federal government's immunity for patent and copyright infringement.[9] A federal agency, therefore, may be sued for infringing acts by its employees. The situation differs for the states, because the Eleventh Amendment to the U.S. Constitution prohibits suits in federal court by an individual against a state without the state's consent. Congress has passed legislation abrogating Eleventh Amendment immunity, but court decisions have held that the legislation did not validly abrogate a state's immunity in copyright infringement suits.[10] Still, a state *employee* may

---

9. 28 U.S.C. § 1498 (2000).
10. 17 U.S.C. § 511 (2000). *Seminole Tribe of Florida v. Florida*, 517 U.S. 44 (1996), *Chavez v. Arte Publico Press*, 139 F.3d 504 (5th Cir. 1998), and *Rodriguez v. Texas Comm'n on the Arts*, 199 F.3d. 279 (5th Cir. 2000) all held that the federal statute did not validly abrogate a state's sovereign immunity against infringement lawsuits.

be sued for infringement, may be subject to damages, and may have his or her activities enjoined by a court.

The Bottom Line: Even if you work for the government and think your employer has immunity, always do what is right.

Chapter Four
FAIR USE
(SECTION 107)

ʒ❀ɞ

Copyright owners' rights are vitally important, but Congress did not put copyrighted works in a lockbox. A copyright owner does not have an absolute monopoly over the use of his or her work; owners' rights are subject to other provisions of the Act that permit certain uses of copyrighted works. For those who work in libraries or schools, the most important of these rights are fair use (section 107 of the Act), the library exemption (section 108), the first sale doctrine (section 109), and the public performance exemptions (section 110).

Section 107 provides the broadest scope of protection for those who use copyrighted works. Unlike other sections of the Act that permit certain types of uses, or the use of certain types of materials, section 107 is an all-purpose exemption, like Fantastik® or 409® brand all-purpose cleaners. Every use should be viewed under the section 107 microscope; when you try to determine whether a use is permitted under other exemptions, also consider whether it is a fair use.[1] And remember that when a use is allowed under section 107 or another exemption, you need not receive permission from the copyright owner nor pay royalties.

Most scholars trace the origin of fair use in the United States to an 1841 case, *Folsom v. Marsh*.[2] Jared Sparks, who had been assigned

---

1. 17 U.S.C. § 108(f)(4) (2000).
2. 2 Story 100, 9 F. Cas. 342 (C.C. Mass. 1841) (No. 4,901).

copyright in the letters of George Washington, edited them into a twelve-volume set. The Reverend Charles Upham used more than 300 pages from Sparks' set in his own 866-page biography of Washington. To determine whether Reverend Upham infringed, Justice Joseph Story decreed that the court had to look at three things: (1) the nature and objects of the selection, (2) the quantity and value of the materials used, and (3) the degree in which the use may prejudice the work, diminish the author's profits, or supersede the objects of the original work. After examining these factors, Justice Story concluded that Upham's use was not fair.

Fair use remained exclusively within the judiciary until Congress codified it in the 1976 Copyright Act. Congress understood the complexity of legislating fair use; the legislative history notes that Congress intended to restate the fair use doctrine as it had developed in the courts, not to change, narrow, or enlarge it.[3] Recognizing the difficulty in defining fair use, the House Judiciary Committee wrote

> Although the courts have considered and ruled upon the fair use doctrine over and over again, no real definition of the concept has ever emerged. Indeed, since the doctrine is an equitable rule of reason, no generally applicable definition is possible, and each case raising the question must be decided on its own facts.[4]

Fair use, then, is an equitable concept that attempts to balance the rights of copyright owners with the needs of those who use copyrighted works. The judiciary ultimately determines which uses are "fair uses." American jurisprudence is guided by precedent, and a court deciding a case today will look at earlier decisions involving similar facts and issues for guidance. But because fair use determinations are fact-specific, it is difficult to generalize what is, and what is not, fair. The Judiciary Committee also noted the freedom courts have in deciding whether a particular use is fair. It wrote

> The statement of the fair use doctrine in section 107 offers some guidance to users in determining when the principles of the doctrine apply. However, the endless variety of situations and combinations of circumstances that can arise in particular cases precludes the formulation of exact rules in the statute.... Beyond a very broad statutory explanation of what fair use is and some of the criteria applicable to it, the courts must be free to adapt the doctrine to particular situations on a case-by-case basis.[5]

---

3. H.R. REP. NO. 94-1476, at 66 (1976).

4. *Id.* at 65.

5. *Id.* at 66.

> ### 4.1. Section 107
> ### Fair Use Purposes
>
>
>
> - Criticism
> - Comment
> - News reporting
> - Teaching (including multiple classroom copies)
> - Scholarship
> - Research
> - Other possible uses

Let's move to the Act. Section 107 begins with the statement that the fair use of a copyrighted work, including reproduction for purposes such as criticism, comment, news reporting, teaching (including multiple copies for classroom use), scholarship, or research is not an infringement. The Supreme Court has written that this list is not intended to be exhaustive, nor intended to single out any particular use as presumptively "fair."[6] And although the uses noted in the preamble are favored, you will see that not all copying done for such purposes is necessarily fair.

The Four Factors

Under the statute, a court deciding whether a use of a copyrighted work is a "fair use" must consider no less than four factors. Section 107 continues:

> In determining whether the use made of a work in any particular case is a fair use the factors to be considered shall include—
>
> (1) the purpose and character of the use, including whether such use is of a commercial nature or is for nonprofit educational purposes;
> (2) the nature of the copyrighted work;
> (3) the amount and substantially of the portion used in relation to the copyrighted work as a whole; and

---

6. Harper & Row v. Nation Enters., 471 U.S. 539, 561 (1985).

(4) the effect of the use upon the potential market for or value of the copyrighted work.[7]

4.2. Section 107 Fair Use Factors

- ๛ Purpose of the use
- ๛ Nature of the copyrighted work
- ๛ Amount and substantiality
- ๛ Effect on potential market or value

- ๛ Non-publication does not bar fair use

The first factor examines two different things—the purpose of the use, and the character of the use. With regard to *purpose*, a court will consider whether the use is of a commercial nature or, instead, for non-profit educational purposes. Although non-profit educational uses are favored over commercial uses, this means neither that all non-profit educational uses are fair, nor that all commercial uses are infringing. For example, a court has held that extensive copying of PBS programs by a public school system for distribution to schools within the system—an obvious educational use—was infringing.[8] Another court ruled that it was not a fair use when a teacher copied eleven pages from a thirty-five-page copyrighted booklet on cake decorating, and incorporated those eleven pages into a twenty-four-page booklet she prepared for her class.[9]

The second part of the first factor requires an examination of the *character* of the use, including whether the use is transformative. The character/transformative issue was discussed at great length in *Campbell v. Acuff-Rose,* where the U.S. Supreme Court found that the band 2 Live Crew's parody of Roy Orbison's "Oh Pretty Woman" was a fair use.[10] The Court wrote that the central purpose of the first factor is whether the new work merely supplants the original—a non-transformative use—or instead

> adds something new, with a further purpose or different character, altering the first with new expression, meaning, or message; it asks, in other words, whether and to what extent the new work is "trans-

---

7. 17 U.S.C. § 107 (2000).

8. Encyclopedia Britannica Educ. Corp. v. Crooks, 542 F. Supp. 1156 (W.D.N.Y. 1982).

9. Marcus v. Rowley, 695 F.2d 1171 (9th Cir. 1983).

10. 510 U.S. 569 (1994).

formative." . . . [T]he more transformative the new work, the less the significance of the other factors, like commercialism, that may weigh against a finding of fair use."[11]

The concept of transforming a work was explored in great detail by a federal appeals court in *American Geophysical Union v. Texaco,*[12] which is discussed below.

The second fair use factor is the nature of the work copied. Because the purpose of copyright is to "promote the progress of science and the useful arts," there is more freedom to copy or otherwise use informational, scientific, or factual works than there is for creative or expressive works.[13] For example, articles on the First Amendment, HIV, and the Middle East may be more freely copied than a short story from the *New Yorker* or a Charles Schultz comic strip. This does *not* mean that a person may copy a "favored" work anytime he or she wants. Nor does it mean that someone may *never* copy a *Peanuts* comic strip. A fair use analysis requires examination of all four factors, and sometimes others.

For example, courts often consider whether the work is published, unpublished, or out of print. In 1987, a federal appeals court ruled that a biographer of J.D. Salinger could not include Salinger's private letters because, even though they were deposited in the archives of several university libraries, they were unpublished.[14] Following the *Salinger* decision, after several other courts also restricted copying from unpublished works, it became apparent that some tinkering with the fair use provision was necessary. Consequently, in 1992 Congress amended section 107 with the following, simple clause: "The fact that a work is unpublished shall not itself bar a finding of fair use if such finding is made upon consideration of all the above factors."

Today, the fact that a work is out-of-print or otherwise unavailable in the marketplace may work for, or against, fair use. That a work is out-of-print may work in favor of the copyright owner because royalties are the only source of income from the work copied.[15] In other situations, however, the fact that a work is unavailable may

---

11. *Campbell,* 510 U.S. at 579.
12. 60 F.3d 913 (2d Cir. 1994).
13. *Harper & Row v. Nation Enters.,* 471 U.S. at 563.
14. Salinger v. Random House, 811 F.2d 90 (2d Cir. 1987), *opinion supplemented and reh'g denied,* 818 F.2d 252 (1987).
15. Basic Books, Inc. v. Kinko's Graphics Corp. 758 F. Supp. 1522 (S.D.N.Y. 1991).

actually work in favor of the user, particularly if the copyright owner has not set up a handy mechanism to collect royalties.[16]

The Bottom Line: The second factor favors the use of informational, scientific, scholarly, or factual works is favored. The use of creative works such as novels, poetry, or cartoons is not. The published or unpublished nature of a work may work for or against a finding of fair use.

The third fair use factor considers the amount of the copyrighted work that was copied, performed, or otherwise used. As a general matter, the more that is copied, the less likely this factor will favor the user. But you must look beyond quantity. A court may very well hold this factor in favor of the copyright owner even when a very small portion of a copyrighted work is used—less than 1%, in some cases—if what is used constitutes the heart of the work.

In *Harper & Row v. Nation Enterprises,*[17] *The Nation* magazine scooped an article on the memoirs of President Gerald Ford that was to appear in *Time* magazine. Harper & Row, which was to publish a book on the Ford memoirs, negotiated a prepublication agreement with *Time* in which the magazine would excerpt 7,500 words from the book dealing with Ford's account of his pardon of former President Nixon. Before the *Time* article appeared in print, someone provided *The Nation* with a copy of the Ford manuscript. A few weeks before the publication of the *Time* article, *The Nation* published a 2,250-word article that included about 300 copyrighted words

---

16. In Maxtone-Graham v. Burtchaell, 803 F.2d 1253, 1264 n. 8 (2d Cir. 1986), the appeals court wrote:

> We also note that *Pregnant by Mistake* was out of print when *Rachel Weeping* was published. While this factor is not essential to our affirmance of the district court's finding of fair use, it certainly supports our determination. The legislative reports have provided some guidance on this issue: "A key, though not necessarily determinative, factor in fair use is whether or not the work is available to the potential user. If the work is 'out of print' and unavailable for purchase through normal channels, the user may have more justification for reproducing it than in the ordinary case, . . . S. Rep. No. 94-473, 94th Cong., 1st Sess. 64 (1965); H.R. REP. NO. 94-1476, 94th Cong., 2d Sess. 67 (1976). . . ."

More recently, in Sony Computer Entm't Am., Inc. v. Bleem, LLC, 214 F.3d 1022, 1028 (9th Cir. 2000), the Ninth Circuit wrote the following:

> For instance, if the copyrighted work is out of print and cannot be purchased, a user may be more likely to prevail on a fair use defense. . . . On the other hand, if the copyrighted material is unpublished and creative while the copy is a commercial publication, courts would be less receptive to the defense of fair use.

17. 471 U.S. 539 (1985).

(verbatim quotes, actually) from the as yet unpublished manuscript. With its article scooped, *Time* cancelled its agreement with Harper & Row, and Harper & Row sued *The Nation*. In terms of quantity, *The Nation* used less than 1% from the Harper & Row manuscript, but still Harper & Row won.

A court may consider not only the amount taken from the first work, but also how much of the new work includes material that was copied from the first one. In other words, if the author of a twenty-page article "borrows" twelve pages from another person's work, 60% of the latter work (twelve of the twenty pages) really is someone else's. Needless to say, "the more the merrier" does not bode well for defendants in these cases.

Because much library copying involves the reproduction of articles, it is important to understand that there are two levels of copyright protection for journals. First, there is copyright in the journal issue as a "collective work," which typically is held in the name of the publisher. Second, there is copyright in each individual article. Copyright in an article is held by its author, unless the author transfers the copyright to another person or entity. If you want to use an article, and that use is *not* permitted by section 107 or another provision of the Copyright Act, you will need permission from whomever holds copyright in the article. In most cases it probably will be the author, but many journals require authors to transfer copyright in their articles to the publisher.

Copying from newsletters is even more problematic. Copying entire issues of newsletters is particularly frowned upon. A library should *not* subscribe to only one copy of a newsletter and use it to make additional copies for others in the organization. Neither should an individual subscribe to a newsletter and make copies for his or her friends or professional colleagues. Three court decisions indicate the risk of making cover-to-cover copies of newsletters, both in the for-profit or non-profit sector.

In 1991, a Washington, D.C.–area law firm was sued for making multiple copies of a newsletter for several attorneys in the firm, even though there were discounts available for multiple subscriptions.[18] The law firm reportedly paid a huge amount of money to settle the

---

18. Washington Bus. Info., Inc. v. Collier, Shannon & Scott, No. 91-CV-305 (E.D. Va., filed Feb. 26, 1991). *See* James Gibbs, *Copyright and Copy Rights*, LEGAL TIMES, May 3, 1993, at S33.

suit.[19] A year later, another newsletter publisher succeeded in getting an injunction against a for-profit corporation that was making cover-to-cover copies for employees in its branch offices.[20] And one year after that, a non-profit association was held to have infringed for doing the same thing.[21]

For newsletters, do not make cover-to-cover copies, even if you work in a non-profit educational institution. This does not mean that you cannot copy *anything* from a newsletter. Occasional, isolated copying of small portions—not a significant portion, and not regularly—would likely be fair. Even an entire newsletter issue may occasionally be copied, within limited circumstances, under the section 108 library exemption. (See Chapter Five.)

Fair Use in the For-Profit Sector: The Texaco Case and Beyond

All right. Time to talk turkey. Time to talk about *Texaco,* a case coordinated by the Association of American Publishers in the name of five publishers. First the facts. In 1992, a federal district court in New York held that Texaco's routing of journals to researchers within the corporation, who subsequently photocopied articles and filed them away for later use, was not a fair use.[22] Two years later the U.S. Court of Appeals for the Second Circuit upheld the lower court decision.[23]

Although Texaco employed hundreds of scientists, before trial the parties agreed that the trial would focus on the activities of one, Dr. Donald H. Chickering, who photocopied eight articles from the *Journal of Catalysis* and placed them in his personal filing cabinet. Let's see how the trial and appellate courts addressed the main issue in *Texaco*: Was the routing of journals to corporate scientists, who copied articles and filed them away for possible later use, a fair use under section 107 of the Act. On to the first fair use factor.

---

19. The *New York Times* wrote that the settlement, including legal fees, "may have cost Collier, Shannon $1 million." David Margolick, *When a Firm Tries to Cut Corners, It Is Caught in Copyright Embarrassment,* N.Y. TIMES, Dec. 6, 1991, at B-7.
20. Pasha Publ'ns, Inc. v. Enmark Gas Corp., 22 U.S.P.Q.2d (BNA) 1076, 1992 Copyright L. Dec. (CCH) ¶ 26,881, 19 Media L. Rep. (BNA) 2062 (N.D. Tex. 1992).
21. Television Digest v. United States Tel. Ass'n, 1994 Copyright. L. Dec. (CCH) ¶ 27,191, 28 U.S.P.Q.2d 1697, 21 Media L. Rep. (BNA) 2211 (D.D.C. 1993).
22. American Geophysical Union v. Texaco, Inc., 802 F. Supp. 1 (S.D.N.Y. 1992).
23. American Geophysical Union v. Texaco, Inc., 60 F.3d 913 (2d Cir. 1994).

The trial (district) court judge spent considerable time examining the first factor—the purpose and character of the use. As for the *purpose* of the use, the judge wrote that because the defendant was a for-profit company, its copying was "commercial." As for the *character* of the use, the judge was struck by the fact that Dr. Chickering did not transform the copyrighted articles in any way. Chickering copied the articles and filed them away for possible later use, but there was no evidence that he ever used the articles in his research.

When the appeals court examined the first fair use factor two years later, it was guided by the Supreme Court's recent decision in the 2 Live Crew case (*Campbell v. Acuff-Rose Music*), discussed earlier in this chapter. The *Campbell* court wrote that when a court looks at the *purpose* of the use it must determine whether the use is non-profit educational, for-profit commercial, or something else. As for the *character* of the use, it wrote that courts must determine "whether and to what extent it is 'transformative,' altering the original with new expression, meaning, or message. . . . [T]he more transformative the new work, the less will be the significance of other factors, like commercialism, that may weigh against a finding of fair use."[24]

As for the *purpose* of the use, the appeals court tried to determine if Dr. Chickering's copying was, as the district court concluded, commercial copying. Noting that Texaco did not directly profit from the copying, the court concluded that the purpose was neither "for-profit" nor "non-profit educational," calling it instead an "intermediate" use.[25] As for the *character* of the use, the appeals court agreed with the district court that the copying was not transformative.

---

24. *Campbell*, 510 U.S. at 579.

25. The court pointedly distinguished copying at corporations such as Texaco from those whose business is to make copies, such as copyshops, when it wrote

> our concern here is that the court let the for-profit nature of Texaco's activity weigh against Texaco without differentiating between a direct commercial use and the more indirect relation to commercial activity that occurred here. Texaco was not gaining direct or immediate commercial advantage from the photocopying at issue in this case, i.e. Texaco's profits, revenues, and overall commercial performance were not tied to making copies of eight *Catalysis* articles for Chickering. . . . Rather, Texaco's photocopying served, at most, to facilitate Chickering's research, which in turn might have led to the development of new products and technology that could have improved Texaco's commercial performance.

> *Texaco*, 60 F.3d at 921.

The appeals court also pointedly called into question the library's systematically routing journals to Texaco scientists so that each person could build a mini-library of photocopied articles. It called this

> "archival"—*i.e*, done for the primary purpose of providing numerous Texaco scientists each with his or her own copy of each article without Texaco having to purchase another additional journal subscriptions. The photocopying "merely supersede[s] the objects of the original creation" [quoting *Campbell* and *Folsom v. Marsh*] and tilts the first fair use factor against Texaco.[26]

Weighing its words carefully, the court continued

> We do not mean to suggest that no instance of archival copying would be fair use, but the first factor tilts against Texaco in this case because the making of copies to be placed on the shelf in Chickering's office is part of a systematic process of encouraging employee researchers to copy articles so as to multiply available copies while avoiding payment.[27]

The second fair use factor, you will recall, examines the nature of the work copied. Both the district and appeals courts characterized the articles in the *Journal of Catalysis* as factual in nature, and concluded that the second factor favored Texaco. As for the third factor—the amount used—both courts concluded that it favored the plaintiffs because entire articles were being copied.

On to the fourth factor, the effect of the use upon the potential market for or value of the copyrighted work. Courts are more likely to find an infringement when the copyright owner incurs financial harm due to unauthorized or uncompensated copying. In 1985, the Supreme Court called the fourth factor "undoubtedly the single most important element of fair use."[28] But since the 1994 *Campbell* decision, as the appeals court noted, the fourth factor no longer is more important than the others.[29]

---

26. *Id.* at 919–20.
27. *Id.* at 920.
28. *Harper & Row,* 471 U.S. at 566.
29. Prior to *Campbell,* the Supreme Court had characterized the fourth factor as "the single most important element of fair use," Harper & Row, 471 U.S. at 566. . . . However, *Campbell's* discussion of the fourth factor conspicuously omits this phrasing. Apparently abandoning the idea that any factor enjoys primacy, *Campbell* instructs that "[a]ll [four factors] are to be explored, and the results weighed together, in light of the purposes of copyright."

    Texaco, 60 F.3d at 926 (1994).

This is good, because courts usually find that a use is not fair when the defendant loses the fourth factor. But do not get too excited, for courts also will consider markets beyond journal subscriptions, such as the secondary market for article and book chapter reprints, and royalty or licensing fees.[30] And the news does not get better. Not only will a court examine the market impact of the individual defendant's copying, but also "whether unrestricted and widespread conduct of the sort engaged in by the defendant . . . would result in a substantially adverse impact on the potential market for the original."[31] In other words, what would be the impact if a lot of other people do what this particular defendant did?

Both the district and appellate courts in *Texaco* noted that the publishers lost sales of additional journal subscriptions, back issues and back volumes, and also licensing revenue and fees. As did the district court, the appeals court also thought it significant that the publishers of the journals from which articles were copied were registered with the Copyright Clearance Center, thereby making it easy to pay royalties.[32] Both the district court and the appeals court found that the fourth factor favored the publishers.

As Texaco lost the first, third, and fourth factors, the appeals court upheld the lower court decision and found that Texaco had infringed. But you should not conclude from the *Texaco* decision that a corporate library can *never* route journals to researchers; the appeals court did *not* say that all copying in for-profit companies is infringing. Indeed, the court limited its ruling "to the institutional, systematic, archival multiplication of copies revealed by the record—the precise copying that the parties stipulated should be the basis for the District Court's decision now on appeal and for which licenses are in fact available."[33]

Remember that fair use is an equitable concept; whether a use is or is not fair depends on the particular facts of each case. A company that fails to purchase as many subscriptions as it needs and uses large-scale copying—either by the library or by employees—as a substitute for subscriptions risks liability as an infringer. This is true not

---

30. *Texaco,* 60 F.3d at 927–29.

31. *Campbell,* 510 U.S. at 590.

32. Though the publishers still have not established a conventional market for the direct sale and distribution of individual articles, they have created, primarily through the CCC, a workable market for institutional users to obtain licenses for the right to produce their own copies of individual articles via photocopying. The District Court found that many major corporations now subscribe to the CCC systems for photocopying licenses.

    Texaco, 60 F.3d at 930.

33. *Id.* at 931.

only in for-profit corporations such as Texaco, but even for non-profit educational institutions. The lesson from *Texaco* is not that fair use doesn't exist in the corporate sector, but instead that there are limits as to what libraries and what employees of an organization may do. Let's take a closer look at fair use in the for-profit sector. We need to recognize first that there are different types of for-profit entities, and that under copyright law, they are not all created equal. Two of the earliest infringement lawsuits against corporations for internal copying were orchestrated by the Association of American Publishers in the early 1980s. Both resulted in out-of-court settlements. American Cyanamid, the defendant in the first suit, relinquished all fair use rights and agreed to make payments to the Copyright Clearance Center for internal copying. The other corporation, Squibb, also joined the CCC, but under its settlement did not have to pay royalties for a small amount (6%) of their copying that was considered fair use.[34]

A decade later, as noted earlier, newsletter publisher Washington Business Information sued the Collier, Shannon & Scott law firm for making cover-to-cover copies of newsletters and sending them to attorneys throughout the firm. And in 1999 LeBoeuf, Lamb, Greene & MacRae, a large New York–based law firm, purchased a multi-year photocopying license with the CCC and paid an undisclosed settlement to avoid an infringement suit brought by four publishers.[35]

Then we have litigation against the for-profit information brokers. In the early 1990s, the West Publishing Company, the largest U.S. legal publisher, sued several for-profit information brokers for infringement as a response to their copying and distributing the proprietary features in West's court reporters.[36] These cases resulted in victories for West, either through injunction or settlement.

We ought not forget litigation against copyshops for producing coursepacks for college students. The first was a successful suit against the Gnomon Corporation, which operated several stores in the Northeast. In 1980 Gnomon entered into a consent decree enjoining the company from making multiple copies of journal articles and book chapters to produce coursepacks unless they had written permission from the copyright owners, or written certification from the

---

34. Michael C. Elmer & John F. Harnick, *In-House Photocopying Subject to New Challenges,* LEGAL TIMES, Apr. 25 1983, at 11.
35. Anna Snider, *Firm Settles Photocopy Charges,* NAT'L L.J., Mar. 22, 1999.
36. West Publ'g Co. v. California Law Retrieval Serv., No. 93-7137 (C.D. Cal., filed Nov. 24, 1993); West Publ'g Co. v. Aaron/Smith, No. 89-CV-2693 (N.D. Ga., filed Dec. 1, 1989); West Publ'g v. Faxlaw, No. 91-CV-293 (S.D. Fla., filed Feb. 12, 1991).

faculty member that the copying complied with the *Classroom Guidelines,* which are part of the legislative history of the 1976 Copyright Act.[37] A year later, Harper & Row brought a successful suit against Tyco Copy Service. Here, the copyshop agreed to settle the case on terms similar to the Gnomon settlement.[38]

A case that received more publicity than either *Gnomon* and *Tyco* involved a lawsuit by Addison-Wesley Publishing against New York University, several members of its faculty, and a private copyshop for creating coursepacks. The parties settled, with NYU agreeing to inform its faculty members of NYU's photocopying policies and to encourage them to comply with the *Classroom Guidelines.*[39]

A few years later came the case with some staying power: Kinko's, the venerable institution seemingly found in every college town, was sued for copying articles and portions of books and compiling them into coursepacks.[40] Kinko's argued that the copying was educational because it was done for students at the request of their instructors. The court did not agree. Not only did the court describe the copying as non-educational and commercial, but it also criticized Kinko's internal policies and procedures and its failure to educate and adequately supervise its employees, and held that Kinko's was a willful infringer.

Michigan Document Services (MDS), an Ann Arbor copyshop, apparently failed to learn any lessons from the *Kinko's* decision. In the MDS case,[41] a decision by a three-judge panel of the U.S. Court of Appeals for the Sixth Circuit in favor of MDS was later reversed by the entire court. The original three-judge appellate panel considered MDS's copying "educational," and held that it was a fair use. But MDS's happiness was short-lived. The entire court reversed the panel's decision, holding that the copyshop's systematic and premeditated copying for commercial motivation was infringing, noting also that MDS's copying went beyond the *Classroom Guidelines.*

Litigation against copyshops did not end with the MDS case. The Copyright Clearance Center coordinated separate lawsuits in 2002 and 2003 against copyshops located near universities, with the earlier suit

---

37. Basic Books, Inc. v. Gnomon Corp., Copyright L. Dec. (CCH) ¶ 25,145, at 15,847 (D. Conn. 1980).
38. Harper & Row, Publishers, Inc. v. Tyco Copy Serv., Inc., Copyright L. Dec. (CCH) ¶ 25,230, at 16,361 (D. Conn. 1981).
39. Addison-Wesley Publ'g v. New York Univ., 1983 Copyright L. Dec. (CCH) ¶ 25,544, at 18,203 (S.D.N.Y. 1983).
40. Basic Books, Inc. v. Kinko's Graphics Corp., 758 F. Supp. 1522 (S.D.N.Y. 1991).
41. Princeton Univ. Press v. Michigan Document Servs., 99 F.3d 1381 (6th Cir. 1996).

filed against Gainesville, Florida's Custom Copies & Textbooks,[42] and the latter against Los Angeles–based Westwood Copies.[43] Westwood Copies quickly settled its case for an undisclosed amount of damages.[44]

On first blush, looking at all of these cases may give those who work in the private sector more shivers than actors performing *Hair* in Central Park in February. But remember that every fact counts in a fair use analysis, and no two cases are the same.

Take, for example, the status of the defendants. In the lawsuits against the pharmaceutical companies, the defendants were corporations that were *not* in the business of directly profiting from making copies. These lawsuits resulted in settlements, not in court decisions. By contrast, the other lawsuits targeted for-profit document delivery companies and for-profit copyshops which directly profit from making copies of copyrighted works. The latter group— companies whose business is making money from making copies—are on much thinner ice than pharmaceutical companies or other businesses that do *not* directly profit from copying copyrighted works.

So what should we make of *Texaco?* The court of appeals did *not* say that all copying in for-profit companies is infringing. The Association of American Publishers and the Copyright Clearance Center might believe—and they also may want librarians to believe—that *all* corporate copying requires permission or payment of royalties. But that is not what the court wrote, and it is not how fair use is applied. The appeals court noted that its decision was limited to the facts before it:

> Our ruling does not consider photocopying for personal use by an individual. Our ruling is confined to the institutional, systematic, archival multiplication of copies revealed by the record—the precise copying that the parties stipulated should be the basis for the District Court's decision now on appeal and for which licenses are in fact available.[45]

The Bottom Line: If you have an identical situation to that in *Texaco*—(1) systematic and extensive routing of journals to corporate researchers; (2) who make copies of entire articles; (3) without even reading them or otherwise using them for any purpose; and (4)

---

42. Steven Zeitchik & Judith Rosen, *CCC Charges Copy Shop with Infringement,* PUBLISHERS WKLY., Oct. 21, 2002, at 9.

43. Steven Zeitchik, *Four Publishers Sue L.A. Copy Shop,* PUBLISHERS WKLY., Jan. 27, 2003, at 113.

44. Judith Rosen, *CCC Settles with Copy Shop,* PUBLISHERS WKLY., Mar. 10, 2003, at 18. For even more recent settlements, see Judith Rosen, *CCC Wins Copy Shop Settlements,* PUBLISHERS WKLY., Nov. 17, 2003, at 16.

45. *Texaco,* 60 F.3d at 931.

merely file them away for possible later use (archiving) such that the effect is to multiply the number of subscriptions without actually subscribing to the needed number of copies; and (5) if there is an easy way to pay royalties, such as through the CCC—then the copying is not a fair use. If you do not have this same factual situation, you should examine *your* facts under the fair use test. *Texaco* did not eliminate fair use in the commercial sector. Now let's see how *Texaco* might play out in the non-profit educational sector.

Fair Use in the Educational Sector

In its decision in *Texaco,* the court of appeals wrote:

> We do not deal with the question of copying by an individual, for personal use in research or otherwise (not for resale), recognizing that under the fair use doctrine or the *de minimis* doctrine, such a practice by an individual might well not constitute an infringement. In other words, our opinion does not decide the case that would arise if Chickering were a professor or an independent scientist engaged in copying and creating files for independent research, as opposed to being employed by an institution in the pursuit of his research on the institution's behalf.[46]

Does a professor act independently of her university when she writes a book or an article? My answer is yes. Unless the professor was hired by the university to create a particular work under circumstances that would make it a "work made for hire," or unless the university otherwise owns or shares copyright with the professor in the work (which, under university policies, is more likely when a professor or researcher uses significant university funding and other resources), I think that a professor does act independently of the

---

46. *Texaco,* 60 F.3d at 916.

university when she writes a book or an article.[47] And as the appellate court in *Texaco* wrote, its opinion did not address that issue.

Would the appeals court have reached a different conclusion if Dr. Chickering was a professor at a university rather than a researcher in a for-profit corporation? As noted above, the court took great pains to limit the decision to the facts before it. Libraries may continue to route journals to their faculty, and their faculty may copy individual articles. But there are limits. A court might very well decide against a university if the copying is systematic, extensive, and archival—if, for example, a university library routes issues to the dozen members of the economics department, and the faculty extensively copy articles from the issues for later use. (Realistically, of course, we know that materials routed to faculty are unlikely to get beyond the first few names on the routing list).

---

47. "Works made for hire" are owned by the employer. Whether a work is a "work made for hire" is more complex than is presented here but, generally, if the creator is an independent contractor, the work must come within one of nine categories listed in section 101 of the Act where "work made for hire" is defined, and there also must be a written agreement specifying that the work is a "work made for hire."

    If the work was prepared by an employee, whether it is a "work made for hire" depends on (1) control by the employer over the work, such as whether the work was prepared at the employer's location, whether the employer determined *how* the work was done, and whether the employer provided equipment or other means that supported the creation of the work; (2) control by the employer over the employee; and (3) the status and conduct of the employer, such as the employer being in the business of producing these kinds of works. *See* U.S. COPYRIGHT OFFICE, CIRCULAR 9: WORKS MADE FOR HIRE UNDER THE 1976 COPYRIGHT ACT (rev'd Dec. 2000).

    Most university policies assume that a professor owns his or her scholarly work unless there is significant investment by the university. *See, e.g.,* UNIVERSITY OF CALIFORNIA, OFFICE OF TECHNOLOGY TRANSFER, COPYRIGHTED WORKS CREATED AT THE UNIVERSITY OF CALIFORNIA, *available at* <http://www.ucop.edu/ott/crworks.html>.

The Classroom Guidelines and the ALA Model Policy

4.3. Agreement on Guidelines for Classroom Copying in Not-for-Profit Educational Institutions

For teachers

   ❧ Single copy for research or teaching

For students

   ❧ One copy
   ❧ Brevity and spontaneity limitations
   ❧ Cumulative effect not harmful,

But

   ❧ No anthologies, compilations, or collective works

House Report No. 94-1476

Section 107 of the Act provides that "the fair use of a copyrighted work . . . for purposes such as criticism, comment, news reporting, teaching (including multiple copies for classroom use), scholarship, or research, is not an infringement." The Act itself sheds no more light on what is fair use in an educational setting. We do have some guidelines, however, courtesy of a 1976 agreement by the Ad Hoc Committee of Educational Institutions and Organizations on Copyright Law Revision, the Authors League of America, and the Association of American Publishers. The *Agreement on Guidelines for Classroom Copying in Not-for-Profit Educational Institutions* was included in the House Report as part of the 1976 Act's legislative history.[48] Following are the highlights of the *Guidelines.*

> (1) A single copy of a journal or newspaper article, a book chapter, or a drawing may be made by or for a teacher for research or to help teach or prepare to teach a class.

---

48. H.R. REP. NO. 94-1476, at 68–70.

(2) A teacher may provide one copy of a copyrighted work to each pupil in his or her class (i.e., multiple copies) under the following conditions:

- A. Brevity: (1) a 2,500 word article, or, if article is greater than 2,500 words, a 1,000 word excerpt or 10%, whichever is less (but at least 500 words).
- B. Spontaneity: (1) The copying is made at the teacher's insistence and inspiration (rather than being directed from above by a principal, department chair, or dean); and (2) There was no time to get permission from the copyright owner.
- C. Cumulative effect: (1) The copying is done for a single course (but multiple sections of the same course are okay); (2) No more than one article from a single author or three articles from a journal volume are copied during a class term; and (3) There are no more than nine instances of copying during a term, and the same materials are not copied from term to term.
- D. You cannot copy to create anthologies, compilations, or collective works (i.e., "coursepacks").

The *Guidelines* are quite restrictive. For example, a teacher may not copy for her students an entire article if it is longer than 2,500 words. Although the typical *Newsweek* or *Time* article will fit comfortably within the 2,500-word limit, that is not true for articles in scholarly journals.

The American Association of University Professors and the Association of American Law Schools criticized the *Guidelines* "particularly with respect to multiple copying, as being too restrictive with respect to classroom situations at the university and graduate level" and would not endorse them.[49] Acknowledging this criticism, the House Judiciary Committee noted that the "purpose of the . . . guidelines is to state the minimum and not the maximum standards of educational fair use," and that "there may be instances in which copying which does not fall within the guidelines . . . may nonetheless be permitted under the criteria of fair use."[50]

You will note that the *Guidelines* do not permit the creation of coursepacks. As you read earlier, many courts agree. You must have permission to use each item, regardless of who does the copying—a for-profit copyshop, a non-profit university copy center, or a teacher. Coursepacks require permission. Period. If a teacher cannot get permission to include an article or book chapter in a coursepack, then it should be left out.

---

49. *Id.* at 72.
50. *Id.*

4.4. ALA Model Policy (March 1982)

Single copy of a chapter or article for research or for reserve

Multiple copies

- ❧ Reasonable: amount of reading, number of students, timing . . .
- ❧ Notice of copyright
- ❧ No detrimental effect

Generally

- ❧ Less than six copies
- ❧ Not repetitive
- ❧ Not for profit
- ❧ Not for consumable works
- ❧ Not anthologize

The *Classroom Guidelines* did not address copying for library "reserve." In response to librarians' wish for some guidance, and also the belief that the Guidelines were unrealistic in the college and university setting, in 1982 the American Library Association prepared a *Model Policy Concerning College and University Photocopying for Classroom Research and Library Reserve Use.*[51] Following are its highlights.

Copies for Instructors

Like the *Classroom Guidelines*, the ALA *Model Policy* provides that an instructor may, for scholarly research or use in teaching or preparing to teach a class, make a single copy of a chapter of a book; a journal or newspaper article; a short story, short essay, or short poem; or a chart, diagram, graph drawing, cartoon or picture.

Copies for Students

The *Model Policy* follows the *Classroom Guidelines*, including permitting distributing a single copy to students in a class without permission so long as (a) the same material is not distributed every semester, (b) the material includes a copyright notice on the first

---

51. MODEL POLICY, *available at* <http:/www.cni.org/docs/infopols/ALA.html>.

page of the item, and (c) students are not assessed a fee beyond the actual cost of the copying.

After repeating the *Classroom Guidelines'* brevity standards, the *Model Policy* notes that they are not realistic in a university setting and that faculty "should not feel hampered by these guidelines, although they should attempt a 'selective and sparing' use of photocopied, copyrighted material." The Policy notes that copying should not have a significant detrimental impact on the market for copyrighted works, and, therefore, that instructors usually should restrict using an item to one course and not repeatedly copy excerpts from one journal or author without permission.

Copies for Reserve

The *Model Policy* views library reserve as an extension of the classroom, and provides that at the request of a faculty member, a library may copy and place on reserve an entire article, a book chapter, or a poem. Multiple copies for reserve are permitted if

- ∞ The amount of material copied is reasonable in relation to the total amount of reading assigned for the course;
- ∞ The number of copies made is reasonable in light of the number of students, the difficulty and timing of the assignment, and other courses which assigned the same material;
- ∞ Each copy includes a notice of copyright; and
- ∞ The effect of the copying is not detrimental to the market (i.e., the library should own one printed copy of the work).

The *Model Policy* adds these caveats:

- ∞ Do not place more than five copies on reserve for a single course;
- ∞ Avoid repetitive copying; do not copy the same materials semester after semester;
- ∞ Do not profit from the copying;
- ∞ Do not copy consumable works (such as workbooks); and
- ∞ Do not create anthologies (including coursepacks).

Electronic Reserves

4.5. E-Reserves

- Legal copy
- Copyright (©) notice and credits
- Reasonable amount
- For teacher and enrolled students
- Non-repetitive
- Course/faculty name retrieval
- Retrieve by course or instructor's name

I think that electronic reserves are not very different from paper reserves, and that the *Model Policy* can provide a framework for e-reserve. We can also borrow some ideas from the Conference on Fair Use's (CONFU) *Fair-Use Guidelines for Electronic Reserve Systems*, even though the conferees never reached consensus on them.[52]

Before offering some e-reserve guidelines, I want to comment on a statement in the draft electronic reserve guidelines: "The complexities of the electronic environment, and the growing potential for implicating copyright infringements, raise the need for a fresh understanding of fair use."[53] Horse Feathers! The issue of electronic reserve is not terribly complex, and it does not require a fresh understanding of fair use. Although it is easy to send a digital copy to lots of people, that does not mean that an entire university community wants to receive—let alone read—the article Professor Quincy Wagstaff assigns

---

52. THE CONFERENCE ON FAIR USE, FINAL REPORT TO THE COMMISSIONER ON THE CONCLU-SION OF THE CONFERENCE ON FAIR USE (Nov. 1988). The *Final Report* notes (at pp. 15–16) that the working group reached an impasse over the scope and language of possible electronic reserve guidelines. However, some members of the working group continued to meet, and drafted for comment proposed guidelines. At the CONFU plenary session on September 6, 1996, several organizations, including the American Association of Law Libraries, the American Council on Learned Societies, the Music Library Association, and the Special Libraries Association, supported the draft. Others, including ASCAP, the Association of American Publishers, the Authors Guild/Authors Registry, and the Association of Research Libraries, did not. It was ultimately decided that the proposed electronic reserve guidelines would not be disseminated as a formal work product of CONFU.

The *Final Report,* which does not include the draft electronic reserve guidelines, can be found at the Patent and Trademark Office website <http://www.uspto.gov>. The proferred draft electronic reserve guidelines may be found at the University of Texas's Office of General Counsel's intellectual property site <http://www.utsystem.edu/ogc/intellectualproperty/rsrvguid.htm>.

53. DRAFT FAIR USE GUIDELINES FOR ELECTRONIC RESERVE SYSTEMS.

to his Huxley College students. Furthermore, with appropriate controls, you can minimize the risk of abuse, unlikely as they may be. Finally, as an equitable concept, fair use is flexible enough to apply to nearly any type of situation and any type of format; that is its elegance.

Incorporating the "best of" the CONFU Guidelines and the ALA *Model Policy*, here are my suggested E-reserve guidelines:

- ᛒ At the request of an instructor, E-Reserves may include entire articles, chapters, and poems;

- ᛒ The amount of material on reserve for a course should be reasonable in relation to the total amount of reading assigned for the course;

- ᛒ Access to E-Reserve documents is limited to the instructors and to students registered in the particular course for which the materials are placed on reserve;

- ᛒ Documents in the E-Reserve system for a particular course may be retrieved by course number or name, or by using the instructor's name;

- ᛒ Documents on reserve for a specific course shall remain in the E-Reserve system only during the semester in which the course is taught, but short-term access to E-Reserve documents may be provided to students who have not completed the course;

- ᛒ Simultaneous access to a particular document is limited to a maximum of five individuals;

- ᛒ The introductory screen to the E-reserve system shall include the following notice:

> WARNING: THE E-RESERVE DATABASE IN-
> CLUDES COPYRIGHTED WORKS. THE MAKING
> OF A COPY MAY BE SUBJECT TO THE UNITED
> STATES COPYRIGHT LAW (TITLE 17 UNITED
> STATES CODE). DO NOT FURTHER DISTRIB-
> UTE COPYRIGHTED WORKS INCLUDED IN THIS
> DATABASE.

- ᛒ If a copyright notice appears on the copy of the work, that notice should be included on the digital copy;

- ᛒ Documents in the E-Reserve system will include accurate copyright management information, including (but not necessarily limited to) the author, source, and date of publication;

- ᛒ The instructor or the library should possess a lawfully made copy of any document placed on E-Reserve;

⁖ Students shall not be charged a fee to access or use the E-reserve system; and

⁖ The university shall set up appropriate control mechanisms to prevent the copying, public display, or public distribution of materials on the E-Reserve system beyond that which is permitted by fair use (section 107) or other provisions of the Copyright Act.

Chapter Five
THE LIBRARY EXEMPTION
(SECTION 108)

໖໐໕

In addition to fair use, libraries and archives have rights under section 108 of the Act. Employees of qualifying libraries who are acting under the scope of their employment may, under certain circumstances, make one copy of a work without needing to receive permission from the copyright owner or pay royalties. But first, the library must qualify for the exemption.

5.1. Section 108(a)
The Library Exemption

A library or employee acting within the scope of employment:

- ໖ One copy
- ໖ No direct or indirect commercial advantage
- ໖ Open or available collection
- ໖ Personal access or interlibrary loan
- ໖ Copyright notice
  - from the copy reproduced, or
  - legend

Qualifying for the Exemption (Section 108(a))

To qualify for the library exemption

- ✌ the library's collection must be open to the public or to researchers;
- ✌ copying or distribution must be made without any purpose of direct or indirect commercial advantage; and
- ✌ the copy must include a notice of copyright.

Each of these requirements merits discussion.

Open or Available Collection

> ...the collections of the library or archives are (i) open to the public, or (ii) available not only to researchers affiliated with the library or archives or with the institution of which it is a part, but also to other persons doing research in a specialized field.[1]

The exemption is not limited to "public" libraries. Permitting visitors to use the collection, or participating in interlibrary loan arrangements under which a library makes its collection available to others, will meet the "open or available" requirement. This means that libraries whose doors are not wide open, such as corporations and law firms, many governmental and trade association libraries, and private college and university libraries, may qualify for section 108.

Direct or Indirect Commercial Advantage

> ...the reproduction or distribution must be made without any purpose of direct or indirect commercial advantage.[2]

The Senate and House committees considering the proposed legislation had different interpretations of this requirement. The Senate Judiciary Committee wrote that this clause prohibited libraries in the for-profit sector from providing copies to their employees unless the copying qualified as a fair use or the organization received permission.[3] The House Judiciary Committee had a very different opinion. It wrote that "the 'advantage' referred to in this clause must attach to the immediate commercial motivation behind the reproduction or

---

1. 17 U.S.C. § 108(a)(2) (2000).
2. *Id.* § 108(a)(1).
3. S. REP. NO. 94-473, at 67.

distribution itself, rather than to the ultimate profit-making motivation of the enterprise in which the library is located."[4] Unlike the
Senate, the House believed that libraries in the for-profit sector *could*
qualify for the library exemption. It wrote

> Isolated, spontaneous making of single photocopies by a library in
> a for-profit organization, without any systematic effort to substitute
> photocopying for subscriptions or purchases, would be covered by
> section 108, even though copies are furnished to the employees of
> the organization for use in their work. Similarly, for-profit libraries
> could participate in interlibrary arrangements for exchange of
> photocopies, as long as the production or distribution was not "sys-
> tematic." These activities, by themselves, would ordinarily not be
> considered "for direct or indirect commercial advantages," since the
> "advantage" referred to in this clause must attach to the immediate,
> commercial motivation behind the reproduction or distribution
> itself, rather than to the ultimate profit-making motivation behind
> the enterprise in which the library is located. On the other hand,
> section 108 would not excuse reproduction or distribution if there
> were a commercial motive behind the actual making or distributing
> of the copies, if multiple copies were made or distributed, or if the
> photocopying activities were "systematic" in the sense that their aim
> was to substitute for subscriptions or purchases.[5]

The House Judiciary Committee's interpretation was supported by
the Conference Committee, which was composed of members of both
the House and the Senate. The Conference Committee concluded

> Another point of interpretation involves the meaning of 'indirect
> commercial advantage,' as used in section 108(a)(1), in the case of
> libraries or archival collection within industrial, profit-making, or
> proprietary institutions. As long as the library or archives meets the
> criteria in section 108(a) and the other requirements of the section,
> including the prohibitions against multiple and systematic copying
> in subsection (g), the conferees consider that isolated, spontaneous
> making of single photocopies by a library or archives in a for-profit
> organization without any commercial motivation, or participation by
> such a library or archives in interlibrary arrangements, would come
> within the scope of section 108.[6]

---

4. H.R. REP. NO. 94-1476, at 75.
5. *Id.* at 75.
6. H.R. REP. NO. 94-1733 (Conf.), at 73–74 (1976), *reprinted in* 1976 U.S.C.C.A.N.
   at 5810.

The Bottom Line: Libraries affiliated with for-profit organizations may qualify for the library exemption. All libraries—those in for- and non-profit institutions—must avoid the § 108(g) prohibitions against multiple and systematic copying, discussed below.

Document Delivery

The direct or indirect commercial advantage prohibition means that a library loses section 108 protection if it profits from making copies. The first question for every library that provides document delivery services is whether it profits from its services. The first step, then, is comparing how much it costs the library to make a copy with how much you charge. You may go beyond the obvious costs of paper and toner, and include all direct and indirect costs, such as equipment, supplies, and personnel.

An Association of Research Libraries (ARL) study from the mid 1990s may help you determine if you are within this mandate.[7] In its report, the ARL noted that it cost research libraries, on average, $18.35 to borrow an item, and $9.48 to lend an item (the average cost for *all* libraries was $12.02 to borrow and $7.25 to lend). Costs obviously vary from one library to the next, and presumably are higher today.

I can hear some librarians saying, "We're not making money on document delivery; the revenue we receive just enables us to enhance our collection." Whoa! If your document delivery activities enable you to "enhance your collection," you are either making money from document delivery (which you cannot do), or you are not counting all of your expenses (which indeed may be the case).

There is no definitive answer as to how much you may charge. But if you press me for an answer, how about these university library document delivery hypotheticals?

ಐ Freedonia State College has a base document delivery transaction charge of $5.00, plus $.25 per page. Freedonia State, then, charges $7.50 for a 10-page article, and $10.00 for a 20-page article. I doubt that the college is making any money from its document delivery services.

---

7. ASSOCIATION OF RESEARCH LIBRARIES, INTERLIBRARY LOAN AND DOCUMENT DELIVERY (ILL/DD) PERFORMANCE MEASURES STUDY, EXECUTIVE SUMMARY LL/DD PERFORMANCE MEASURES STUDY (May 1998), *available at* <http://www.arl.org>.

ᴥ The University of Freedonia charges $5.00 plus $.50 per page. If UF has determined that it costs $10 to supply a 10-page article and $15 to supply a 20-page article, it will not violate the "direct or indirect advantage" prohibition.

ᴥ The library at the Freedonia School of Medicine charges non-profit institutions $10 per article, and for-profit institutions $20. Again, if this merely recovers actual costs, the pricing structure is fine. The library may choose to subsidize document delivery to the non-profit sector, but it cannot profit from its services to the for-profit sector.

ᴥ The University of Freedonia Law Library has a minimum copying charge of $15 for individuals and non-profit institutions, and $20 for businesses. To that add a $.50 per-page photocopying charge. For business requests it also adds a $1 per-minute search fee, with a minimum search charge of $15.00. In other words, a ten-page article costs a business $40.00. The law library's charges certainly appear to be beyond what is permitted under section 108. This does not mean that the library cannot provide document delivery services. It may, but it must pay royalties. The library would be wise to register with the Copyright Clearance Center, and pay royalty fees to the CCC.

ᴥ The Freedonia Institute of Technology (FIT) Library sets up a fee-based document delivery unit (FIT-DOC). It has its own budget and hires its own staff. It advertises its document delivery services throughout the state and the region, especially to the corporate scientific community. It charges non-profits a flat $25 per article charge, and for-profit organizations $35 per article, plus whatever royalties it pays for copying. It also does online research at a charge of $50 per half hour. FIT-DOC is a member of the CCC and pays royalties to the CCC. This certainly looks and smells like a business, even though it operates out of a state-supported university. It certainly seems appropriate for FIT-DOC to pay royalties and belong to the CCC.

The typical library (if one exists) photocopies documents—mostly journal articles—for other libraries, and occasionally for the commercial sector. Other libraries operate extensive document delivery services that may operate as a separate division within their institution (typically a university library), with their own budget and staff. Some question whether their activities may qualify as a fair use or under the section 108 library exemption, or instead require payment of royalties.

The Association of American Publishers has stated that the activities of "fee-based and technology-enhanced copying and distribution services of libraries . . . are indistinguishable in purpose and effect from those of commercial document delivery suppliers."[8] The AAP's position echoed an earlier opinion from a former Register of Copyrights, who wrote that large scale library photocopying services that employ full time photocopying staff, advertise, and make lots and lots of copies engage in systematic copying.[9]

In fact, there is no definite answer when a library document delivery service becomes systematic, and we have only one court decision—an old one at that—that involves library document delivery. In *Williams & Wilkins Co. v. United States,*[10] the U.S. Supreme Court upheld, by a four-to-four vote, a U.S. Court of Claims decision holding that large scale copying by the National Library of Medicine and the National Institute of Health was a fair use. Although the NIH copied only for their own staff, about 12% of NLM's requests came from private or commercial organizations, drug companies in particular.

How *William & Wilkins* would be decided today is anyone's guess. You may consider what the appellate court in *Texaco* wrote about the advent of licensing since the 1973 *Williams & Wilkins* decision:

> Whatever the situation may have been previously, before the development of a market for institutional users to obtain licenses to photocopy articles [citing *Williams & Wilkins*] . . . it is now appropriate to consider the loss of licensing revenues in evaluating "the effect of the use upon the potential market for or value of" journal articles. It is especially appropriate to do so with respect to copying of articles from *Catalysis,* a publication as to which a photocopying license is now available. We do not decide how the fair use balance would be resolved if a photocopying license for *Catalysis* articles were not currently available.[11]

The dissenting judge in *Texaco* had a very different opinion. Referring (as did the majority) to *Williams & Wilkins,* he wrote that he disagreed with the majority that "a reasonable and customary use becomes unfair when the copyright holder develops a way to exact an additional price for the same product," and that what Dr. Chickering (the Texaco scientist) did was a customary fact of copyright life that should be considered a fair use.[12]

---

8. ASSOCIATION OF AMERICAN PUBLISHERS, STATEMENT OF THE ASSOCIATION OF AMERICAN PUBLISHERS ON DOCUMENT DELIVERY (Apr. 1994).

9. U.S. COPYRIGHT OFFICE, REPORT OF THE REGISTER OF COPYRIGHTS: LIBRARY REPRODUCTION OF COPYRIGHTED WORKS (17 U.S.C. § 108) 140 (1983) [hereinafter REGISTER'S REPORT].

10. 487 F.2d 1345 (Ct. Cl. 1973) (*aff'd* by an equally divided Court, 420 U.S. 376 (1975)).

11. *Texaco,* 60 F.3d 913, 931.

12. *Id.* at 934 (Jacobs, J., dissenting).

Thirty years after it was decided, what remain instructive about *Williams & Wilkins* are the NIH's and NLM's policies and practices. You may want to consider them when you create ILL/document delivery policies for your library.

NIH made only single copies of articles, and generally would copy only forty or fifty pages, although longer articles would be copied with permission of a high level supervisor. As a general rule they copied only a single article from a journal issue. Exceptions were routinely made, but NIH would not copy more than half of an issue.[13]

NLM would make only single copies of articles, and would not copy an entire issue. Nor would they copy articles from 104 journals that were included on a "widely available" list. NLM would not honor what it considered an excessive number of requests from an individual or an institution: not more than twenty requests from an individual or thirty from an institution, within a month. NLM would copy no more than one article from a single issue, or three from a volume. Generally, they would not copy more than fifty pages.[14]

With NIH's and NLM's policies in hand, here are document delivery guidelines you may want to consider for your library. If they seem too liberal or conservative to you, adjust them to suit your taste.

Document Delivery Guidelines[15]

1. The library pays royalties whenever appropriate, regardless of whether a title is registered with the Copyright Clearance Center (CCC) or another licensing organization. Royalties may be paid to the CCC or directly to the copyright owner.

2. The library will not make more than one copy of an item at a time.

3. The library will make multiple copies of an item for the same user (including the institution with which the user is affiliated) whether made simultaneously or over a period of time, only with permission of the copyright owner or upon payment of royalties.

4. The library will copy no more than two articles from a periodical issue, and never more than one-third of an issue, without permission.

5. The library will not fill a request if it knows that the requestor plans to sell the copy.

---

13. *Williams & Wilkins,* 487 F.2d at 1348.
14. *Id.* at 1348–49.
15. Guidelines adapted from James S. Heller, *The Impact of Recent Litigation on Interlibrary Loan and Document Delivery,* 88 L. LIBR. J. 158, 176–77 (1996).

6. If the library first photocopies materials for subsequent fax transmission, it will destroy the photocopy after the transmission is complete.

7. If the library downloads or scans an document to transmit it to a requestor, it will destroy the electronic copy after the transmission is complete.

8. The library will not honor an excessive number of requests from an individual or an institution for articles from the same journal title. The CONTU Guidelines may provide some guidance as to when requests are excessive.

9. The library may fill requests from other libraries that include an attestation that the request complies with the Copyright Act or the CONTU Guidelines. The library will not provide copies if it knows that the request exceeds fair use or the section 108 exemption.

10. The library will include with the copy it makes, if readily available, the "notice of copyright" from the work copied. The library will include on every copy it makes the following notice: "THIS MATERIAL IS SUBJECT TO THE UNITED STATES COPYRIGHT LAW; FURTHER REPRODUCTION IN VIOLATION OF THAT LAW IS PROHIBITED."

Notice of Copyright

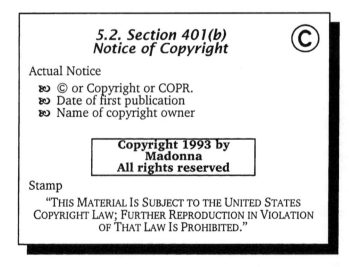

5.2. Section 401(b) Notice of Copyright ©

Actual Notice
- © or Copyright or COPR.
- Date of first publication
- Name of copyright owner

Copyright 1993 by
Madonna
All rights reserved

Stamp
"THIS MATERIAL IS SUBJECT TO THE UNITED STATES COPYRIGHT LAW; FURTHER REPRODUCTION IN VIOLATION OF THAT LAW IS PROHIBITED."

...the reproduction or distribution of the work includes a notice of copyright that appears on the copy or phonorecord that is reproduced under the provisions of this section, or includes a legend stating that the work may be protected by copyright if no such notice can be found on the copy or phonorecord that is reproduced under the provisions of this section.[16]

First, understand that you may not always be able to find a formal copyright notice. Since the United States joined the Berne Convention in 1989, a work does not need the notice to be copyrighted. If a work qualifies for protection, it is copyrighted when it is created, whether or not it has the formal notice.

As enacted in 1976, section 108(a)(3) required a library to include "a notice of copyright" on the material copied. It was unclear, however, whether that meant the section 401 statutory notice (for example, "© 2004, James S. Heller"), or merely a statement that the work copied may be protected by copyright. Section 108(a)(3) was amended by the 1998 Digital Millennium Copyright Act; the copy that you make should include a notice of copyright that appears on the document you are copying, or, if you cannot find the notice, a legend that the work may be protected.

Here is my take. When you copy journal articles, and the article itself includes a copyright notice, include it. If you are lucky, the copyright notice will appear on the first page of the article, either right after the author's name, or perhaps as a footnote. Unfortunately, many journal publishers do not include a copyright notice with each specific article, but instead only a general notice at the beginning of the issue, or elsewhere.

Finding the notice may not be easy. The U.S. Copyright Office lists ten places where a copyright notice may appear in a book, and an additional three places for periodical issues.[17] The truth is, looking for the copyright notice could be like spending a day at the circus: There are so many options it can make you dizzy. Make a diligent search for the formal notice, but do not make yourself crazy trying to find it.

If you cannot readily locate the formal copyright notice, stamp the article: "THIS MATERIAL IS SUBJECT TO THE U.S. COPYRIGHT LAW; FURTHER REPRODUCTION IN VIOLATION OF THAT LAW IS PROHIBITED." In fact, you should use the stamp *every time* your library makes a copy under the section 108 exemption. Here is what you should do:

∞ Prepare this notice in large (13-point) type;

∞ Put a box around it so it looks like this:

---

16. 17 U.S.C. § 108(a)(3) (2000).
17. 37 C.F.R. § 201.20 (2002).

> **THIS MATERIAL IS SUBJECT TO THE U.S. COPYRIGHT LAW; FURTHER REPRODUCTION IN VIOLATION OF THAT LAW IS PROHIBITED**

ಐ Send this to a stamp company and ask them to make you a stamp (in fact, make an extra stamp);

ಐ Purchase a red ink pad and extra red ink;

ಐ Whenever you make a copy—even when you *do* include the formal copyright notice—stamp the copy in the upper right hand corner.

What about chapters from books? The copyright notice can usually be found on the verso of the title page (although as you read above, Copyright Office regulations permit an Easter egg-like hunt). Whenever you copy a book chapter, look for the formal notice and include it with the copy you are making. I also would include the title page from the book, as it indicates where the chapter came from. Therefore, in addition to the chapter that you want to copy, also copy the title page and the copyright notice, which usually appears on the verso of the title page.

It helps to understand the distinction between copyright in books and articles. A book invariably is copyrighted in the name of the author or authors, or by the publisher. Except for collective works, the whole book generally has that single copyright. Finding the formal copyright notice for the book usually identifies correctly who has copyright in its chapters.

If a book consists of a variety of chapters written by different authors, it is a collective work, and each author may have copyright in his or her own chapter. The Copyright Office notes that a single notice applicable to the entire collective work indicates copyright protection for all of the contributions, regardless of who owns copyright in each separate contribution.[18] Therefore, treat all books the same: When you copy a chapter, also copy the title page and the general copyright notice. And use the red stamp, too.

Journals are different. A journal article will be copyrighted in the name of its author unless there is an express agreement to the contrary.[19] Copyright in the journal issue or volume—a *collective work—*

---

18. U.S. COPYRIGHT OFFICE, CIRCULAR 3: COPYRIGHT NOTICE (rev'd June 1999).
19. 17 U.S.C. § 201(c) (2000). For example, see U.S. COPYRIGHT OFFICE, FORM TX (registration form for nondramatic literary works).

is different from copyright in each individual article. Although the publisher typically has copyright in the collective work, the authors have copyright in their articles unless they signed those rights away. Although many publishers do in fact require authors to transfer copyright to them, you should not assume that the publisher of a journal holds copyright in the articles.

What about digital information? Copyright Office regulations provide several acceptable methods of affixing the copyright notice on what they call "works reproduced in machine-readable copies," and what we call digital works: (1) When the work is reproduced in visually perceptible printouts, affix the notice either with or near the title, or at the end of the work; (2) When the work appears on a terminal, affix the notice at sign-on, or keep it continuously displayed on the terminal; (3) When a container is used "as a permanent receptacle for the copies," affix the notice on a label.[20]

Here are two simple pieces of advice:

1. If you want to make a paper copy of a document that you find on a computer, look for the copyright notice on the screen, just as you would if the article was in print. If you find the notice, copy it, too. And use the red stamp.

2. If you electronically forward the digital article to someone, in your introductory e-mail message include the "THIS MATERIAL IS SUBJECT TO THE U.S. COPYRIGHT LAW; FURTHER REPRODUCTION IN VIOLATION OF THAT LAW IS PROHIBITED" notice. If you include this notice on a generic "Here is the article you requested" e-mail message that you send to everyone who requests copies, this will be automatic.

The Bottom Lines on section 108(a):

∞ The copying or distribution must be done with no purpose of direct or indirect commercial advantage. You may not profit, but you may recoup your costs. These may include direct factors such as the cost of photocopying and mailing the document, but also staff time.

∞ The library collection must be open to the public or available to researchers in a specialized field. Your library qualifies if it offers in-person access to the collection, or if you make your collection available through interlibrary lending. A library need not be open to the general public to fulfill this requirement.

∞ Include a notice of copyright on all copies provided, or a legend that the work may be protected. You will not always be able to

---

20. 37 C.F.R. § 201.20(g)(4) (2002).

find the statutory notice on the work copied. Whether you find the formal notice or not, use the "This Material Is Subject to the U.S. Copyright Law; Further Reproduction in Violation of That Law Is Prohibited" stamp (red, 13-point typeface, upper-right- hand corner of the first page of each document copied). Stamp . . . Stamp . . . Stamp. . . .

Copying Unpublished Works (Section 108(b))

5.3. Section 108(b) Copying Entire Unpublished Works

- ൠ Three copies
- ൠ For preservation and security, or for deposit for research use in another § 108(a) library

If
- ൠ The work is owned by the library asked to make the copy, and
- ൠ The digital version is used internally

As originally enacted in 1976, section 108(b) permitted a library to reproduce an unpublished work for the purpose of preservation and security, or for deposit for research use in another library, if the library making the reproduction owned a copy of the work. The copy had to be a facsimile copy, either in paper or microform. It could not be digital.

The 1998 Digital Millennium Copyright Act[21] amended 108(b). Among the changes was the elimination of the word "facsimile." Today a library may make up to three copies of an unpublished work in *any* format—including digital—for preservation and security or for deposit for research use in another library or archives.

But when Congress gives, it sometimes takes away. Expressing concern that "uncontrolled public access to the copies or phonorecords in digital formats could substantially harm the interests of the copyright owner by facilitating immediate, flawless and widespread reproduction and distribution of additional copies or phonorecords of the work,"[22] Congress included some restrictions regarding further distribution of digital copies, and where digital copies may be accessed.

Under section 108(b)(2), copies reproduced in digital format may not be "otherwise distributed in that format," nor "made available to the public in that format outside the premises of the library or archives." The provision prohibiting further distribution in digital format might seem to preclude a library that owns an unpublished work from sending a digital copy to another library for research

---

21. Pub. L. No. 105-304, 112 Stat. 2860 (Oct. 28, 1998).
22. S. REP. NO. 105-190, at 61 (1998).

purposes. The legislative history, however, indicates otherwise. In its report on the DMCA, the Senate Judiciary Committee wrote that

> [t]he amendment to subsection (b) permits a library or archive to make (for itself or another library or archive of the type described by clause (2) of subsection (a)) up to 3 copies or phonorecords for these purposes, rather than just one, and permits such copies or phonorecords to be made in digital as well as analog formats."[23]

It seems pretty clear that a library that owns a copy of an unpublished work may make an analog *or* a digital copy "for deposit for research use in another library."

The language mandating that digital copies may be used only within the library premises seems less ambiguous. A library that has made or received a digital copy of an unpublished work under 108(b) apparently may not make it available in that format to the public outside the premises. A library patron may use a digital copy onsite, but the library should not send a digital copy to an individual, nor permit access to a digital version, outside the walls of the library.

If a library receives a copy of an unpublished work under 108(b), may a researcher copy the work? The answer depends on the results of a section 107 analysis. Whether a use is a "fair use" depends on the facts, so the answer is a definite maybe. There probably is less room to copy an entire unpublished work than there is to copy a published work,[24] but section 107 itself says that "the fact that a work is unpublished shall not itself bar a finding of fair use if such a finding is made upon consideration of all the above factors."[25] And in some cases, a library may copy an unpublished work for a patron under section 108(e), which is discussed later in this chapter.

---

23. *Id.*
24. In 1983, a former Register of Copyrights, citing the Senate Judiciary Committee's report (S. REP. NO. 94-473, at 106), wrote that "there is *no* fair use copying [of unpublished works] permitted beyond that authorized by 108(b)." REGISTER'S REPORT, *supra* note 9, at 106. However, one of the premier treatises on copyright law includes this passage: "The scope of the fair use doctrine is considerably narrower with respect to unpublished works that are held confidential by their copyright owners. Note that 'confidential' differs subtly from 'unpublished.' If the author does not seek confidentiality, fair use is not necessarily precluded as to an unpublished work." MELVILLE B. NIMMER & DAVID NIMMER, NIMMER ON COPYRIGHT § 13.05[A][2][b] (2003). Nimmer continues: "The amendment thus reaffirms the holding in the *Nation* case—in particular, that the unpublished nature of a work is a 'key, though not necessarily determining factor tending to negate a determination of fair use'..." *Id.*
25. Section 107 was amended in 1992 to address the problem users had copying from unpublished works after the *Salinger* decision, discussed earlier. Pub. L. No. 102-492, 106 Stat. 3145 (Oct. 24, 1992).

The Bottom Line: A library may copy an unpublished work it already owns for preservation and security. The library may make up to three digital copies of the work, but the digital copies may only be used on-site. A library that owns an unpublished work may send a digital copy to another section 108 library. A library that receives a digital copy under 108(b) for research use similarly must limit access to the digital copy to within the library's walls.

Replacing Lost, Stolen, Damaged, or Deteriorating Copies of Published Works (Section 108(c))

> ### 5.4. Section 108(c) Copying Entire Published Works
>
> ໒ Three copies
> ໒ To replace a damaged, deteriorating, lost or stolen copy, or
> ໒ Obsolete format
>
> If
> ໒ Unused replacement unobtainable at a fair price
> ໒ Digital version is used internally

Section 108(c) permits a library, under some circumstances, to replace a lost, stolen, damaged, or deteriorating copy of a published work by photocopying if, after reasonable efforts, it determines that an unused replacement cannot be obtained at a fair price. Like 108(b), the 1976 Act required that the copy had to be a "facsimile." The DMCA eliminated the facsimile limitation, and now three digital copies may be made to replace a damaged, deteriorating, lost, or stolen copy. Like § 108(b), the digital version may be used only within the library premises.

Before a library may make a copy under 108(c) it must have made a reasonable effort to acquire an unused replacement copy, and must not have been able to find such a copy at a fair price. The legislative history notes that a reasonable effort varies according to the circumstances, but that a library should contact commonly-known trade sources such as dealers and jobbers, and generally the publisher or other copyright owner.[26] You do not need to contact *used* book dealers; you must only determine that you cannot get an unused copy at a fair price.

What is a fair price? A former Register of Copyrights wrote that a fair price for a book or periodical is that which is charged by a publisher, a dealer specializing in remainders, or a jobber or dealer in bulk issues of periodicals, but not if the only unused copies are available at high prices from rare or antique dealers.[27] The Register's statement makes more sense for books than for journals when you consider the following scenarios.

Example 1. The Case of the Missing Issue

You are ready to bind the six issues from a scholarly journal, and discover that the July/August issue is missing. The subscription price was $40 for six issues, or about $7.00 per issue.

Comment

If the publisher or jobber charges $10 to $15 to replace the July/August issue, the price seems fair. If it costs $20 or more to replace one issue, you might conclude that it is not. (Of course if you consider what it costs two libraries to request, reproduce, receive, and do the bookkeeping for an ILL request, it *may* make sense to bite the bullet and just buy the issue.)

Example 2. The Case of the Missing Article

Someone cut out one article from the same journal. Each of the six issues has eight to ten articles. In other words, you "lost" about 2% of the volume.

Comment

If it will cost $15 to $20 to replace the issue in which the article appeared, or $10 for a reprint of the article, you may conclude that the price is not fair and ask another library to copy the article for you under section 108(c).

The 1998 DMCA also amended 108(c) by adding a provision that enables a library to copy a published work "if the existing format in which the work is stored has become obsolete." A format is obsolete "if the machine or device necessary to render perceptive a work stored in that format is no longer manufactured or is no longer reasonably available in the commercial marketplace." If you cannot see or hear the work because you are unable to acquire the equipment

---

26. H.R. REP. NO. 94-1476, at 75–76; S. REP. NO. 94-473, at 68.
27. REGISTER'S REPORT, *supra* note 9, at 107–08.

that enables you to see or hear it—if the equipment is no longer manufactured or not reasonably available—then you can make a copy of it.

Example 3. Sound Recordings

Your library owns some Bessie Smith 78 r.p.m. records but only one ancient record player.

Comment

Under the statute, if you cannot acquire at a reasonable price a record player that plays 78s, you can copy the records onto a different format. This ought not end the inquiry, however. If you can buy the Bessie Smith recordings in a different format—if they are available on CD or audiocassette—then do so, and do not make a copy.

Example 4. Videos

Your library has some old videos in Betamax format and you only have one very old Betamax machine.

Comment

If you cannot purchase at a reasonable price Betamax equipment, you can copy the videos onto a different format unless, as in Example 2, you can purchase a video in a "current" format such as VHS or DVD.

The Bottom Line: If at a reasonable price a library can buy the equipment that enables it to play its old format "stuff," or if it can buy the old "stuff" in a current format, it should. If the library cannot do either, then it may make a copy under 108(c).

Articles or Excerpts for Users (Section 108(d))

5.5. Section 108(d) Articles and Excerpts

- ಲು Single copy
- ಲು Becomes user's property
- ಲು No notice of impermissible purpose
- ಲು Warning of copyright
  - where orders are accepted
  - on order form

Most section 108 copying by libraries takes place under subsection (d). Section 108(d) permits a library to make a single copy of an article, or of another contribution to a collection or periodical issue such as a book chapter, for a patron. It also permits library-to-library copying to fill a patron's request—what we call interlibrary loan, or perhaps more appropriately, document delivery. There are four conditions.

First, you can only make one copy. What if the requestor asks for two copies, one to read and mark up, and one for her files? Follow Nancy Reagan's advice, and just say no.[28]

Second, the copy must become the property of the user. You may not add it to the library's collection. Say, for example, that African explorer Jeffrey T. Spaulding[29] is hired to teach courses at your university. Professor Spaulding asks a reference librarian for an article from the *Ghana Journal of Science,* and also one from *JASSA: Journal of Applied Science in South Africa,* neither of which the library owns. The reference librarian asks the ILL librarian to get copies of the two articles from another library. The professor really likes one of the articles. He gives it back to the reference librarian and asks her to add it to the library's collection. Just say no.

Third, the library must have no notice that the use will be for a purpose other than private study, scholarship, or research. Congress

---

28. *See* <http://www.reaganfoundation.org/reagan/nancy/>.
29. "At last we are to meet him, the famous Captain Spaulding. From climates hot and scalding, the Captain has arrived. . . ." "Hooray for Captain Spaulding," from the film *Animal Crackers* (music and Lyrics by Bert Kalmar & Harry Ruby (1936)).

did not explain what this means, but it is reasonable to conclude that a library may do for a library patron what that person could do for him or herself as a fair use. You may decide—wisely, I think—that your library will not make copies for fee-based information brokers. Information brokers do not request copies for "private study, scholarship, or research." To the contrary, they are in the business of supplying copies to others. Even if the information broker says "We will pay royalties," it is *your* library that is making the copy. If you feel more comfortable not offering document delivery services to fee-based information brokers—and that is how I feel—just say no.

The final condition under 108(d) requires the library to display prominently at the place orders are accepted, and include on its order forms, a warning of copyright as prescribed by the Register of Copyrights. Here is what you have to do: (1) Copy the warning below and tape it near the door of the office where people request copies; (2) include the warning on the form people fill out when they ask for copies; and (3) if you accept electronic ILL requests, include the warning on your electronic ILL form.

Section 108(d) Warning
Copyright Restrictions

The copyright law of the United States (Title 17, United States Code) governs the making of photocopies or other reproduction of copyrighted material.

Under certain conditions specified in the law, libraries and archives are authorized to furnish a photocopy or other reproduction. One of these specified conditions is that the photocopy or reproduction is not to be "used for any purpose other than private study, scholarship, or research." If a user makes a request for, or later uses, a photocopy or reproduction for purposes in excess of "fair use," that user may be liable for copyright infringement.

This institution reserves the right to refuse to accept a copying order if, in its judgment, fulfillment of the order would involve violation of copyright law.

Source: 37 C.F.R. § 201.14

Out-of-Print and Unavailable Works (Section 108(e))

5.6. Section 108(e)
Copying Entire Works for Patrons

From the collection of a library where the user makes the request or from another library if:

- ဢ New or used copy is unobtainable at a fair price
- ဢ Becomes the user's property
- ဢ No notice of impermissible purpose
- ဢ Warning of copyright

Section 108(e) permits in some situations the copying of an entire work (a complete book, a substantial part of a book, or a journal issue) for a library patron if the library cannot obtain either a new or used copy at a fair price, and if the library meets the other requirements of subsection (d) discussed above (the copy becomes the property of the user; the library has no notice that the copy will be used for a purpose other than private study, scholarship, or research; and the library displays the copyright warning).

Like section 108(c) subsection (e) similarly requires that the library make a reasonable effort to find a copy at a fair price. However, the "unavailable copy" requirement for 108(e) is stricter than it is under 108(c). Under 108(c), Library A may ask Library B to make a copy of a damaged, deteriorating, lost, or stolen work if Library A cannot find a *new* copy at a fair price. Under 108(e), however, Library A must be unable to find either a new *or* used copy. The library, therefore, must contact both new and used dealers.

Example 1

Professor Spaulding finds out that a certain journal recently published a symposium issue devoted to a single topic, and asks the library to photocopy every article from that issue for him.

Comment

You cannot do this under 108(e). You could, of course, tell the professor that he may keep the library's issue, and then order another issue for the library. The professor will love you, he will love the library, and he will support you when the library wants something really important, like $100,000 to replace its fraying carpeting. If you cannot afford to purchase another issue, check out the issue to the professor and give him plenty of time to read it.

Example 2
Professor Spaulding wants to read a book published in 1983 on architectural ruins in north Africa. You borrow the book from another library, and when it needs to be returned the professor tells you it is the best book he ever read on that topic and he wants to purchase a copy. Unfortunately, the book is out of print. You contact numerous new and used book dealers, but none have the book, nor can they locate one.

Comment
Under these circumstances, a copy of the book may be made for the professor under 108(e).

Library Reproducing Equipment (a.k.a. Photocopiers) (Section 108(f)(1) and (2))

A library is not liable for infringing activities done on library-owned equipment that is not "supervised."[30] Joe Student checks out a book from the Reserve Desk. He begins reading it, and decides to copy the entire book. We will assume that Joe's actions are infringing. The library is not liable as a contributory infringer if (1) Joe's copying is unsupervised, and (2) there is a notice on the machine that says:

> WARNING: THE MAKING OF A COPY MAY BE
> SUBJECT TO THE UNITED STATES COPYRIGHT
> LAW (TITLE 17 UNITED STATES CODE)

Your equipment does not come with this warning, so you must create a label yourself. Make it prominent—use large, bolded typeface—and tape it to the machine, close to the "copy" button. You should put a label on every copier in the building, even copiers in staff-only areas.

A library is absolved from liability only for the use of "unsupervised use of reproducing equipment located on its premises." If the equipment is available for walk-up use and the library merely adds toner or paper, replaces cartridges, and fixes paper jams, the copying is not supervised. Copying *is* supervised when library staff (or agents

---

30. 17 U.S.C. § 108(f)(1) (2000).

of the library) make the copies, or when the equipment is under such close supervision that the library can control what patrons actually copy. The most obvious example is a copy center in a university or corporate library that makes copies for students and employees. If the copying is infringing, then the library can be liable.

Do the same rules apply in both for- and non-profit organizations? The legislative history to the 1976 Act says that "a library in a profit-making organization could not evade these obligations by installing reproducing equipment on its premises for unsupervised use by the organization's staff."[31] In other words, if an employee in a for-profit organization infringes copyright, both the employee and the institution can be held liable because businesses and corporations are assumed to have control over the actions of their employees.

One who makes unauthorized copies on an unsupervised walk-up machine could be liable for infringement, of course. Section 108(f)(2) provides that a person who uses unsupervised equipment to make copies that exceed fair use is not excused from liability for infringement. Furthermore, a person who *requests* that the library make a copy for him or her under 108(d) is not excused from liability for infringement if the copying exceeds fair use.[32]

Contracts, Licenses, and Fair Use (Section 108(f)(4))

Tiny subsection (f)(4) of section 108 has a lot of oomph, just like Maria Callas or Leontyne Price at a night at the opera. Here is what it says:

> Nothing in this section [108] in any way affects the right of fair use as provided by section 107, or any contractual obligations assumed at any time by the library or archives when it obtained a copy or phonorecord of a work in its collections.

First, this means that libraries, in addition to having rights under the section 108 exemption, also have fair use rights. This interpretation is supported by the legislative history of the 1976 Act.

> Nothing in section 108 impairs the applicability of the fair use doctrine to a wide variety of situations involving photocopying or other reproduction by a library of copyrighted material in its collections,

---

31. H.R. REP. NO. 94-1476, at 75.
32. 17 U.S.C. § 108(f)(2) (2000).

where the user requests the reproduction for legitimate scholarly or research purposes.[33]

You should be wary of contrary messages from the publishing industry. Soon after passage of the 1976 Act, the Association of American Publishers and the Authors League of America asserted that libraries could copy materials *only* under section 108.[34] The then Register of Copyrights also had a restrictive, although somewhat different, interpretation of the relationship between sections 107 and 108. The Register wrote that library photocopying beyond section 108 may be permitted as a fair use, but only if the copying would be a fair use absent section 108, and then, only if the library first accounted for any section 108 copying that already took place.[35]

The AAP/Authors' League and the Register were wrong. Section 108(f)(4) cannot be clearer: "Nothing in this section in any way affects the right of fair use as provided by section 107." The legislative history is equally clear. Library copying may be permitted under section 107 even if it does not come within the section 108 exemption.

But there is another side of subsection (f)(4): Section 108 rights do not affect any contractual obligations assumed by a library when it obtained a copy of a work. In plain English, this means that, by signing a license, a library may agree to give up specific rights provided for in the Act, such as fair use and the section 108 exemption. Licenses and contracts are addressed in greater detail in Chapter Seven. For now, just remember this: you *may* contract away your rights. Review carefully all license agreements, and do not sign what you do not understand.

---

33. H.R. REP. NO. 94-1476, at 78–79.
34. ASSOCIATION OF AMERICAN PUBLISHERS & THE AUTHORS LEAGUE OF AMERICA, PHOTO-COPYING BY ACADEMIC, PUBLIC AND NONPROFIT RESEARCH LIBRARIES 4, 16 (1978).
35. REGISTER'S REPORT, *supra* note 9, at 98–99.

The Section 108(g) Provisos

5.7. Section 108(g)

Section 108 rights do not apply to:

- ▷ Related or concerted reproduction
  - • Multiple copies
  - • Same material

- ▷ Systematic reproduction
  - • Single or multiple copies
  - • Same or different material

Related or Concerted Copying or Distribution (Section 108(g)(1))

Fasten your seatbelts, secure your tray tables, and place your seats in an upright position. If you think that libraries can do most anything under section 108, you are wrong. Section 108(g)(1) and (2) govern section 108. No monkey business is allowed. There are two parts to subsection (g), and we begin with the first part.

Section 108(g)(1) prohibits related or concerted copying or distribution of multiple copies of the same material, whether at one time or over a period of time, either for aggregate use by one or more individuals or for separate use by individual members of a group. Congress did not define what "related or concerted" means, so we will use some examples.

Example 1

Mary N. Librarian reads an article on insurance bad faith (when an insurance company places its own interests above those of its insured clients and unreasonably denies a claim). Mary thinks the article might interest several people: professors if she works in a law school, attorneys if she is in a law firm, or agents if she works for an insurance company.

Comment

The "related or concerted" limitation in 108(g)(1) may be implicated if, on her own initiative, Mary copies the articles for numerous individuals. The easy (and also effective) alternative would be to notify them of the article. If any ask to see the article, Mary could route them the issue, or she may be able to make a copy under section 108(d).

Example 2

Mary is on a listserv and receives an e-mail message about the insurance bad faith article. The message has a link to the article, which the author posted on the Web.

Comment

Mary should not download the article and send digital copies to professors, attorneys, or insurance agents. She should instead send an e-mail message that includes the link to the article.

Example 3

Mary presents continuing education workshops for several different library and education associations each year. She wants to give every attendee a packet of materials that includes several copyrighted articles.

Comment

This certainly looks and smells like related copying and distribution of multiple copies of the same material at one time (for a specific workshop) *and* over a period of time (the different workshops). It is precisely what subsection (g)(1) proscribes, and Mary needs to get permission from the copyright owners.

Systematic Copying or Distribution (Section 108(g)(2))

Section 108(g)(2) is a bit different from (g)(1). Subsection (g)(1) addresses related and concerted copying of the *same* copyrighted work. Subsection (g)(2), however, prohibits the systematic making of multiple copies, and in some cases even *single* copies, of articles or short excerpts from the same publication. Here is the precise language.

The rights of reproduction and distribution under this section . . . do not extend to cases where the library or archives, or its employee—

(2) engages in the systematic reproduction or distribution of single or multiple copies or phonorecords of material described in subsection (d): Provided, That nothing in this clause prevents a library or archives from participating in interlibrary arrangements that do not have, as their purpose or effect, that the library or archives receiving such copies or phonorecords for distribution does so in such aggre-

gate copies as to substitute for a subscription to or purchase of such work.[36]

Subsection (g)(2) addresses copying for library users, and also copying *between* libraries. It expressly permits library-to-library copying, but there are limits. The big question: When is library copying systematic? A generation ago the Register of Copyrights wrote that

> [t]he fundamental concern with respect to (g)(2) has been and continues to be the lack of statutory precision or common consensus about what copying is (and is not) 'systematic.' The meaning of that term has been vigorously debated since before the enactment of the statute, but not even the rudiments of agreement have emerged.[37]

The Senate Judiciary Committee offered specific examples of what it considered systematic copying.[38] Do not take these as gospel; the Senate Committee was more conservative than the House Committee with regard to library copying. That said, here are the Senate Committee's examples, and my comments.

Senate Example 1

A library with a collection of journals in biology informs other libraries with similar collections that it will maintain and build its own collection and will make copies of articles from these journals available to them and their patrons on request. Accordingly, the other libraries discontinue or refrain from purchasing subscriptions to these journals and fulfill their patrons' requests for articles by obtaining photocopies from the source library.

Comment

The real test is one of degree: How many copies are being requested by the libraries that cancel their subscriptions? Each library certainly may request copies within the CONTU Guidelines (see below). Also remember that section 108 is not implicated if the library with the subscription *lends* an issue to another library, rather than makes copies for it.

Senate Example 2

A research center employing a number of scientists and technicians subscribes to one or two copies of needed periodicals. By reproducing photocopies of articles the center is able to make the materials in these periodicals available to its staff in the same manner which otherwise would require multiple subscriptions.

---

36. 17 U.S.C. § 108(g)(2) (2000).
37. REGISTER'S REPORT, *supra* note 9, at 130.
38. S. REP. NO. 94-473, at 70.

Comment

This sounds like *Texaco,* except here the library makes the copies rather than the scientist. If the library makes so many copies that copying does, indeed, substitute for additional subscriptions—if but for the copying the library would need additional subscriptions—then the copying is systematic.

Reactive is better than proactive. A library that actively promotes its photocopying services is engaging in risky business. If your library sends out weekly or monthly tables of contents from recently published journals to professors or lawyers, you would be wise not to advertise that the library will photocopy articles upon request. A library that becomes a copying factory will run afoul of the related or concerted copying prohibitions of 108(g)(1), and perhaps the systematic copying proscribed by 108(g)(2). Remember that section 108(g) begins with these words: 'The rights of reproduction and distribution under this section extend to the isolated and unrelated reproduction or distribution of a single copy or phonorecord of the same material on separate occasions."

Senate Example 3

Several branches of a library system agree that one branch will subscribe to particular journals in lieu of each branch purchasing its own subscriptions, and the one subscribing branch will reproduce copies of articles from the publication for users of the other branches.

Comment

This differs from the first example in that it involves a single library system that decides to reduce its number of subscriptions to the same title. Should transactions between libraries within a single library system be considered "interlibrary" transactions? I think the answer is yes. If the central library sends lots of copies to its branches—so many that the single subscription substitutes for subscriptions the branches really should have—the copying is systematic. As in Senate Example 1, consider lending the issue rather than making copies.

Subscriptions to most periodicals subscribed to by city and county public libraries are not expensive. Do not be penny-wise and pound-foolish. Money saved by cancelling a subscription to a $50 magazine will be quickly eaten up by photocopying or shuttle costs. If a title is used frequently in each branch of a library system, you should have multiple subscriptions. You will make your users happy, and probably will save money in the long run.

The CONTU Guidelines

> ### 5.8. Section 108(g)(2)
> ### The CONTU Guidelines
>
>
> "such aggregate quantities as to substitute for a subscription . . ."
> ഏ Journal published within last five years
> ഏ Maximum of five articles from same title in one year
> ഏ Exceptions
>   • issue is missing
>   • journal is on order
> ഏ Attestation by requesting library
> ഏ Maintain three years of "borrowing" records

After writing that section 108 struck the appropriate balance between the rights of creators and the needs of users, the Senate Judiciary Committee continued

> However, neither a statute nor legislative history can specify precisely which library photocopying practices constitute the making of "single copies" as distinguished from "systematic reproduction." Isolated single spontaneous requests must be distinguished from "systematic reproduction." The photocopying needs of such operations as multi-county regional systems must be met. The committee therefore recommends that representatives of authors, book and periodical publishers and other owners of copyrighted material meet with the library community to formulate photocopying guidelines to assist library patrons and employees.[39]

The House Judiciary Committee's Report, submitted nine months after the Senate Report, noted the "storm of controversy" provoked by the addition of subsection (g)(2) proscribing the "systematic reproduction or distribution of single or multiple copies or phonorecords," and that 108(g)(2) was then amended to include the proviso "that nothing in this clause prevents a library or archives from participating in interlibrary arrangements that do not have, as their purpose or effect, that the library or archives receiving such copies or phonorecords for distribution does so in such aggregate quantities as to substitute for a subscription to or purchase of such work."[40] The Committee wrote that the National Commission on New Technological Uses of Copyrighted Works offered to help develop "more or less specific guidelines establishing criteria to govern various situations."[41]

---

39. *Id.* at 70–71.
40. H.R. Rep. No. 94-1476, at 77–78.
41. *Id.* at 78.

The CONTU Guidelines, which were included in the Conference Report to the 1976 Act,[42] follow.

Guidelines for the Proviso of Subsection 108(g)(2)

1. As used in the proviso of subsection 108(g)(2), the words ". . . such aggregate quantities as to substitute for a subscription to or purchase of such work" shall mean:

(a) with respect to any given periodical (as opposed to any given issue of a periodical), filled requests of a library or archives (a "requesting entity") within any calendar year for a total of six or more copies of an article or articles published in such periodical within five years prior to the date of the request. These guidelines specifically shall not apply, directly or indirectly, to any request of a requesting entity for a copy or copies of an article or articles published in any issue of a periodical, the publication date of which is more than five years prior to the date when the request is made. These guidelines do not define the meaning, with respect to such a request, of ". . . such aggregate quantities as to substitute for a subscription to [such periodical]".

(b) With respect to any other material described in subsection 108(d), (including fiction and poetry), filled requests of a requesting entity within any calendar year for a total of six or more copies or phonorecords of or from any given work (including a collective work) during the entire period when such material shall be protected by copyright.

2. In the event that a requesting entity—

(a) shall have in force or shall have entered an order for a subscription to a periodical, or

(b) has within its collection, or shall have entered an order for, a copy of phonorecord of any other copyrighted work, materials from either category of which it desires to obtain by copy from another library or archives (the "supplying entity"), because the material to be copied is not reasonably available for use by the requesting entity itself, then the fulfillment of such request shall be treated as though the requesting entity made such copy from its own collection. A library or archives may request a copy or phonorecord from a supplying entity only under those circumstances where the requesting entity would have been able, under the other provisos of section 108, to supply such copy from materials in its own collection.

---

42. H.R. REP. NO. 94-1733 (Conf.), at 72–74.

3. No request for a copy or phonorecord of any materials to which these guidelines apply may be fulfilled by the supplying entity unless such request is accompanied by a representation by the requesting entity that the request was made in conformity with these guidelines.

4. The requesting entity shall maintain records of all requests made by it for copies or phonorecords of any materials to which these guidelines apply and shall maintain records of the fulfillment of such requests, which records shall be retained until the end of the third complete calendar year after the end of the calendar year in which the respective request shall have been made.

5. As part of the review provided for in subsection 108(i), these guidelines shall be reviewed not later than five years from the effective date of this bill.

The CONTU drafters seem to have had grand illusions of being in Congress. Let's use plain English, and some examples and comments, to explain what the Guidelines really say.

∞ The Guidelines apply only to journal articles published within the last five years.

∞ In any one year, the Guidelines expressly permit a library to request from another library copies of five articles from the same journal title (some call this as the "Rule of 5" or "Suggestion of 5").

Example 1

You work in a college library. Professor Spaulding, a visiting professor for one semester, needs articles from several journals your library does not own. Are you absolutely limited to requesting from other libraries no more than five copies from each title?

Comment

No. Here is what the Conference Committee wrote about the Guidelines:

> The conference committee understands that the guidelines are not intended as, and cannot be considered, explicit rules or directions governing any and all cases, now or in the future. It is recognized that their purpose is to provide guidance in the most commonly encountered interlibrary photocopying situations, that they are not intended to be limiting or determinate in themselves or with respect to other situations, and that they deal with an evolving situation that will undoubtedly require their continuous reevaluation and adjustment. With these qualifications, the conference committee agrees that the guidelines are a reasonable interpre-

tation of the proviso of section 108(g)(2) in the most common situations to which they apply today.[43]

As for Professor Spaulding's request, remember that these are guidelines. You may exercise some judgment. I think that a short-term project is a good example of when you may go beyond the "five article" guideline. Requesting six articles from other libraries does not bother me and, frankly, neither does a few more. I do not feel the least bit queasy until it moves into double figures.

Example 2
The requestor is an attorney who is working on a quick turnaround, one-time project.

Comment
Same answer as above.

ᗡ You do not need to count requests if your library subscribes to the journal and the issue you need happens to be unavailable.

ᗡ You do not need to count requests if your library has entered an order for a subscription to the journal.

ᗡ The requesting library must attest that the request conforms to the guidelines.

Example 3
The requesting library confirms that the request complies with another provision of the Act, such as section 108(c)—to replace a damaged or lost copy.

Comment
This is fine. The American Library Association's Interlibrary Loan Request Form requires that the requesting library check off one of the following selections.

Request complies with
❑ 108(g)(2) Guidelines (CCG), or
❑ other provisions of the copyright law (CCL).[44]

---

43. *Id.* at 71–72.
44. The ALA reminds requesting libraries that they are responsible for complying with section 108(g)(2) and the CONTU Guidelines. AMERICAN LIBRARY ASSOCIATION, INTERLIBRARY LOAN CODE FOR THE UNITED STATES, EXPLANATORY SUPPLEMENT § 4.8 (Jan. 2001). The ALA's interlibrary loan request form is available at <http://www.ala.org> [hereinafter ALA INTERLIBRARY LOAN CODE].

Example 4

The requesting library does not include any attestation.

Comment

Just say no.

   ⁚ The requesting library should keep records of its document delivery requests for three full calendar years, plus the current year.

Example 5

Your interlibrary loan clerk read the USA Patriot Act[45] and is concerned about privacy. She wants to discard all borrowing records more than three months old.

Comment

The ALA notes that ILL transactions are confidential library records, but that it does not violate their Interlibrary Loan Code to include a user's name on an ILL request.[46] To monitor requests, I suggest that libraries record (1) the date of the request; (2) the title and author of the article; and (3) the title of the journal, its volume number, and the publication date. Three full calendar years plus the current year means just that: Keep records for the entire time period.

The 2001 Patriot Act treats library records, including borrowing transactions, as business records that must be disclosed to law enforcement officials who present a subpoena or search warrant from a duly authorized court as part of a criminal investigation. After an ILL transaction has been completed, libraries may want to delete from their records the name of the person who requested the item.

In the end, there is no exact answer as to how much copying is permitted under section 108. Even non-profit academic libraries that arguably have "gold club" status cannot make copies for faculty or students, or use document delivery, in quantities such that the copying substitutes for needed subscriptions or purchases. Because section 108 really is a fair use–like provision that permits a library to, in effect, act as an agent for the person who needs a copy, the answer to the question "How much may I copy?" depends on the facts.

So here you are, in the gray zone. What is the bottom line when you receive a request from a library patron—a teacher, a judge, a corporate CEO, whomever—and are unsure whether the use is permitted under section 108 or as a fair use? If you thought about

---

45. Pub. L. No. 107-56, 115 Stat. 272 (2001) ("USA Patriot Act" is an acronym for Uniting and Strengthening America by Providing Appropriate Tools Required to Intercept and Obstruct Terrorism).

46. ALA INTERLIBRARY LOAN CODE, *supra* note 44, § 4.2.

this a lot and *still* think it is a close call, you may recall that the primary purpose of copyright is not to reward copyright owners but instead to enhance knowledge and promote the creation of other works, and resolve it in favor of the use.

Preservation and Term Extension (The Return of Sonny Bono) (Section 108(h))

5.9. Section 108(h) Preservation and Term Extension

May copy, distribute, display, or perform the work during last twenty years of term for preservation, scholarship, or research

- ೞ The work is not exploited commercially
- ೞ A copy is unobtainable at a fair price
- ೞ No owner notification

The Sonny Bono Copyright Term Extension Act added twenty years to the copyright term. Congress tried to appease the library and academic communities with a tiny bone: During the last twenty years of copyright of a published work, a library or archives, or a non-profit educational institution that functions as a library or archives, may copy, distribute, display, or perform a work—in either facsimile or digital form—for preservation, scholarship, or research if (a) the work is not subject to normal commercial exploitation, and (b) a copy cannot be obtained at a reasonable price. The library may not take advantage of the exemption if the copyright owner notifies the Copyright Office that either (a) or (b) apply.[47]

The "normal commercial exploitation" language appears to mean that the copyright owner has decided there is no commercial value in the work. If the copyright owner makes the work available on the Web for a fee—either as part of a database or as a stand-alone product—or if the library can purchase reprints, the work *is* being commercially exploited and the exemption does not apply. And even

---

47. 17 U.S.C. § 108(h)(1)–(3) (2000).

if the work is not being commercially exploited, the exemption only applies if the library cannot acquire a copy at a reasonable price.

The Bottom Line: This exemption probably is not worth the paper it was printed on or the bits and bytes it takes up in the digital world. Works that have value will be commercially exploited. And in any event, by the time a work is in the last twenty years of its term, it is pretty darn old.

Non-Print Works (Music, Pictures, Graphs, and Sculptural Works) (Section 108(i))

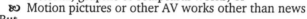

5.10. Section 108(i) Non-Print Works

Except for subsections (b) and (c), Section 108 does not apply to:

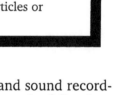

⁜ Musical works
⁜ Pictorial, graphic or sculptural works, or
⁜ Motion pictures or other AV works other than news
But
  ⁜ May include illustrations and diagrams within articles or chapters

Section 108 is designed primarily for print works and sound recordings. Most of the library exemption does not apply to the following: (1) musical works, (2) pictorial works, (3) graphical works, (4) sculptural works, (5) motion pictures, and (6) audiovisual works that do not deal with the news.[48]

Section 108(i), however, provides that each of these six types of works may be reproduced or distributed under certain circumstances. First, section 108(b), which permits the copying of an unpublished work for purposes of preservation, security, or for deposit for research use in another library, applies to works in these non-print formats. Second, section 108(c) also applies to these types of works, thereby permitting the copying of a published work in these formats to re-

---

48. 17 U.S.C. § 108(i) (2000). A "musical work" is different from a "sound recording." The musical work is the composition; the sound recording is what we hear by playing a disk, tape, phonorecord, etc.

place a damaged, deteriorating, lost, or stolen copy if the library cannot obtain an unused replacement copy at a fair price. Third, section 108(c) also permits the making of a copy if the format in which the work is stored is obsolete and you cannot acquire an unused replacement of the work at a fair price.

Articles and book chapters often are accompanied by illustrations, diagrams, graphs and charts. You *may* include illustrations, diagrams, etc., when you copy an article or book excerpt under section 108(d) or (e).

Section 108 and Fair Use (Reprise) (Section 108(f)(4))

Section 108, as you have seen, has its limitations. But remember that fair use may still apply. Section 108(f) reads "[n]othing in this section . . . in any way affects the right of fair use as provided by section 107. . . ." This is reinforced by the House Judiciary Committee:

> Nothing in section 108 impairs the applicability of the fair use doctrine to a wide variety of situations involving photocopying or other reproduction by a library of copyrighted material in its collections, where the user requests the reproduction for legitimate scholarly or research purposes.[49]

---

49. H.R. Rep. No. 94-1476, at 78–79.

Chapter Six
DIGITAL INFORMATION AND DATABASES

ක්‍රෝ

In the last century, libraries could actually purchase information in digital format. Today, software and digital products generally are transferred under license. As you will see below, courts are split on the validity of unilateral "shrinkwrap" or "click" licenses when consumers cannot really bargain over the terms.

Shrinkwrap and click licenses refer to unsigned agreements between a purchaser of digital products or software and the creator or vendor that define the respective rights of the parties. Shrinkwrap refers to the plastic wrap that encases software; upon opening the program the first thing the user sees is the license agreement that sets out the terms of use. A purchaser who opens the shrinkwrap or other packaging, or begins using the software, is presumed to have read the license and assented to its terms.

Click licenses are found on Web-based products. The user cannot access the information or use the program until he or she agrees to the terms by clicking "yes." Licenses frequently include terms that prohibit uses otherwise permitted under federal copyright law or state consumer protection law, such as the right to make fair use of the work. Courts are split on whether shrinkwrap or click licenses are enforceable.

Compare *Vault v. Quaid,*[1] a 1988 decision of the United States Court of Appeals for the Fifth Circuit, with *Pro-CD v. Zeidenberg,*[2] a 1996 decision from the Seventh Circuit. In *Vault,* the court held unenforceable a license provision that was not disclosed to the

---

1. 847 F.2d 255 (5th Cir. 1988).
2. 86 F.3d 1447 (7th Cir. 1996).

purchaser at the time of purchase. By contrast, the *Pro-CD* court held that shrinkwrap licenses *are* enforceable unless their terms are objectionable on grounds applicable to contracts in general. The fact that federal copyright law permits uses that might be precluded under a license did not convnce the court to reach a different conclusion.

A library *can* contract away its rights, so read licensing agreements carefully. Also pay attention to how the contract affects those who use the digital products. A license agreement between a library and a vendor may limit a library patron's right to copy or otherwise use an article in the licensed database, even though the use would be a permissible fair use. We will get into licensing issues in greater depth a little later. For now, here are answers to several basic questions.

Question 1

Is information on the World Wide Web subject to copyright protection?

Answer

Yes.

Question 2

Do the same rules apply to digital information, and information in book or magazine format?

Answer

Generally, yes, but there are exceptions, such as sections 108(b) (unpublished works duplicated for purposes of preservation and security or for deposit for research use in another library or archives) and (c) (a replacement copy of a damaged, deteriorating, lost, or stolen published work) which restrict the places where digital copies may be read.

Question 3

May I send information from the Web to anyone I want, such as members of a listserv?

Answer

Think about the print world. You may not, under either fair use or the library exemption, photocopy a copyrighted journal article and send paper copies to an untold number of people without permission. That you can easily distribute digital articles to lots of people via e-mail, a listserv, or a bulletin board does not mean that you can legally do so. This is true even when an an author posts his or her article on the Web. Rather than download the text, send an e-mail message that includes a link. You achieve the same result, but you have not made any copies. Even e-mail messages are copyrightable. There may be an unwritten assumption that someone who sends an e-mail message to a huge listserv impliedly gives his or her permission to send it to the rest of the world, but this may not always be the case.

Question 4

I receive the *New York Times* online for free every morning. When I link to an article on nytime.com, there is an "E-mail This Article" button. Does this mean I may send the article to anyone I want?

Answer

No. The *New York Times* does permit you to send the article to others via e-mail, but you are "limited to 20 addresses."[3] You should also note that the online articles are accompanied by advertisements, and that only recent articles are free.

Question 5

John Bit and I are fellow members of listserv A. John sends a draft article to the list, and invites everyone to share their comments with other members. May I send a reply to the list, along with John's article?

Answer

Yes. Everyone on the list already received John's article, and he invited comments.

Question 6

I am a member of listserv B. My colleague Mary Byte subscribes to both listserv A and listserv B. Mary received a copy of John's article from listserv A and forwarded it to me. May I share John's article with other members of listserv B.

Answer

No. John did not share his article with the members of listserv B, and neither should you.

---

3. *See* <http://www.nytimes.com>.

Computer Programs
(Section 117)

6.1. Section 117
Computer Programs

Owner may make a copy or adapt the program

  ဢ To utilize it, or
  ဢ For archival purposes, or
  ဢ To repair or maintain equipment

Section 117 permits the owner of a computer program—"a set of statements or instructions to be used directly or indirectly in a computer in order to bring about a certain result"[4]—to make a copy under three circumstances. First, the owner may make a new copy of the program, or an adaptation of the program, if it is an essential step in order to use the program in conjunction with a machine. For example, if the software you purchased cannot run on your equipment or operating system, you may make a copy in order to adapt it to make it work. This section also permits the automatic loading of a copy onto a computer's random access memory (RAM).

A software owner may also make a copy for archival purposes, so long as the archival copy is destroyed if possession ceases to be rightful. Remember that the archival copy is just that. You may not make an archival copy under section 117 for use on another computer. Furthermore, when possession is no longer rightful—for example, if you give the original software to someone else—you must destroy the archival copy.

Finally, the Digital Millennium Copyright Act amended section 117 to permit someone who owns or leases a computer to make a temporary copy of a program that was loaded on the machine for the purpose of repairing or maintaining the equipment. The new copy must be destroyed after the maintenance has been completed.

Enough of section 117. Let's move on to what really engages libraries and information providers, the matter of licenses. We are going where the wild things are, so let the wild rumpus begin.[5]

---

4. 17 U.S.C. § 101 (2000).
5. Maurice Sendak, Where the Wild Things Are (1963).

Single-User and Site Licenses

The typical single-user license agreement prohibits use of software on more than one piece of equipment at one time. Unless the license so provides, you should not load the software on a network accessible to several different users, even if only one person can access the software at a time. However, installing software on a single computer that is used by several different people is permissible.

Site licenses permit group access to software, to databases, or to other digital information. Because cost is directly proportional to the number of users, you should determine how many people really need access. Although a public library may serve a population of 50,000 and a law firm library 500 attorneys, this does not mean that the information needs to be accessible to everyone at one time. The public library may do quite well with a site license to a genealogy database that allows a few patrons simultaneous access to the database. Similarly, the firm's license to a labor law database need only reflect the needs of those who do labor-related work, a small fraction of the 500 attorneys in the firm.

Downloading

Downloading involves transmitting online data to a local storage medium. Copying the results of a LexisNexis search onto a hard drive is a good example. When you download, a copy is being made. Copyright principles, including fair use, apply, so you will want to answer the following questions: Is the work being used for private study, scholarship, or research? Is the use for a commercial or a non-profit educational purpose? Is the use transformative? Is the information factual or creative? How much is being downloaded? Will the copying significantly affect the market for the original work? And, of course, what does the license say?

I can sense you are not satisfied, so here are some guidelines.

- Downloading information, not changing it at all, and then selling it would be frowned upon. Very frowned upon.

- The more you transform the data that you downloaded, the more likely the use is fair. If after downloading textual and bibliographic data from a few searches you delete the information that is not relevant to the end user, reformat the information to make it easier to use, and add some comments of your own, that is good.

ɞ Temporarily downloading data so that you can use it later, and then discarding the information after you have completed your work, should be fine.

ɞ Check your license. If the license reads "Downloading and storing in any format and in any portion any information from this database is prohibited," you may be stuck. If this was a negotiated contract, you may have placed fair use on the sacrificial contract altar. Do not agree to such terms.

Database Protection (Redux)

We know that some information—facts and works of the U.S. government, for example—are not protected by copyright. However, *databases* of federal governmental works and other works in the public domain, such as facts, might receive protection as compilations.

As noted in chapter one, in *Feist v. Rural Telephone Service*[6] the U.S. Supreme Court discredited the "sweat of the brow" doctrine and held that a white pages telephone directory could not be copyrighted because it lacked originality. However, a database may be eligible for protection if the compiler exercised sufficient skill and judgment in selecting, organizing, and arranging the data.

Although many database providers thought that *Feist* would bring the apocalypse to their businesses, subsequent to that decision many courts have held that databases consisting of factual information (a Yellow Pages directory,[7] or a database with information on the value of used vehicles,[8] for example) may be copyrightable compilations. Remember that compilation copyright extends only to the material contributed by the author, not to the underlying materials actually compiled. You may use some of the content, but taking a significant portion of the information— especially as it appears in the compilation—and using it in your own work may very well be infringing.

The Bottom Line: You may use unprotected factual information from a printed work (like an almanac) or an online database that is copyrighted as a compilation. But if you copy or download a significant amount of that information—more than that which is allowed

---

6. 499 U.S. 340 (1991).
7. *See, e.g.*, BellSouth Adver. & Publ'g Corp. v. Donnelly Info. Publ'g, Inc., 999 F.2d 1436 (11th Cir. 1993); Key Publ'ns, Inc. v. Chinatown Today, Publ'g, 945 F.2d 509 (2d Cir. 1991).
8. CCC Info. Servs., Inc. v. Maclean Hunter Mkt. Reports, Inc., 44 F.3d 61 (2d Cir. 1994).

under fair use—you may violate the copyright that protects how the information is selected, arranged, and presented.

The First Sale Doctrine (Reprise) (Section 109)

Section 109 of the Copyright Act—the First Sale Doctrine—is the statutory provision that enables libraries to lend their materials. We discussed this earlier in chapter two, but let's visit it again in the context of digital information.

> ### 6.2. Lending Software and Sound Recordings
>
> ᔔ May not lend for direct or indirect commercial advantage
>
> But
>
> ᔔ Nonprofit library or educational institution may lend
> • to another educational institution
> • to faculty, staff, or students
> ᔔ For-profit entity may lend internally
> ᔔ Include copyright notice for software

Lending Software

Remember that the copyright owner has the right to copy, to publicly distribute, and to publicly display the copyrighted work. The Computer Software Rental Amendments Act of 1990[9] amended section 109 to prohibit the owner of computer software from lending software for a purpose of direct or indirect commercial advantage. The prohibition does not, however, bar a non-profit library or a non-profit educational institution from lending software to another educational institution, or to faculty, staff or students, so long as the software has the requisite notice prescribed by the Register of Copyrights.[10] Affix the notice (which you can find in Chapter Two) on the computer disk or

---

9. Pub. L. No. 101-650, Title VIII, §§ 802, 803, 104 Stat. 5134 (1990).
10. 37 C.F.R. § 201.24 (2002).

its container, whether it is a stand-alone product or if the software comes with a book.

Public Display (Section 109(c))

Section 109(c) provides that notwithstanding the right of a copyright owner to display the work publicly, the owner of a lawfully made copy may, without permission, display the copy publicly, either directly or by projection, of no more than one image at a time, to viewers present at the place where the copy is located.

Question
The library subscribes to a Web-based product. Absent a license agreement that specifically permits or prohibits any of the following uses, which of these is permitted under 109(c)?

A. A group of people may view the image at the same computer terminal or from a projection device.
B. The image may be transmitted simultaneously to computers throughout the library so lots of people may see it at the same time.
C. You may transmit the image throughout the library to multiple pieces of equipment, but no more than one computer can show the image at any one time.

Answer
"A."

Analogize this to a painting in a museum. Dozens of people may contemplate the farmer and his daughter in Grant Wood's *American Gothic* at the Art Institute of Chicago. In the library setting, § 109(c) allows half a dozen students to crowd around a terminal while the librarian demonstrates a new database, and you also may project the image onto a large screen at a training session. But § 109(c) does not permit you to project the image to numerous computers throughout the library or elsewhere. If you want multiple, simultaneous access, get those terms in the license.

The Digital Millennium Copyright Act

> ### 6.3. Digital Millennium Copyright Act
> ∞ Digital copies for preservation
> ∞ Online service provider protections
> ∞ Anti-circumvention provisions

The 1998 Digital Millennium Copyright Act (DMCA)[11] addresses several matters that affect librarians and educators. In addition to the amendments to sections 108(b) and (c) that permit some digital copying, the DMCA provides some protection for service providers (SP's) who have infringing materials on their websites, or temporarily store or link to such materials. The DMCA also includes two important prohibitions: One proscribes the circumvention of devices that limit access to digital works, and the other bans interference with copyright management information.

Under the DMCA, a service provider is "an entity offering the transmission, routing, or providing connections for digital online communications, between or among points specified by a user, of material of the user's choosing, without modification to the content of the materials sent or received."[12] This would include libraries and institutions that maintain websites. (Feel free to use "Internet service provider (ISP) or "online service provider" (OSP) rather than "service provider.") The DMCA uses "service provider" (SP), and that is what is used here.

In a nutshell, there are four situations where the DMCA protects service providers: (1) transitory digital communications, (2) caching, (3) materials stored on a network at the direction of a user (including hosting websites), and (4) information location tools (linking). Very generally, under certain circumstances an SP that infringes because its website routes, stores, or links to infringing material will neither be liable for monetary damages nor subject to injunctive relief.[13]

---

11. Pub. L. No. 105-304, 112 Stat. 2860 (1998).
12. 17 U.S.C. § 512(k) (2000).
13. 17 U.S.C. § 512(j) (2000) (spells out the limited injunctive relief available to a plaintiff).

Transitory Digital Network Communications (Section 512(a))

Section 512(a) of the Act addresses a service provider (SP) that "merely acts as a data conduit, transmitting digital information from one point on a network to another at someone else's request" when the information transmitted happens to be infringing.[14] This protects the SP for simply routing or providing connections that enable the information to be transmitted, and also for any intermediate and transient copies that are made automatically during regular network operations.

The key is passivity, and several things must (or must not) take place: (1) the SP does not initiate the transmission; (2) the transmission, routing, connecting, or copying is automatic (i.e., the SP did not select the materials transmitted); (3) the SP does not determine who receives the materials transmitted; (4) intermediate copies are accessible only to anticipated recipients of the transmission; (5) the SP does not retain the materials transmitted; and (6) the SP does not modify the materials that are transmitted.

System Caching (Section 512(b))

System caching is an automatic process that stores data from other networks temporarily on the service provider's system so that data need not be retrieved over and over again from the original source. Caching, which technically involves making a copy, saves bandwidth. Section 512(b) provides some protections for a SP if (1) the caching process is automatic; (2) the content of the data was not modified; (3) the data is refreshed with more current materials according to industry standards; (4) the SP does not interfere with "hit" information (which is used for advertising revenue); and (5) the SP limits or blocks access to the data when the original poster uses access control devices, such as passwords.[15]

---

14. UNITED STATES COPYRIGHT OFFICE, THE DIGITAL MILLENNIUM COPYRIGHT ACT OF 1998: U.S. COPYRIGHT OFFICE SUMMARY at 10 (Dec. 1998), *available at* <http://www.copyright.gov> [hereinafter DMCA SUMMARY].
15. 17 U.S.C. § 512(b) (2000).

Information Residing on Systems or Networks at the Direction of Users (Section 512(c))

6.4. DMCA Service Provider Protections

Generally limits liability for infringing content or links to infringing content if:

- No actual knowledge
- No financial benefit
- Designated institutional agent
- Take down

The DMCA also provides some protection for a service provider that has infringing material stored on its system or network—including hosting a website—at the direction of a user. If the service provider does not have the right and ability to control the infringing activity, the protection kicks in if the SP did not have actual knowledge that the material or the activity using the material on the network was infringing. If the service provider *can* control the infringing activity, the protections apply if the SP does not receive a financial benefit due to the infringing activity. Should the SP receive notice that infringing materials are on its system or network, it must remove or block access to that material.[16]

Designated Agent, and Notice and Takedown

The service provider is protected under section 512(c) only if it has filed with the U.S. Copyright Office the name and contact information for someone who can receive complaints from copyright owners.[17] Neither Congress nor the Copyright Office specifies what role the designated agent must have in your organization. A university, for example, may appoint its director of information technology or its provost, a law firm its managing partner, a public library its chief librarian, and a corporation its general counsel.

The designated agent will receive complaints from copyright owners, such as a poet who discovers her poem on your website, or that your website links to her poem. Section 512(c) also spells out the required elements of notification of a claimed infringement, including that the notification must be in writing with a physical or electronic

---

16. 17 U.S.C. § 512 (c)(1) (2000).
17. 17 U.S.C. § 512(c)(2) (2000).

signature; identify the infringing work or materials; include information how to contact the complainant; and include statements that the complainant has authority to act on behalf of the copyright owner, has a good faith belief that the use complained of is not authorized, and that the information in the complaint is accurate.

This begins the "notice and takedown" process. Assuming that the copyright owner follows the statutory notification requirements, the service provider must remove or block access to the material, and also notify the subscriber who posted the allegedly infringing materials of the complaint. The subscriber may then file a counter notification. If that happens, the service provider must restore the materials unless the complainant notifies the provider that it has sought a court order to enjoin the alleged infringement.[18]

Information Location Tools (Linking) (Section 512(d))

Finally, the DMCA protects a service provider that provides information location tools. A service provider will not be liable for referring or linking users to a website that contains infringing content if the SP did not have knowledge of the infringing link and, if the SP had the right and ability to control the activity, it does not receive a financial benefit from doing so. As in 512(c), the provider must remove the link if it receives notice that it is linking to a site that has infringing content.[19]

---

18. 17 U.S.C. § 512(c) and (g) (2000). *See* DMCA SUMMARY, *supra* note 14, at 12; Casey Lide, *What Colleges and Universities Need to Know about the Digital Millennium Copyright Act,* 22 CAUSE/EFFECT (1999), *available at* <http://www.educause.edu>.
19. 17 U.S.C. § 512(d) (2000).

Non-Profit Educational Institutions (Section 512(e))

Non-profit educational institutions are included in the DMCA's definition of "service provider." However, provisions for educational institutions in section 512(e) clarify that some activities of faculty or graduate students who are employees performing teaching or research functions will not be considered activities of the institution itself. A faculty member's or graduate student's knowledge or awareness of his or her infringing activity will not be attributed to the institution if: (1) the activity does not involve access to instructional materials that are or were required or recommended, within the last three years, for a course taught by that person; (2) within the last three years the institution did not receive more than two notifications of infringement by the instructor, and (3) the institution provides informational materials that accurately describe and promote compliance with federal copyright law.[20]

Anti-Circumvention (Section 1201)

The DMCA also prohibits the circumvention of technological protective measures used by the copyright owner to prevent unauthorized access to the information.[21] Copyright owners (or their authorized vendors) often use technological tools, such as passwords or encryption, to block access to digital information. You cannot circumvent—or override—those technological measures. If Moses carried tablets down from Mount Millennium, they might say:

- Thou shall not decrypt an encrypted work.
- Thou shall not descramble a scrambled work.
- If one needest a password to access a digital work, thou shall not override password access.
- Thou shall not avoid, bypass, remove, or deactivate a technological protective measure that limits access to a protected work without permission.
- Thou shall not traffic in devices that have a primary purpose of circumvention.
- Thou shall not covet thy neighbor's databases.

---

20. For various polices, simply do a Google search using terms such as "DMCA copyright compliance."
21. 17 U.S.C. § 1201 (2000).

The DMCA actually addresses two types of technology—that which prevents unauthorized *access to* a work, and that which prevents unauthorized *copying of* a work—by prohibiting the making or selling of devices (including software) or services that circumvent either. The DMCA prohibits the manufacturing or selling of devices that prevent unauthorized access to or the copying of a work. But when it comes to circumvention, Congress distinguished between devices that control *access* to a work from those which control *copying*.

The DMCA prohibits you from circumventing *access-control* technological protective devices—those that prevent you from accessing protected digital information. The Act does *not*, however, prohibit the circumvention of devices that control *copying* because, according to the Copyright Office, copying may be a fair use.[22] In other words, you cannot override technology that prevents you from accessing a protected work. However, once you have legitimately accessed a work, you *may* override technology that prevents copying that would otherwise be permitted, such as if it is a fair use.

Congress did toss a tiny bone to the library and educational communities. A non-profit library or educational institution may circumvent technologies that prevent access to a work in order to make a decision whether to acquire it.[23] How meaningless is this? Publishers are delighted to give libraries temporary passwords to sample their products. If your library has a techie with lots of time on her hands, let her try to figure out how to circumvent an access-control technological protective measure so you can make a decision whether to subscribe to a product. If you do not have that luxury, pick up the phone and dial the toll-free 800 number or send the vendor an e-mail message. Figuring out how to override the access-control technology could take weeks, months, or forever. Picking up the phone or sending an e-mail message takes minutes. You decide what you want to do.

Copyright Management Information (Section 1202)

The final entree on our DMCA dim sum menu is copyright management information. Copyright management information includes the copyright notice, the title of the work and other information that identifies it, identifying information about the author, performer, or

---

22. UNITED STATES COPYRIGHT OFFICE, THE DIGITAL MILLENNIUM COPYRIGHT ACT OF 1998: U.S. COPYRIGHT OFFICE SUMMARY at 3–4 (Dec. 1998), *available at* <http://www.copyright.gov/legislation/dmca.pdf>.
23. 17 U.S.C. § 1201(d) (2000).

director of a work, and the terms and conditions of use. The DMCA makes it illegal to knowingly falsify, alter, or remove any copyright management information with the intention of inducing or enabling infringement.[24]

The Bottom Line: Do not mess with copyright management information. This is only a snapshot of some of the DMCA provisions that may affect libraries. For more information on the DMCA, the websites of the Library of Congress,[25] the Association of Research Libraries,[26] EDUCAUSE,[27] and the University of Texas[28] are particularly helpful.

---

24. 17 U.S.C. § 1202 (2000).
25. DMCA SUMMARY, *available at* <http://www.copyright.gov>.
26. ASSOCIATION OF RESEARCH LIBRARIES, DIGITAL MILLENNIUM COPYRIGHT ACT: STATUS AND ANALYSIS, *available at* <http://www.arl.org>.
27. EDUCAUSE, CURRENT ISSUES: THE DIGITAL MILLENNIUM COPYRIGHT ACT, *available at* <http://www.educause.edu>.
28. UNIVERSITY OF TEXAS, COPYRIGHT CRASH COURSE: COMPLYING WITH THE DIGITAL MILLENNIUM COPYRIGHT ACT, *available at* <http://www.utsystem.edu/ogc/intellectualproperty>.

Chapter Seven
LICENSING

ଈଠ୦ଔଓ

The Uniform Computer Information Transactions Act (UCITA)

The 1976 Copyright Act, as passed by Congress, was for the most part technologically neutral. For example, in defining the types of works eligible for copyright protection, Congress spoke of "original works of authorship *fixed in any tangible medium of expression, now known or later developed. . . .*"[1] The Pythia—the Oracle of Delphi— could not foresee the digital information revolution, and certainly not the topsy turvy world where *accessing* digital information has become more common than *owning* it.

7.1. UCITA
(Uniform Computer Information Transactions Act)

Default: Transaction to acquire software is a license

- ଈଠ Seller can unilaterally limit or control use
- ଈଠ Threatens Copyright Act rights
- ଈଠ Includes mass-market transactions
- ଈଠ Endorses shrinkwrap and click licenses for software
- ଈଠ User's breach is library's breach

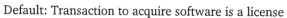

---

1. 17 U.S.C. § 102(a) (2000) (italics added).

The change from ownership to access through licensing takes us first to the Uniform Computer Information Transactions Act, more commonly known as UCITA.[2] The scope of UCITA is very broad. According to the National Conference of Commissioners on Uniform State Laws (NCCUSL), UCITA "provides a comprehensive set of rules for licensing computer information, whether computer software or other clearly identified forms of computer information."[3] NCCUSL makes clear its goal of the pre-eminence of the contract:

> Freedom of contract is a dominating underlying policy for UCITA, exactly as that principle is the foundation for the law of commercial transactions, generally, and exactly as that law has served all commercial transactions in the United States and has contributed to the economic growth and health of the United States.[4]

Although freedom of contract may be a noble goal, you may reasonably question how well it works when the marketplace is for information, rather than for goods such as cars or washing machines. Unlike a corporeal good, information is *not* fungible. A scientist, a lawyer, a professor, or a student who wants to read a book or an article written by a particular author wants *that* book or *that* article. Unfortunately, vendors have the edge over licensees; the vendors draft the contracts. You also should recognize the fundamental difference between owning something and merely having a license to use it.

NCCUSL wrote that "[t]he difference between a licensing contract and a sale contract is that the license generally contains restrictions on use and transfer of the computer information by the licensee during the life of the contract, and it may or may not transfer title to the licensee."[5] Licenses have the potential to dilute—perhaps even eliminate—critical rights for libraries and users, including the first sale doctrine, the library exemption, and fair use.

The section 107 fair use exemption permits a library patron, in most circumstances, to copy an article from a journal or a chapter from a book. But a patron may be out of luck if the library subscribes only to a digital version of the journal when the license precludes copying even small parts of articles. There could be problems for the

---

2. In a surprise move, on August 1, 2003, the National Conference of Commissioners on Uniform State Laws announced that it would "not expend any additional Conference energy or resources in having UCITA adopted." Letter from K. King Burnett, President, NCCUSL, to the Commissioners, *available at* <http://www.nccusl.org>.

3. NATIONAL CONFERENCE OF COMMISSIONERS ON UNIFORM STATE LAWS, Uniform Computer Information Transactions Act—A Summary, *available at* <http://www.nccusl.org>.

4. *Id.*

5. *Id.*

library, too. UCITA provides that "[i]f a license expressly limits use of the information or informational rights, use in any other manner is a breach of contract."[6] The library patron's breach—even if his or her conduct would be a fair use—becomes the library's breach. And if the library breaches the licensing agreement, the licensor may terminate the contract *and* recover the information.[7]

UCITA does have some safeguards, but they may prove meaningless for libraries. First, unconscionable contract terms are voidable.[8] Unfortunately, going to court is not a viable solution for libraries,[9] and proving unconscionability is not easy.[10] Second, sections of UCITA that are preempted by federal law are unenforceable to the extent of the preemption.[11] You might think that federal copyright law trumps contracts, but the official comments to UCITA provide that "no general preemption of contracting arises under copyright or patent law."[12] Third, UCITA provides that courts may refuse to enforce terms of a contract that violate a fundamental public policy.[13] In real life, your chance of arguing successfully that a clause in a license (prohibiting library-to-library copying, for example) violates a fundamental public policy is less than your chance of winning a $100 million Powerball lottery.

Still not convinced? Professor Wagstaff, who will speak at a national conference, wants to share with the other panelists copies of

---

6. UCITA § 307(b) (Aug. 2002). All references to UCITA are to the August 2002 version.
7. UCITA §§ 618, 814–815.
8. UCITA § 111.
9. UCITA § 117(a) summarizes questions to be determined by courts, including whether contractual terms are conspicuous, and whether terms are unenforceable either because they violate fundamental public policy or if they are unconscionable.
10. *See, e.g.,* JOHN E. MURRAY JR., MURRAY ON CONTRACTS § 96 (Michie, 1990). Murray quotes the following statement from Judge Skelley Wright in the case, Williams v. Walker-Thomas Furniture Co., 350 F.2d 445, 449 (D.C. Cir. 1965): "Unconscionability has generally been recognized to include an absence of meaningful choice on the part of one of the parties together with contract terms which are unreasonably unfavorable to the other party."
11. UCITA § 105(a).
12. Comments to UCITA § 105. NCCUSL cites National Car Rental Sys., Inc. v. Computer Assocs. Int'l, Inc., 991 F.2d 426 (8th Cir. 1993) and ProCD v. Zeidenberg, 86 F.3d 1447 (7th Cir. 1996) as support for this approach—that licenses are enforceable because rights created by contract are not equivalent to any of the exclusive rights within the general scope of copyright. But other courts have held otherwise, such as in Vault v. Quaid Software Ltd., 847 F.2d 255 (5th Cir. 1988) and American Movie Classics Co. v. Turner Entm't Co., 922 F. Supp. 926 (S.D.N.Y. 1996).
13. UCITA § 105(b).

federal statutes and court decisions relevant to the program. The professor finds the documents on a licensed electronic database, and, after removing any proprietary information, downloads the cases and laws or makes a print copy of them. But then he discovers that the license agreement permits him only to "transfer and store temporarily insubstantial amounts of downloadable data."

Under the Copyright Act, works of the federal government are not protected by copyright.[14] Professor Wagstaff certainly may copy selected laws and court decisions from print codes and case reporters that sit on the library's shelves. However, a license to an electronic database may prohibit him from copying that same information, even thought is in the public domain. Although the information is the same, it is treated differently because the book version is owned by the library, while the electronic version is subject to a license.

The License under the Microscope

7.2. Licensing Agreement

 🕮 Read the contract
 🕮 Permanent or temporary access
 🕮 No barriers to authorized users
 🕮 Preserve Copyright Act rights
 🕮 Respect user's privacy and confidentiality
 🕮 Hold-harmless clause
 🕮 Read the contract again

The word is vigilant. You must be vigilant when you sign a license for digital information. According to the legislative history to the Act, "[n]othing in the bill derogates from the rights of parties to contract with each other and to sue for breaches of contract. . . ."[15] You must look out for your library, and for those who use it. This includes *other* libraries too, for librarians share information through interlibrary lending and document delivery as permitted under section 108.

Probably the best way to examine the good, the bad, and the ugly that you may find in license agreements is to take a look at a license.

---

14. 17 U.S.C. § 105 (2000).
15. H.R. Rep. No. 94-1476, at 132.

Let's look at the online subscription agreement for journals from the American Meteorological Society,[16] with my comments added.

Terms and Conditions

1. Scope of License

Institutional Subscriber Use Restrictions. Under this Agreement, Subscribing Institution is granted a nonexclusive, revocable, nontransferable right and license to access and use the subscribed AMS journals made available to Subscribing Institution on the World Wide Web via the Subscribing Institution's Internet protocol addresses (IP addresses) up to the authorized number of workstations and, in connection with the foregoing, to permit Subscribing Institution's Authorized Users to access the journals and:

> *Comment*
> Access via IP address is good. By using a proxy server—a local computer that serves as an intermediary between off-site users and restricted online resources—authorized users can access the information from any computer, anywhere.

a. make searches of the subscribed journals;

> *Comment*
> Users obviously need to be able to search through the licensed information.

b. download search results to hard disk or diskette;

> *Comment*
> Absolutely. You want to be able to download. Make sure the license does not limit you to a specific technology. Today you may be using CDs, tomorrow Memory Sticks, and a few years from now something completely different.

c. make one hard copy of the output of any search;

> *Comment*
> Very good. This license permits the making of a single print copy, and there is no limitation as to size (such as "a small portion," or "a 500-word excerpt").

---

16. The AMS Journals Online Subscription Agreement may be found at <http://www.ametsoc.org/pubs/elicense.pdf>.

d. to share such hard copy with third parties to the same extent as
    the print edition or to the extent permitted under fair use provi-
    sions of the Copyright Act of 1976;

Comment
This treats the digital product as the same as the print version. It expressly recognizes fair use. Although by implication I think it also
recognizes the section 108 library exemption, you should add that to
the contract.

e. to use, with appropriate credit, figures, tables, and brief excerpts
    from the journals in scientific and educational works or similar
    work product of the Authorized User, except those portions there-
    of that are so noted as in the public domain or are U.S. Govern-
    ment works, for which no permission to copy is required.

Comment
Very good. Users should always give credit when it is due. It is nice
to see the publisher expressly acknowledge no copyright in content
that is in the public domain, including works of the U.S. government.

Except as expressly permitted herein, all other uses of the journals
or any portion thereof, including republication, resale, systematic
reproduction, or storage in a searchable, machine-readable database,
or time-share of the AMS journals database require written permission of the AMS.

Comment
It is not a bad idea to spell out the uses that are *not* allowed under
the license. If you do not understand the meaning of the terms (such
as "time-share") ask for clarification before you sign.

Authorized Users must be employees, faculty, staff, and students
officially affiliated with the Subscribing Institution and patrons of the
Subscribing Institution's library facilities. This includes occasional
users who access AMS journals through stations physically located on
the site and under the control and administration of the Subscribing
Institution. Authorized Users also includes persons affiliated with
remote sites or campuses of the Subscribing Institution that are
administered from the Subscribing Institution's site or campus, but
not persons affiliated with remote sites or campuses that have separate administrative staffs.

Comment
This is a very inclusive clause that addresses virtually every type of user and both on- and off-site use. You may need to clarify the distinction "between persons affiliated with remote sites or campuses administered from the Subscribing Institution's sites or campus" (who may access the journals) and those affiliated with "remote sites or campuses with separate administrative staffs" (who may not). Many universities have multiple campuses, and AMS wants to license the information separately for each campus. AMS probably will negotiate terms for a multi-campus license.

This Agreement is enforceable only against and by the parties who have executed it; the Agreement neither creates nor restricts rights to third parties. AMS understands that the Subscribing Institution is unable to practically enforce the terms of the Agreement for third parties. However, AMS asks that the Subscribing Institution agree to make reasonable efforts to take appropriate action should they become aware of any misuse that would violate the terms of the Agreement and that the Subscribing Institution continue to promote an environment that does not allow for abuse of the terms of the Agreement.

Comment
AMS reasonably asks that the library take "appropriate action" if it becomes aware of conduct that violates the license. AMS does not mandate what that action should be. Library staff should promote compliance with the license agreement.

2. Terms and Fees
The agreement will last through the end of the calendar year in which the subscription first becomes effective. This Agreement will remain in effect thereafter for successive subscription years so long as annual subscription fees are paid, subject to any new terms and/or conditions required by AMS at that time and shared with Subscribing Institution 30 days in advance. Both AMS and Subscribing Institution have the right to terminate this Agreement at the end of a subscription year by written notice given at least 30 days before the end of the subscription year.

Comment
You should specify that you are to be informed of new terms or conditions in writing. You do not want new terms or conditions conveyed merely via e-mail or a notice on the publisher's website. For planning and budget purposes, you may want 60- or even 90- day notice.

Upon termination for non-renewal of a subscription, Subscribing Institution may continue to use and access those journals to which it previously subscribed, subject to the terms and conditions contained herein. In the event that AMS determines that it will no longer provide the journals over the World Wide Web, AMS may provide Subscribing Institution with access to said subscribed journals in another searchable media format selected by AMS at its sole option.

Comment
The cup is more than half full. It is great that AMS offers perpetual access to the materials to which you subscribed during the term of the license, even if the license is not renewed. You might prefer some alternatives regarding the format in which the materials can be searched in the event AMS discontinues Web access.

AMS reserves the right to suspend or terminate access to the AMS journals under this Agreement without prior notice if the Subscribing Institution violates any term of this Agreement.

Comment
You really want the vendor to notify you of suspected violations of the contract before they suspend or terminate access to the content. You should insist on written notice, and the right to respond. You may even want to include in the agreement how disputes will be handled, including arbitration, and who will pay for it.

3. Technical Assistance and Customer Support
Technical assistance solely related to the online technical aspects of the AMS journals database can be obtained by sending e-mail to. . . . Monday through Friday, excluding holidays, from 9:00 A.M. to 4:30 P.M. ET. . . .

Comment
You want and need support. AMS provides both an e-mail address and a phone number. Both are desirable.

4. Copyright
The Subscribing Institution acknowledges that it has no claim to ownership by reason of its use of or access to the subscribed AMS journals. Except as otherwise provided herein, the journals, their content, and the database are owned by the AMS and are protected by the U.S. Copyright Laws and International Treaty provisions. Downloading or copying of content is permitted to allow Subscribing Institution and its Authorized Users to exercise its rights under this Agreement to the same extent as the print edition of the journal.

Other recompiling, copying, publication, or republication of the content, or any portion thereof, in any form or medium whatsoever, may be done only with the specific written permission from AMS.

Comment

No surprises here. The "ownership v. access" dichotomy is clear. AMS makes sure you know that you do not own the journals, but merely have a license to access them. For the most part, this section repeats what we read earlier in Section 1 (Scope of License).

5. Disclaimer of Warranties—Limitation of Liability

THE SUBSCRIBED JOURNALS ARE PROVIDED "AS IS" WITHOUT ANY WARRANTIES OF ANY KIND, EITHER EXPRESS OR IMPLIED, INCLUDING BUT NOT LIMITED TO, WARRANTIES OF DESIGN, MERCHANTABILITY OR FITNESS FOR A PARTICULAR PURPOSE, OR ARISING FROM A COURSE OF DEALING, USAGE, OR TRADE PRACTICE.

Comment

No surprise. AMS will not assume responsibility for the content of the information on the database.

Further, AMS does not warrant that the Subscribing Institution's or any Authorized User's use of the subscribed journals will be uninterrupted or error free, or that the results obtained will be useful or will satisfy the Subscribing Institution's or any Authorized User's requirements.

Comment

We all understand that there may be glitches. The real question is whether they are serious, and how long they last. I have no problem agreeing that AMS will not be responsible for "minor or occasional interruptions in service," or for "minor or occasional" errors in the data.

Sometimes vendors will try to disclaim all warranties, both express and implied. If the vendor will not agree to any express warranties, you at least want the contract to not negate implied warranties of merchantability and fitness for a particular purpose. The warranties of merchantability and fitness for a particular purpose can provide important protections in the event that the vendor or the product does not perform as promised or expected. If the database or some part of it cannot be used for the purpose for which it was acquired, the library may want to terminate the contract.

Subscribing Institution's sole and exclusive remedy for damages and/or loss in any way connected with this License shall be limited to the amount of the License Fee. UNDER NO CIRCUMSTANCES SHALL AMS BE LIABLE TO SUBSCRIBING INSTITUTION OR ANY OTHER PERSON, INCLUDING BUT NOT LIMITED TO AUTHORIZED USERS, FOR ANY SPECIAL, INCIDENTAL, OR CONSEQUENTIAL DAMAGES OF ANY CHARACTER, INCLUDING WITHOUT LIMITATION, DAMAGES ARISING OUT OF INABILITY TO ACCESS AMS'S JOURNALS OR ERRORS OR INACCURACIES IN THE JOURNAL CONTENT.

Comment

The library's remedy, in the event of the vendor's breach or other problems, is limited to the monies tied in with the license fee. This should mean that the vendor will credit you for the time you cannot access the service beyond the "minor or occasional interruptions" noted in the prior paragraph. That AMS will not be liable for special, incidental, or consequential damages is standard fare in a contract of this nature. For example, if an article in the database has erroneous information, and a lawyer relies on that information in representing a client and suffers some harm due to that reliance, the lawyer cannot blame (or recover consequential damages from) AMS.

Additionally, AMS shall not be liable or deemed to be in default for any delay or failure in performance or interruption resulting directly or indirectly from any cause or circumstance beyond the reasonable control of AMS; equipment or telecommunications failure; labor dispute; or failure of any third party to perform any agreement with AMS that adversely affects AMS's ability to perform its obligations hereunder.

Comment

More standard fare that protects the licensor from matters not under its control.

6. General

a. This Agreement constitutes the entire Agreement between the parties hereto and supersedes all prior oral and written and all contemporaneous oral negotiations, commitments, and understandings. The various headings in this Agreement are informational only and do not limit the scope or content of the subject matter contained therein. No waiver, amendment, or modification of this Agreement shall be effective unless it is in writing and signed by the parties hereto.

Comment

Yes, this is the entire agreement. It does not matter what was said over the phone or via e-mail during contract negotiations. If you do not like the written contract—this contract—you must change it now.

b. The Subscribing Institution may not assign or transfer its rights under this Agreement.

Comment

The contract is solely between the institution and AMS. You cannot transfer the license to another institution. No problem.

c. Should any provision of this Agreement be held to be void or unenforceable, the remaining provisions shall remain in full force and effect to read and [sic] construed as if the void or unenforceable provisions were originally deleted.

Comment

Standard fare. If, for example, the "disclaimer of warranty" language was held to be unenforceable because it violates public policy or is preempted by federal or state law, the rest of the contract is still valid.

d. The validity, interpretation, and performance of this Agreement shall be governed by the laws of the Commonwealth of Massachusetts, excluding that body of laws dealing with conflict of laws. Venue shall be the courts of competent jurisdiction located in Massachusetts.

Comment

You usually want the contract to be interpreted under the laws of your home state. If the library is publicly funded, your state may have laws requiring that contracts be interpreted under the laws of your home state. Although in most cases this probably is good for the library, that is not always true. For example, if your state enacted UCITA you may be better off interpreting the contract under the laws of a state that did not. If you are operating under laws that prohibit a contract from stating that disputes will be governed by laws other than that of your home state, you may want to simply delete the "choice of law" section of the contract.

The last steps are to sign and date the contract. Both parties should have original copies that include original signatures, not a photocopy or an electronic version.

You could look at other licenses for ideas about terms to include or exclude. One of the best sources, Licensingmodels.com, suggests model licenses for private libraries, public libraries, single academic institutions, and academic consortia. Licensingmodels.com puts in [square brackets] optional language for contracting parties to consider. Below you will find selected clauses from Licensingmodels.com's

"Academic Single User License" that are not included in or are addressed differently than in the AMS license.[17]

Licensingmodels.com Academic Single Institution License: Version 2.0 14/4/00

1. Key Definitions

Comment
The license defines ten or so terms. Clarity is good.

Commercial Use. Use for the purposes of monetary reward (whether by or for the Licensee or an Authorised User) by means of sale, resale, loan, transfer, hire or other form of exploitation of the Licensed Materials. For the avoidance of doubt, neither recovery of direct costs by the Licensee from Authorised Users, nor use by the Licensee or by an Authorised User of the Licensed Materials in the course of research funded by a commercial organization, is deemed to be Commercial Use.

Comment
I would prefer that cost recovery include both direct and indirect costs.

Course Packs. A collection or compilation of materials (e.g., book chapters, journal articles) assembled by members of staff of the Licensee for use by students in a class for the purposes of instruction.

Comment
If you want to use the database to create coursepacks, it is good to address them—and define them—in the agreement.

Electronic Reserve. Electronic copies of materials (e.g., book chapters, journal articles) made and stored on the Secure Network by the Licensee for use by students in connection with specific courses of instruction offered by the Licensee to its students.

Comment
Good.

---

17. This website originates in the United Kingdom, thus the British spelling of some words.

2. Agreement
2.3. On termination of this License, the Publisher shall provide continuing access for Authorised Users to that part of the Licensed Materials which was published and paid for within the Subscription Period, either from the Server [or from the archive . . .] or by supplying [electronic files] [CD-ROMs] [printed copies] to the Licensee [subject to payment of such fees as the parties may agree] [except where such termination is due to a breach of the License by the Licensee which the Licensee has failed to remedy as provided in . . . of this License {, in which case such continuing access shall be provided in respect of Licensed Materials published up to the date of such breach}].

Comment
What's not to like? Note the different options for continued access: (1) from the Server, (2) from the archive, (3) electronic files, (4) CD-ROMs, or (5) print copies.

3. Usage Rights
3.1.2. [Make such back-up copies of the Licensed Materials as are reasonably necessary.]

Comment
Good.

3.1.3. Make such [temporary] local electronic copies [by means of caching {or mirrored storage}] of all or part of the Licensed Materials as are necessary solely to ensure efficient use by Authorised Users [and not to make available to Authorised Users duplicate copies of the Licensed Material].

Comment
Making a cache copy provides quicker access to the online data.

3.1.6. Provide single printed or electronic copies of single articles at the request of individual Authorised Users.

Comment
Yes. Section 108.

3.2. Authorised Users may, in accordance with the copyright laws of [jurisdiction] and subject to clause 6 below:

Comment
The uses that follow are expressly permitted under the license. Make sure you read clause 6 carefully.

3.2.4. Distribute a copy of individual articles or items of the Licensed Materials in print or electronic form to other Authorised Users [; for the avoidance of doubt, this sub-clause shall include the distribution of a copy for teaching purposes to each individual student Authorised User in a class at the Licensee's institution].

Comment
You could be more succinct (and a little more encompassing) by using the following language: "Distribute a copy of individual articles or items of the Licensed Materials in any format to other Authorised Users, including copies to students enrolled in a class or those who attend educational programs sponsored by the Licensee's institution."

3.3. [Nothing in this Licence shall in any way exclude, modify or affect any of the Licensee's rights under Copyright Revision Act 1976 as amended . . . provided that such rights are exercised in accordance with Section 108 of the Act and with the guidelines developed by the National Commission on New Technological Uses of Copyrighted Works (CONTU Guidelines) and published in U.S. Copyright Office Circular 21.]

Or

[Nothing in this Licence shall in any way exclude, modify or affect any of the Licensee's statutory rights under the copyright laws of {jurisdiction}.]

Comment
You want the license to expressly acknowledge user rights. I prefer the broader second clause, which would include other library and user-friendly sections of the Act, especially sections 107-110.

4. Supply of Copies to Other Libraries
4.1. [The Licensee may, subject to clause 6 below, supply to an Authorised User of another library {within the same country as the Licensee}(whether by post or fax [or secure transmission, using Ariel or its equivalent, whereby the electronic file is deleted immediately after printing]), for the purposes of research or private study and not for Commercial Use, a single paper copy of an electronic original of an individual document being part of the Licensed Materials.]

Or

[The Licensee may, subject to clause 6 below, supply to an Authorised User of another library {within the same country as the Licensee} a copy of an individual document being part of the Licensed Materials by post, fax or electronic transmission via the Internet or otherwise, for the purposes of research or private study and not for Commercial Use.]

Or

[Notwithstanding the provisions of Clauses 3.1 and 3.3, it is understood and agreed that neither the Licensee nor Authorised Users may provide, by electronic means, to a user at another library a copy of any part of the Licensed Materials for research or private study or otherwise.]

Comment

I prefer the following language: "Consistent with section 108 of the Copyright Act, the Licensee may provide to another library, in either print, fax, or digital format, a single copy of an individual document that is part of the licensed materials.

5. Course Packs and Electronic Reserve

5.1. [The Licensee may, subject to clause 6 below, incorporate parts of the Licensed Materials in printed Course Packs [and Electronic Reserve collections] for the use of Authorised Users in the course of instruction at the Licensee's institution, but not for Commercial Use. Each such item shall carry appropriate acknowledgment of the source, listing title and author of the extract, title and author of the work, and the publisher. Copies of such items shall be deleted by the Licensee when they are no longer used for such purpose. Course packs in non-electronic non-print perceptible form, such as audio or Braille, may also be offered to Authorised Users who, in the reasonable opinion of the Licensee, are visually impaired.]

Or

[For the avoidance of doubt, the Licensee may not incorporate all or any part of the Licensed Materials in [Course Packs] [and] [Electronic Reserve collections] without the prior written permission of the Publisher {Publisher's Representative}, which may set out further terms and conditions for such usage.]

Comment

If you can get permission to include coursepacks in your license, as is provided for in the first clause, more power to you. You definitely want to include licensed digital information in the library's electronic reserve system.

6. Prohibited Uses

6.1. Neither the Licensee nor Authorised Users may:

6.1.1. remove or alter the authors' names or the Publisher's copyright notices or other means of identification or disclaimers as they appear in the Licensed Materials;

> *Comment*
>
> No problem. We agree not to mess with Copyright Management Information as a matter of conscience, and as a matter of law (DMCA).

6.1.2. systematically make print or electronic copies of multiple extracts of the Licensed Materials for any purpose [other than back-up copies permitted under clause 3.1.2];

> *Comment*
>
> Systematic copying is not permitted under section 108(g). This language does not bother me, as we all agree to comply with section 108.

6.1.3. mount or distribute any part of the Licensed Material on any electronic network, including without limitation the Internet and the World Wide Web, other than the Secure Network

> *Comment*
>
> We agree not to make the licensed information available to the rest of the world.

6.2. The Publisher's [Representative's] explicit written permission must be obtained in order to:

6.2.1. use all or any part of the Licensed Materials for any Commercial Use;

> *Comment*
>
> This does not bother me. "Commercial Use" is defined earlier as selling or transferring the licensed information for money. If you are in a for-profit institution, make sure that "Commercial Use" does not include the day-to-day operations of the enterprise. In other words, if you are the librarian for Texaco, "Commercial Use" does not include the research activities of Texaco employees.

6.2.4. alter, abridge, adapt or modify the Licensed Materials, except to the extent necessary to make them perceptible on a computer screen [or as otherwise permitted in this Licence,] to Authorised

Users. For the avoidance of doubt, no alteration of the words or their order is permitted.

Comment
I would like to delete this. You should be able to "alter, abridge, adapt, or modify" the materials so long as you are not creating a derivative work that requires the copyright owner's permission. This broad prohibition may be more important in Europe where there has been longstanding protection of authors' moral rights.

7. Publisher's Undertakings
7.1. The Publisher warrants to the Licensee that the Licensed Materials used as contemplated by this Licence do not infringe the copyright or any other proprietary or intellectual property rights of any person. The Publisher shall indemnify and hold the Licensee harmless from and against any loss, damage, costs, liability and expenses (including reasonable legal and professional fees) arising out of any legal action taken against the Licensee claiming actual or alleged infringement of such rights. This indemnity shall survive the termination of this Licence for any reason. This indemnity shall not apply if the Licensee has amended the Licensed Materials in any way not permitted by this Licence.

Comment
I like the "hold harmless clause" because it protects the library if the digital product includes infringing content.

The Publisher shall:

7.2.1. make the Licensed Materials available to the Licensee from the Server in the media, format and time schedule specified in Schedule 1. The Publisher will notify the Licensee [and the Agent] at least [ninety (90)] [sixty (60)] days in advance of any anticipated specification change applicable to the Licensed Materials. If the changes render the Licensed Materials less useful in a material respect to the Licensee, the Licensee may within thirty days of such notice treat such changes as a breach of this License under clause 10.1.2 and 10.4.

Comment
This clause requires the publisher to notify you of changes well in advance, and permits the library to terminate the contract if the changes make the licensed materials less useful. The more notice you have, the better.

7.2.5. use all reasonable endeavors to make the Licensed Materials available to the Licensee and to Authorised Users at all times and on a twenty-four-hour basis, save for routine maintenance (which shall be notified to the Licensee in advance wherever possible), and to restore access to the Licensed Materials as soon as possible in the event of an interruption or suspension of the service.

Comment
Yes.

7.3. The Publisher reserves the right at any time to withdraw from the Licensed Materials any item or part of an item for which it no longer retains the right to publish, or which it has reasonable grounds to believe infringes copyright or is defamatory, obscene, unlawful or otherwise objectionable. The Publisher shall give written notice to the Licensee of such withdrawal. If the withdrawal [represents more than ten per cent (10%) of the book, journal or other publication in which it appeared, the Publisher shall refund to the Licensee that part of the Fee that is in proportion to the amount of material withdrawn and the remaining unexpired portion of the Subscription Period] [results in the Licensed Materials being no longer useful to the Licensee, the Licensee may within thirty days of such notice treat such changes as a breach of this License under clause 10.1.2 and 10.4].

Comment
Licensors often do not own the content. If the licensor does not have permission to publish or distribute the works, it cannot do so. This helpful clause provides for refunds to the library for withdrawn materials. The bracketed text, which I like, permits the library to treat withdrawals as a breach if the remainder "is no longer useful."

7.5. Collection and analysis of data on the usage of the Licensed Materials will assist both the Publisher and the Licensee to under-stand the impact of this License. The Publisher shall provide to the Licensee or facilitate the collection and provision to the Licensee and the Publisher by the Licensee [or by the Agent] of such usage data on the number [of titles] [of abstracts and] of articles downloaded, by journal title, on [a monthly] [a quarterly] [an annual] basis for the Publisher's and the Licensee's private internal use only. Such usage data shall be compiled in a manner consistent with applicable privacy [and data protection] laws [and as may be agreed between the parties from time to time], and the anonymity of individual users and the confidentiality of their searches shall be fully protected. In the case that the Publisher assigns its rights to another party under clause

11.3, the Licensee may at its discretion require the assignee either to keep such usage information confidential or to destroy it.

Comment
Collecting data helps you know how much the databases is being used, which will help you determine whether to renew the contract. You may want monthly reports, but quarterly ones should suffice. The license must preserve the privacy and confidentially of users.

8. Licensee's Undertakings
8.1. The Licensee shall:

8.1.3. use all reasonable endeavors to monitor compliance and immediately upon becoming aware of any unauthorized use or other breach, inform the Publisher and take all reasonable and appropriate steps, including disciplinary action, both to ensure that such activity ceases and to prevent any recurrence;

Comment
Ouch! Librarians should monitor the use of licensed materials, but I would not agree to inform the publisher of unauthorized uses. The library should decide the reasonable and appropriate steps it will take, not the vendor.

8.2. [{Subject to applicable law,} The Licensee agrees to indemnify, defend and hold the Publisher harmless from and against any loss, damage, costs, liability and expenses (including reasonable legal and professional fees) arising out of any claim or legal action taken against the Publisher related to or in any way connected with any use of the Licensed Materials by the Licensee or Authorised Users or any failure by the Licensee to perform its obligations in relation to this Licence, provided that] nothing in this Licence shall make the Licensee liable for breach of the terms of the Licence by any Authorised User provided that the Licensee did not cause, knowingly assist or condone the continuation of such breach to continue after becoming aware of an actual breach having occurred.

Comment
I do not like the first part [in brackets], and would eliminate it. I do like the language relieving the library of liability for breaches by its users unless the library knowingly assisted or condoned the continuation of the breach.

9. Undertakings by Both Parties

9.1 Each party shall use its best endeavours to safeguard the intellectual property, confidential information and proprietary rights of the other party.

Comment

Absolutely!

10. Term and Termination

10.1. In addition to automatic termination (unless renewed) under clause 2.2, this Licence shall be terminated:

10.1.1. if the Licensee [wilfully] defaults in making payment of the Fee as provided in this Licence and fails to remedy such default within [thirty (30)] [sixty (60)] days of notification in writing by the Publisher;

Comment

Sixty is better than thirty, and insist on written notice. Sometimes your parent institution may be a little slow paying its bills.

10.1.2. If the Publisher commits a material or persistent breach of any term of this Licence and fails to remedy the breach (if capable of remedy) within [thirty (30)] [sixty (60)] days of notification in writing by the Licensee;

Comment

Breaches can go both ways. Make sure you notify the vendor promptly—and repeatedly—of any problems.

10.1.3. if the Licensee commits a wilful material and persistent breach of the Publisher's copyright or other intellectual property rights or of the provisions of clause 3 in respect of usage rights or of clause 6 in respect of prohibited uses;

Comment

Make sure you get written notice of any suspected breaches of the agreement or copyright violations, and time to respond and to remedy the problem.

10.1.4. if either party becomes insolvent or becomes subject to receivership, liquidation or similar external administration.

Comment

This type of "ipso facto" clause may not be enforceable in bankruptcy.

11. General

11.2. Alterations to this Licence and to the Schedules to this Licence are only valid if they are recorded in writing and signed by both parties.

Comment

A good clause that prevents the licensor from modifying the contract simply by sending the library an e-mail message or by posting amendments on its website. Changes in the contract should be in writing, and signed.

11.4. If rights in all or any part of the Licensed Materials are assigned to another publisher, the Publisher shall [use its best endeavors to] ensure that the terms and conditions of this Licence are maintained.

Comment

If the licensor assigns rights to another publisher, the assignee should be bound by the agreement. If the new publisher cannot comply with the contractual terms or conditions, the library has a right to renegotiate the contract, or terminate it and get a pro rata share of the contract price returned to it.

12. Use of an Expert to Resolve Disputes

12.1. If any difference arises between the parties on the meaning of this Licence or their rights and obligations, it shall first be referred to an independent expert appointed by agreement of the parties, or, in default of an agreement, by the [President] [Chair] for the time being of the [Institute of Chartered Accountants] [professional or academic body].

Comment

Alternative dispute resolution provisions enable the licensor and licensee to try to resolve disputes without using the courts.

12.2. Any expert so appointed shall act as expert and not as an arbitrator and his decision (which shall be given by him in writing stating the reasons for his decision) shall be final and binding on the parties.

Comment

This clause makes the decision of the expert final.

The Bottom Line on Licenses: Read a license carefully, and then read it again. If you do not like what you see, write in the changes (deletions, additions, modifications) and initial them. Send two signed copies to the licensor, and ask the licensor to send one back to you with his or her signature.

Licensors sometimes will not send back the amended agreement. Therefore, in your cover letter and on the license itself, write that if the licensor provides the product after you mailed the amended agreement, you understand that the licensor has assented to your terms.

Chapter Eight

AUDIOVISUAL WORKS AND NON-PRINT MEDIA

⊱⊰

According to the Copyright Act, audiovisual works "are works that consist of a series of related images which are intrinsically intended to be shown by the use of machines, or devices such as projectors, viewers, or electronic equipment, together with accompanying sounds, if any, regardless of the nature of the material objects, such as films or tapes, in which the works are embodied."[1] In other words, audiovisual works mix visual images and sound, and include items such as films, videocassettes, and DVDs.

The use of audiovisual works under the Act, like the use of copyrighted works in other formats, is not always clear. In fact, sometimes it can be pretty muddy. This chapter addresses issues such as the copying and showing of audiovisual works, including the copyright owners's right of public display and performance.

---

1. 17 U.S.C. § 101 (2000).

Taping

> ### 8.1. Guidelines for Off-Air Taping of Copyrighted Works for Educational Use
>
> ఴ Broadcast programs
> ఴ Non-profit educational institutions
> ఴ For instruction
> ఴ At instructor's request
> ఴ Local transmission
> ఴ Use for first ten days only
> ఴ Thirty-five more days for evaluation, then destroy
> ఴ Institutional controls
>
> 127 Cong. Rec. 24048-49 (October 14, 1981)

It has been nearly a generation since the U.S. Supreme Court decided *Sony Corp. of America v. Universal City Studios, Inc.,*[2] or the "Betamax" case. In 1984, the Court held that off-air taping of broadcast television programs in one's own home for the non-commercial purpose of time-shifting is not infringing. A few points about the Betamax case: First, the decision applies only to programs broadcast on free television; pay television programs such as HBO or Showtime are not included. Second, it does not address taping outside the home. Third, it focuses on taping for the purpose of time-shifting, or watching a program subsequent to the original broadcast. What all of this means is that if you know how to program your VCR, then you may tape NBC's *The West Wing.*

Institutional taping in libraries or schools is a very different story. Take, for example, *Encyclopedia Brittanica Educational Corp. v. Crooks,*[3] where a federal district court held that extensive and systematic off-air taping of educational programs, even for non-profit educational purposes, was infringing. In what is often called the "BOCES" case (for Board of Educational Services for Erie County, New York) a non-profit organization funded by nineteen school districts offered a videotaping service for schools. BOCES's Videotape and Instructional Television Service (VITS) had a nine-person staff, and a library that contained 4,500 videotaped television programs for the 1976–77 school year. VITS's equipment was able to produce sixty videotape copies of a single program in a twenty-four-hour period, and they transmitted about 14,000 programs to schools during that

---

2. 464 U.S. 417 (1984).
3. 542 F. Supp. 1156 (W.D.N.Y. 1982).

year. VITS even created a 345-page catalog of 5,000 "master" video-tapes, divided into twenty-six separate subject areas. A school that requested and received tapes from VITS could keep them. Jerry Lee Lewis might have sang that there was a whole lot of tapin' goin' on.

Not surprisingly, the court concluded that BOCES's "highly organized and systematic practice of making off-the-air videotapes of plaintiffs' copyrighted works for use in later years and the making of numerous derivative copies of plaintiffs' copyrighted works does not constitute fair use. . . ."[4] Even though BOCES was a non-profit educational organization, the court reached the right decision.

The BOCES case does not mean that you can *never* tape programs for educational purposes. You can find some guidance from the *Guidelines for Off-Air Recording of Copyrighted Works for Educational Use.*[5]

A few things about the *Guidelines*. First, they apply to non-profit educational institutions. A school or academic library that helps its parent institution meet its instructional needs certainly qualifies. A for-profit library, such as one in a corporation or law firm, does not come within the *Guidelines*, and neither does a city or county public library unless it is part of an educational institution. Second, the *Guidelines* apply to programs broadcast to the general public without charge, not to pay-TV programs. (Today this would include basic cable, but probably would not include premium channels such as HBO or Showtime). Third, the purpose of the taping must be instructional, rather than for entertainment or recreational purposes. Fourth, requests to tape must be made by the instructor, rather than ordered from above by, say, the school system. Here are the details.

- ಸು You may tape a program only once at the request of the same teacher.
- ಸು You may play a recorded program for students only in the course of teaching, and again for reinforcement, within the first ten consecutive school days after the taping.
- ಸು You may retain a recording for up to forty-five days after it is recorded, after which time it must be erased or destroyed. After the first ten school days, the recordings may be used up to the end of the forty-five day period only for teacher evaluation purposes.
- ಸು You may use a taped program in classrooms and other places in the institution devoted to instruction (presumably including the library), and also in homes of students receiving formalized home instruction.

---

4. *Id.* at 1185.
5. 127 Cong. Rec. 24,048–49 (Oct. 14, 1981) (statement of Rep. Kastenmeier).

› You may make a limited number of copies of each recording to meet the needs of teachers. These copies are subject to the same rules that govern the original recording.

› You need not use a program in its entirety, but may not alter it from its original content so as to change its meaning.

› You may not physically or electronically combine or merge a recording to create a teaching anthology or compilation.

› You must include on all copies the copyright notice as it appeared on the broadcast program as it was recorded.

› An educational institution must establish control procedures that enable it to comply with the *Guidelines*.

The *Guidelines* provide a safe harbor. Taping within them would certainly be permissible, but some uses outside the *Guidelines* also may be permitted as a fair use.

Example 1

Madison High School teacher Connie Brooks tapes a program to show to her class. Student Walter Denton saw the program in class, and asks to see it again three weeks after the first showing because he is working on a term paper.

Comment

The *Guidelines* provide that after the first ten school days, the tape may only be used for teacher evaluation purposes. This is pretty silly. If a student wants to watch the tape again, let him. This sure seems like fair use to me.

Example 2

Walter (the student) is laid up in a hospital for two weeks and asks to see the tape when he returns to school.

Comment

Technically, the *Guidelines* say no. But they are guidelines, not the law. This seems like a perfect case of fair use.

Example 3

Miss Brooks tapes a program to show to her class. She holds on to the tape for a month or so, in accordance with the *Guidelines*. She tells the principal, Mr. Conklin, how good the tape is, and Mr. Conklin tells the school librarian to add the tape to the library's collection.

Comment

Just say no. No matter how much you like the teacher or fear the principal, do not add tapes of recorded television programs to the library's collection. If you want it, buy it.

As noted in Chapter Five, the section 108 library exemption also address copying audiovisual works. However, unless it is a news program, copying is limited to the purposes enumerated in subsections (b) and (c).[6] Under section 108(b), a library may copy an *unpublished* audiovisual work it owns for the purpose of preservation and security, or for deposit in another library for research purposes. Section 108(c) permits copying to replace a lost, stolen, or damaged *published* audiovisual work if the library determines that it cannot obtain an unused replacement at a fair price.

What about news programs? Section 108(f)(3) provides that audiovisual news programs may be copied (i.e., taped) and lent, subject to the limitations in subsection 108(a): There is no purpose of direct or indirect commercial advantage; the library's collections are open to the public or available to researchers; and the reproduction includes a notice of copyright. Unlike the *Off-Air Recording Guidelines*, section 108 rights are not limited to non-profit educational institutions. The legislative history to the 1976 Act sheds a bit more light on taping news programs.

> The conference committee is aware that an issue has arisen as to the meaning of the phrase "audiovisual news program" in section 108(f)(3). The conferees believe that, under the provision as adopted in the conference substitute, a library or archives qualifying under section 108(a) would be free . . . to reproduce, on videotape or any other medium of fixation or reproduction, local, regional, or network newscasts, interviews concerning current news events, and on-the-spot coverage of news events, and to distribute a limited number of reproductions of such programs on a loan basis.[7]

A word of caution here: Congress is referring to straight news, not to documentary, magazine format, nor other public affairs programs. In other words, not *60 Minutes*, *Meet the Press*, nor *Face the Nation*. But always remember that some uses may be permitted as a section 107 fair use.

As you may recall, section 117 permits the making of an archival copy of a computer program. Does this mean that a library may make a copy of a video-recording or a sound-recording because of the possibility that the original may deteriorate or be destroyed? The answer is no. A library that purchases audiotapes, CDs, videotapes, or DVDs for its collection may not make a backup copy "just in case." If you need two copies, then buy two copies.

The story is a little different for obsolete formats. Remember that under section 108(c) a library *may* make a copy if the format in

---

6. 17 U.S.C. § 108(i) (2000).
7. H.R. REP. No. 94-1733 (Conf.), at 73.

which the work is stored is obsolete and the library cannot obtain an unused replacement at a fair price. In other words, if the library purchased a Beta version of a continuing education program back in 1982, and if it cannot locate a VHS or DVD version today, then it may copy the Beta version onto a different format. After you do this, you should discard your old Beta copy.

Public Performances

8.2. Public Performance

- ➥ A place open to the public
- ➥ Where a substantial number of persons gather, or
- ➥ Available to the public via a transmission
  - • same or separate places
  - • same or different times

Take a deep breath and hold on to the reins; we are off to a day at the races. Recall that a copyright owner has several different rights, one of which is the right to perform the copyrighted work publicly. But U.S. copyright law does not protect *all* performances, only *public* performances. According to the Copyright Act:

> To perform or display a work "publicly" means—
>
> (1) to perform or display it at a place open to the public or at any place where a substantial number of persons outside of a normal circle of a family and its social acquaintances is gathered; or
> (2) to transmit or otherwise communicate a performance or display of the work to a place specified by clause (1) or to the public, by means of any device or process, whether the members of the public capable of receiving the performance or display receive it in the same place or in separate places and at the same time or at different times.[8]

In plain English, a public performance occurs under either of three circumstances: (1) when the place where the work is performed is open to the public; (2) if the performance occurs at a place where a large number of people (exclusive of one's family and friends) may

---

8. 17 U.S.C. § 101 (2000).

gather; or (3) if there is a transmission that allows the public to see or hear the work.

The public performance right is designed to prevent large numbers of people from seeing the same copy of the work, whether at one time or over a period of time. Determining when public performances take place is not always easy. Consider, for example, what different state attorneys general wrote during the 1980s as to whether state prisons could show purchased or rented videos to inmates.

In 1982 the Attorney General of California ruled that showing a purchased video that had a "For Home Use Only" notice on it was a public performance, and that showing such tapes to prisoners without a public performance license would be infringing.[9] That same year, Utah's Attorney General wrote that the Utah State Prison could not show videotapes of movies to groups of up to twenty inmates,[10] and the Alaska Attorney General similarly held that their Department of Health and Social Services could not show rented videos to inmates.[11] In 1985, however, the Attorney General of Louisiana ruled that their Department of Corrections *could* show films rented from local stores to groups of between twenty to thirty prisoners, reasoning that those performances were not public.[12] Then, in 1988, the Louisiana Attorney General reaffirmed the 1985 ruling, but held that showing tapes to audiences of 200-300 inmates would be infringing.[13]

To summarize, performances are public if a substantial number of people have the *potential* to see or hear a protected work over the course of time, regardless of how many people actually see or hear it at a particular place or at a particular time. A few cases from the 1980s illustrate how courts determine when a performance is public.

---

9. California Op. Att'y Gen. No. 81-503 (Feb. 5, 1982).
10. Utah Op. Att'y Gen. No. 82-03 (Sept. 22, 1982).
11. Alaska Op. Att'y Gen. No 366-404-82 (June 11, 1982).
12. Louisiana Op. Att'y Gen. No. 84-436 (Jan. 10, 1985) (Laissez les bon temps rouler).
13. Louisiana Op. Att'y Gen. No. 88-576 (Dec. 19, 1988). In another interesting "non-case," in the mid-1980s an attorney representing motion picture copyright owners wrote the Arkansas Department of Corrections (ADC), warning that the showing of films licensed only for home use was infringing. The ADC did not contest this interpretation, and proceeded to contract with two companies to provide films with public performance licenses. The prisoners filed a lawsuit seeking a declaration that prison showings were either not public performances, or that they were permitted as a fair use. (They also pointed out that it cost much more to acquire films with public performance rights than to rent the films: $9,600 versus $2,100 for 121 films.) The case was not decided on the merits because the Eighth Circuit ruled that the district court did not have jurisdiction to decide the case. Diagnostic Unit Inmate Council v. Films, Inc., 39 U.S.P.Q.2d 1371 (8th Cir. 1996).

The first case involved a video store that played tapes rented by their customers in small two- to four-person viewing booths. The U.S. Court of Appeals for the Third Circuit felt that this arrangement was similar to a movie theater with the added feature of privacy, and concluded that such performances were public.[14] Two years later, the same court, ruling in a case with a slightly different twist, held that a video store could not rent videotapes and allow the *renters* to play the tapes in small viewing rooms in the store.[15]

A line was drawn in 1989 when the Ninth Circuit held that a rented hotel room is not a public place, and that a hotel *could* rent videotapes to their guests for viewing on equipment in their room.[16] However, two years later a district court held that the electronic delivery of films to hotel rooms through a bank of video players did create public performances.[17]

If you are wondering why you can find an On Command system at your favorite Hilton, the answer is simple: copyrighted works may be performed publicly when permitted under the Copyright Act, or with the copyright owner's permission or payment of royalties. On Command's website tells you that it licenses films directly from the studios.[18]

These court decisions illustrate that in determining whether a performance is public, look at the place as a whole where the performance takes place, not at a particular room or location within a building. Video stores, restaurants, and hotels (though not a particular room, once it is rented) are open to the general public or to a large number of people outside of one's family and friends. They are public places, and performances that take place in these places are public performances. What about libraries?

You may want to contend that some libraries—those in law firms, corporations, or trade associations, for example—are not open to the public, and that performances to groups of attorneys or to board members are not public performances. You are right. As noted earlier, the legislative history states that "[r]outine meetings of businesses and governmental personnel would be excluded because they do not represent the gathering of a 'substantial number of persons.'"[19]

---

14. Columbia Pictures Indus., Inc. v. Redd Horne Inc., 749 F.2d 154 (3d Cir. 1984).
15. Columbia Pictures Indus., Inc. v. Aveco Inc., 800 F.2d 59 (3d Cir. 1986).
16. Columbia Pictures Indus., Inc. v. Professional Real Estate Investors, Inc., 866 F.2d 278 (9th Cir. 1989).
17. On Command Video Corp. v. Columbia Pictures Indus., 777 F. Supp. 787 (N.D. Cal. 1991) (for some reason, the court left out the "Inc." after "Columbia Pictures").
18. *See* <http://www.ocv.com>.
19. H.R. Rep. No. 94-1476, at 64.

What about city or county public libraries, and public *or* private university libraries? These certainly appear to be places where a substantial number of persons outside of a normal circle of a family and its social acquaintances gather. According to the legislative history, Congress considers performances in these venues to be public performances: "[P]erformances in 'semipublic places' such as clubs, lodges, factories, summer camps, and schools are 'public performances' subject to copyright control."[20]

Two questions come to mind. First, does a copyright owner's public performance right prohibit a public library from showing an audiovisual work to large groups? I think the answer is yes. Unless otherwise permitted under the Copyright Act (as a fair use, for example, or under the section 110 exemptions, which are discussed below) a library cannot show audiovisual works to large groups. There is an alternative, of course: a public performance license.

Public performance licenses may be acquired from the copyright owner, or, more likely, from a distributor. Some distributors of educational materials, such as Films for the Humanities and Sciences, automatically include public performance rights with films they lease or sell.[21] By contrast, popular film vendor MoviesUnlimited includes the following notice on the order page of their catalog: "All programs licensed for home and non-theatrical use only. Broadcast in any form and duplication are prohibited." Many studios authorize the Los Angeles–based Motion Picture Licensing Corporation to convey umbrella public performance licenses to both for and not for-profit organizations and institutions.[22] The license cost depends on the amount of usage, the size of the institution's patron base, and the number of viewing sites.

The second question asks whether a library patron may watch a video in a public library or at a college or university library. The motion picture industry says no. In response to a 1986 article in *Information Technology and Libraries*,[23] and also to videotape and software guidelines published that year in *American Libraries*,[24] a law

---

20. *Id.*
21. *See* <http://www.films.com>.
22. *See* <http://www.mplc.com>.
23. Debra Stanek, *Videotapes, Computer Programs and the Library,* 5 INFO. TECH. & LIBRS. 42 (1986).
24. Mary Hutchings Reed & Debra Stanek, *Library and Classroom Use of Copyrighted Videotapes and Computer Software,* AM. LIBRS. (insert) (Feb. 1986).

firm representing the major U.S. motion picture production and distribution companies[25] wrote the following:

> (1) We agree with the Article's conclusion that all performances on library premises are public performances under the Section 101 definition of "publicly." However, if unauthorized, such performances are infringing and are not protected by the "fair use" doctrine.
> (2) Sales of videocassettes to libraries do not imply any licence to the library to perform publicly or authorize the public performance of those videocassettes.
> (3) Libraries which knowingly rent equipment or videocassettes to patrons for unauthorized copying or public performance are infringers; they cannot insulate themselves from liability merely by posting warning notices.
> (4) Educational performances in libraries must satisfy each and every requirement of §110(1) to be exempt from liability.[26]

According to the film industry, the sale of a videotape to a library does not give the library the right of public performance. The industry asserts that libraries may not show videos to their patrons in small groups, or set up private viewing areas in the library, absent permission or a public performance license.

A former Attorney General of Ohio shared this view when, in 1987, he wrote that patrons of an Ohio school district public library could not view videotapes in library viewing rooms. The Attorney General reasoned that because a public library is accessible to the public, performances of videotapes on the premises—even in individual viewing rooms—were infringing public performances.

> [I]t is the public accessibility of the location where the videotape is shown that determines whether the playing of the tape is a public performance of the copyrighted work for the purposes of section 106(4). A school district public library is, as its name suggests, a place which is open to the public. Therefore, I conclude that the viewing of a copyrighted videotape on the premises of a school district public library constitutes a public performance of the work . . . .[27]

---

25. The companies were Buena Vista Distribution Co., Columbia Pictures, DeLaurentiis Entertainment Group, MGM, New World Pictures, Paramount, Twentieth Century Fox, United Artists, Universal, Walt Disney, and Warner Brothers.

26. Letter from Burton H. Hanft and Harvey Shapiro (Law Offices of Sargoy, Stein & Hanft) to Robert Wedgeworth, Executive Director, American Library Association 2 (Oct. 2, 1986) (on file with author).

27. Ohio Op. Att'y Gen. No. 87-108 (Dec. 29, 1987), Copyright L. Rep. (CCH) ¶ 26,240.

It appears from these writings that the Madison Avenue attorneys and the Ohio A.G. really do not understand fair use. Fair use applies to all types of copyrighted works, in all types of formats, in all kinds of places—even in that venerable (but obviously very scary to some people) institution we call the public library.

Libraries do *not* always need to acquire public performance licenses when they purchase a video or DVD for their collections. If the New York Public Library lends Woody Allen a VHS tape of the 1938 Marx Brothers' film *Room Service* so he can watch it at home while eating take-out Chinese food, why can't he watch it in a library viewing room? Indeed, watching a library-owned video in a small viewing room seems little different from using a library's microform reader to read microfiche, or a library computer to access digital information. In each case, the library is merely providing the equipment that enables someone to use library materials within library premises.

What about allowing small groups to view videotapes in the library? This may be a bit more problematic, but if a group consisting of one's family or friends may watch a rented video at home, they should be able to watch it in a small viewing room in the library. There *are* limits to how many people can watch a video, but there is no magic number. I feel very comfortable with the number four, and quite comfortable with six.

The Bottom Line: A single library patron should be able to watch a library-owned video on a modest-sized television in a private viewing room in the library. A small group should be able to do the same, in a small viewing room. Why? Fair use. How many people? Certainly four, but arguably no more than six. At the end of this chapter are some guidelines for the use of videos in libraries. Right now, however, you should know that you need not rely on fair use alone: The Copyright Act also includes a section that specifically permits certain public performances without the need to receive permission, to pay royalties, or to acquire public performance rights.

8.3. Section 110 Public Performance Exemptions

1. Classroom teaching
2. Educational broadcasting
3. Religious services (non-dramatic literary or musical works, or dramatico-musical religious works)
4. Charitable purposes (non-dramatic literary or musical works)
5. Small businesses (radio or television transmission)
6. Agricultural or horticultural fairs (non-dramatic musical works)
7. Promote sale of non-dramatic musical works or equipment
8. Blind or otherwise handicapped persons (non-dramatic literary works)
9. Handicapped persons (dramatic literary works less than ten years old)
10. Non-profit veterans or fraternal organizations (non-dramatic literary or musical works)

Section 110 of the Act sets forth ten situations in which public performances are expressly permitted. The section 110 exemptions include certain classroom performances,[28] some educational instructional broadcasting,[29] and certain performances at religious services,[30]

---

28. 17 U.S.C. § 110(1) (2000).
29. *Id.* § 110(2) (2000). The instructional broadcast exemption was broadened when Congress passed the Technology, Education, and Harmonization Act (TEACH) in late 2002. Distance education and the TEACH Act are discussed later in this chapter.
30. *Id.* § 110(3) (2000). The exemption applies to a "performance of non-dramatic literary work, musical work, or dramatico-musical work of a religious nature, or display of a work, in the course of services at a place of worship or other type of religious assembly." The exemption would exclude performances of musicals such as *Jesus Christ Superstar*.

for charitable purposes,[31] in small commercial establishments,[32] at agricultural or horticultural fairs,[33] in music stores,[34] transmissions to handicapped audiences,[35] and by fraternal organizations.[36]

Remember this: There is no automatic exemption for non-profit public performances.[37] Just because a performance takes place in a university library or your local public library does not necessarily make it exempt. Also remember that section 110 rights do not attach if the work that is performed is an infringing copy.

Videos purchased or rented from commercial vendors are legitimate copies, and generally may be used for section 110 performances. This should be true even if the tape has a "For Home Use Only" warning label, for that warning by itself does not create a contract.[38]

---

31. *Id.* § 110(4) (2000). A public performance of a non-dramatic literary or musical work is allowed under the following circumstances: (1) the performance must be without any purpose of direct or indirect commercial advantage; (2) fees cannot be paid to performers, promoters or organizers directly for the performance (but performers, directors, or producers may be paid salaries for duties encompassing the performance); (3) there may be no admission charge (or if there is, the net proceeds are used exclusively for educational, religious, or charitable purposes); and (4) the copyright owner has not objected in writing to the proposed performance at least seven days before the date of the performance. This exemption applies to live performances given directly in the presence of the audience.

32. 17 U.S.C. § 110(5) (2000) permits performances of regular (non-pay) radio or television programs (including dramatic and audiovisual works) in small commercial establishments, so long as customers are not charged for the performance and commercial amplification equipment is not used.

33. *Id.* § 110(6) (2000).

34. *Id.* § 110(7) (2000).

35. *Id.* § 110(8), (9) (2000).

36. 17 U.S.C. § 110(10) (2000). This exemption applies to performances of non-dramatic literary or musical works if the performance occurs in the course of a social function organized by a non-profit fraternal organization, and proceeds are used exclusively for charitable purposes. The exemption is available only to groups whose primary purpose is to provide charitable service to the community. College fraternities and sororities may qualify if an event is held for the sole purpose of raising funds for a specific charitable purpose.

37. The 1909 Copyright Act provided that non-profit public performances of musical or non-dramatic works was not an infringement of copyright. 17 U.S.C. § 1(c) and (e) (1976) (repealed). The legislative history of the 1976 Act is not so kind to non-profits. The House Judiciary Committee wrote: "The lines between commercial and non-profit organizations are increasingly difficult to draw. Many 'non-profit' organizations are highly subsidized and capable of paying royalties, and the widespread public exploitation of copyrighted works by public broadcasters and other noncommercial organizations is likely to grow." H.R. REP. NO. 94-1476, at 62–63.

38. As noted earlier, courts are split as to whether restrictions discovered after purchase or rental are enforceable. Some courts enforce these agreements (ProCD, Inc. v. Zeidenberg, 86 F.3d 1447 (7th Cir. 1996) (license terms

Renters and purchasers *can*, however, contract away their rights under the Copyright Act. Signing a contract that permits or prohibits certain uses of a rented or purchased videotape is enforceable, so read carefully any contract that accompanies a work your library purchases or leases. Furthermore, when your library orders a video or DVD, you may want to indicate on the purchase order that it is being purchased by the library for lending and onsite use by library patrons.

Performances for Educational Purposes (Section 110(1))

8.4. Section 110(1)
Performances and Displays for Teaching

&ø Any type of work
&ø Nonprofit educational institution
&ø Classroom or similar place
&ø Face-to-face teaching
&ø Instructors and pupils present
&ø Non-infringing copy

The remainder of this chapter focuses on two of the section 110 public performance exemptions: the 110(1) face-to-face teaching exemption, and 110(2), which addresses instructional broadcasting or what we now call distance education. We begin with 110(1).

Section 110(1) permits the performance or display of both dramatic and non-dramatic works (including audiovisual works) by instructors or pupils that take place in the course of face-to-face teaching activities of non-profit educational institutions. Sometimes called the "face-to-face teaching exemption," 110(1) requires that there be an educational purpose to the performance; showing a video for recreation or entertainment, such as rewarding a class for good

---

displayed on a screen when the purchaser used the software), and Hill v. Gateway 2000, Inc., 105 F.3d 1147 (7th Cir. 1997) (terms in a printed contract that accompanied a computer are enforceable when the purchaser keeps and uses the equipment)), while others have not (Vault Corp. v. Quaid Software Ltd., 847 F.2d 255 (5th Cir. 1988) (state statute that would enforce a software licensing agreement is unenforceable because it is preempted by the Copyright Act)).

behavior, does not qualify for this exemption. What might occur in a law school offers a good example of the educational/entertainment dichotomy.

Example 1

A student group wants to begin a "Thursday Night at the Movies" series. The group will use films that are part of the library collection, or rent them from a local video store. The films will be shown free of charge.

Comment

Because the showings are solely for entertainment purposes, the film series is outside the 110(1) exemption.

Example 2

The school offers a "Law in Film" course, which is taught by an instructor as part of the regular curriculum.

Comment

This educational use is fine. Section 110(1) permits you to show everything from *The Accused* to *Twelve Angry Men* (and even comedies such as *My Cousin Vinny*) so long as you meet the requirements of that section.

Example 3

Several professors want to begin a "Law and Film" series open to any law student who wishes to attend. On the first Tuesday of each month a law-related film will be shown, and a professor will introduce and lead a discussion of the film.

Comment

This too is permitted under 110(1) because the purpose is educational, rather than entertainment.

Let's look a bit more at this exemption. First, what does "face-to-face teaching activities" mean? According to the legislative history of the Act, the instructor and students must be in the same general area in the building, but not necessarily in the same room.[39] And although the teacher and students do not have to be within eyesight, they must simultaneously be in the same general place. Furthermore, although broadcasts or other transmissions from outside locations into

---

39. H.R. Rep. No. 94-1476, at 81.

classrooms are not allowed, amplification devices or visual enhancing equipment may be used within the building.[40]

As for who may attend 110(1) performances, and where can they take place, the exemption requires that attendance be limited to pupils, a guest lecturer, or the instructor. Performances permitted under 110(1) cannot be open to others, such as students' friends or the general public. Although performances must take place in a classroom or a similar place devoted to instruction, any room that can function as a classroom, including the library, may be used.

In a perfect world, everyone who is entitled to attend a section 110(1) performance would be able to see and hear it at the time and place when it takes place, and every such performance would take place in a classroom. In other words, every showing would fit literally, and perfectly, within the exemption. But we do not live in a perfect world. What if

- A student misses the History of Film class where *Citizen Kane* was shown. The student wants to check out the DVD version owned by the library, and watch it in a library viewing room.
- A student saw the film in class, but wants to see it again, this time in a library viewing room, to understand it better.
- The instructor recommends that students see two films directed by and starring Orson Welles, and a student wants to watch them in a library viewing room.

The American Library Association's Model Policy,[41] discussed earlier, considers the reserve room an extension of the classroom for the purpose of photocopying and distributing materials to students. It is equally fair to view a school or university library as an extension of the classroom for purposes of the 110(1) exemption, thereby permitting an otherwise qualifying use to take place in a library viewing room.

The motion picture industry would not agree. The Sargoy, Stein & Hanft attorneys (yes, the same ones you read about a few pages earlier) wrote that "students who miss a classroom performance may not view a videocassette of a motion picture in a library and be within the classroom exemption, since the instructor and pupils are not in

---

40. *Id.*
41. AMERICAN LIBRARY ASSOCIATION, MODEL POLICY CONCERNING COLLEGE AND UNIVERSITY PHOTOCOPYING FOR CLASSROOM RESEARCH AND LIBRARY RESERVE USE (1982), *available at* <http://www.cni.org>.

the same building or general area."[42] Hogwash. Go West, young men—far West, well beyond L.A.

Even if one supports such a narrow interpretation of the face-to-face teaching exemption—which this author does not—we still have fair use. A student who wants to watch a library-owned video in a library viewing room, in support of a school related project, should be able to do so under section 107. If the student could borrow the video from the library and watch it at home, he or she should be able to watch it in the library room. Jack Valenti's Motion Picture Association of America does not have the authority to proclaim the ten commandments of section 107 or 110.[43]

Performances in For-Profit Institutions

The face-to-face teaching exemption applies only to non-profit educational institutions. Performances of educational or training videotapes in organizations such as for-profit schools or corporations are not permitted under section 110(1). However, as noted earlier, the legislative history indicates that routine business meeting showings are not public performances because they do not involve the gathering of a substantial number of people.[44] Consequently, under most circumstances educational or training videotapes may be performed in commercial business settings, without payment of royalties, if the number of people attending the performances, at one time or over a period of time, is not substantial.

Equipment and Institutional Liability

Enough about performances of audiovisual works. What about the equipment needed to play those works? Should—or *may*—a library lend video playing or recording equipment to its patrons? You should proceed with caution. If the library chooses to lend equipment, it would be advisable to provide "play only" devices that cannot record. And because the library has no control over what may happen when equipment is removed from the library, you may want to prohibit the

---

42. Letter from Burton H. Hanft and Harvey Shapiro, Law Offices of Sargoy, Stein & Hanft, to Robert Wedgeworth, Executive Director, American Library Association 11 (Oct. 2, 1986) (on file with author).
43. For policy positions of the MPAA, see <http://www.mpaa.org>.
44. H.R. REP. NO. 94-1476, at 64.

equipment from being taken outside the facility. Of course, you may choose not to lend equipment at all.

What should a library employee who has reason to believe that John Public plans to copy a videotape or show it to a large audience do? If the following conversation takes place, you may wisely decide not to lend the film, or the equipment to play it.

> College Student: "I'd like to check out *Animal House* and also some video equipment."
> Library Staff Member: "That's a pretty neat movie."
> Student: "Yeah. I plan to show it at a frat party during homecoming. We have this huge 72" screen. We're gonna have about 300 people in the House. Don't worry about us spilling beer on the tape. We're gonna copy it first, and if we ruin it, I'll just give you back the copy. Cool?"
> Staff: "I think you need to speak to my supervisor."

You *should* be concerned about the library's possibly being liable as a contributory infringer. The library's policy manual must encourage compliance with the Copyright Act, and it will help if it includes some guidance for the staff. Here, then, are my guidelines for using audiovisual works in libraries. In the unlikely event that a lawyer appears at your door and accuses you of contributing to an unlawful public performance, show her these guidelines.

Guidelines for the Use of Audiovisual Works in Libraries

- ✌ Viewing rooms should be small, with seating for no more than six persons.
- ✌ The equipment on which videos are shown should be of the kind typically used in a private home, generally no larger than a 30" diagonal screen.
- ✌ Do not charge patrons for loans of videos.
- ✌ Make available "play-only" equipment; do not supply equipment that can record.
- ✌ Library-owned equipment may be used only within the library.
- ✌ Do not lend videos or equipment to a person or organization that you have reason to believe will engage in an unauthorized public performance.

ຂ Affix the following notice to videos: "THIS MATERIAL MAY BE PROTECTED BY UNITED STATES COPYRIGHT LAW. UNAUTHORIZED COPYING OR PUBLIC PERFORMANCES ARE PROHIBITED."

ຂ Affix the following notice to equipment: "WARNING: THE MAKING OF A COPY AND PUBLIC DISTRIBUTION, PERFORMANCES OR DISPLAYS MAY BE SUBJECT TO THE UNITED STATES COPYRIGHT LAW (TITLE 17 UNITED STATES CODE)."

ຂ Large groups (more than six persons) may not view videos on library premises unless

  ຂ The use meets the criteria of a section 110 exemption;

  ຂ The library has received permission to publicly perform the work or has paid royalties; or

  ຂ The library has a public performance license for the work.

Distance Education (Section 110(2))

As enacted by Congress in 1976, the Copyright Act imposed limits on the types of materials that could be used for distance education, and to whom those materials could be transmitted. The "old" section 110(2) instructional broadcasting exemption applied only to performances or displays of non-dramatic literary or musical works as part of systematic instructional activities of a governmental body or non-profit educational institution. The performance had to be related to and materially assist instruction; the content of the work had to be educational or instructional; and the transmission had to be made primarily for reception in a classroom or other place devoted to instruction, to the disabled, or for public employees as part of their duties. Broadcasts of dramatic works, films, and audio visual works were outside the scope of the instructional broadcasting exemption.[45]

---

45. 17 U.S.C. § 110(2) (2000).

> ### 8.5. Section 110(2)
> ### The TEACH Act
>
> ❧ Mediated instruction
> ❧ Accredited non-profit educational institution
> ❧ Most categories of works
> ❧ Anywhere
> ❧ Prevent re-transmission
> ❧ Institutional policies

All of this changed in November 2002, with the signing of the Technology, Education, and Copyright Harmonization Act, known colloquially as the TEACH Act.[46] The TEACH Act broadened the section 110(2) instructional broadcasting exemption to permit the transmission of more materials to more people in more places.

In a nutshell, revised section 110(2) now permits performances of non-dramatic literary or musical works, and also reasonable and limited portions of most other types of works. As for displays, the amount of a work is limited to what typically is displayed in the course of a live classroom transmission. Such performances or displays are permitted when:

❧ The performance or display is made by, at the direction of, or under the supervision of an instructor as an integral part of a class session that is a regular part of systematic mediated instructional activities or a governmental body or accredited nonprofit educational institution.

  Post-secondary schools must be accredited by a regional or national accrediting agency recognized by the Council of Higher Education or the U.S. Department of Education. As for elementary and secondary schools, accreditation refers to those which are recognized by state certification or licensing procedures. In the context of digital transmissions, "mediated instructional activities" refers to activities that use the work as an integral part of the class experience that are controlled by or under the supervision of the instructor, and which are analogous to the type of performance or display that take place in a live classroom. In other words, if you would not use the work in face-to-face teaching, do not transmit it digitally. Furthermore, you cannot transmit textbooks, coursepacks, or other materials that are typically purchased or acquired by students.

❧ The performance or display is directly related to and of material assistance to the teaching.

---

46. Pub. L. No. 107-273, § 13301(b), 116 Stat. 1758, 1910-12 (2002).

ಐ The transmission is limited to students enrolled in the course for which the transmission is made, or to governmental employees as part of their official duties or employment.

ಐ The transmitting body (a school, for example) must institute copyright policies that provide some measure of guidance, and must also provide information to its faculty, students, and staff that describe and promote compliance with U.S. copyright law. Furthermore, the institution must notify students that the materials transmitted may be subject to copyright protection.

ಐ If a work is transmitted digitally, the institution must apply technological measures that prevent those who receive it from retaining the work beyond the time the class is in session. The institution also must make sure that the work is not further disseminated. In addition, it must not do anything that interferes with technological measures a copyright owner uses to prevent permanent retention or further unauthorized dissemination.

Congress made it clear that, with the expansion of the types of materials that may be transmitted, there must be some institutional controls. First, materials that are stored on systems or networks cannot be accessible to anyone other than anticipated recipients. (Not only must you have a secure network, but you must also ensure that no one other than the intended recipients can access the information transmitted.) Second, copies cannot reside on networks any longer than is necessary to facilitate the transmissions.

There are other provisions of the TEACH Act that may be of interest, such as the provisions permitting the making of a temporary ("ephemeral") copy of a work in order to transmit it, and permitting the conversion of a print or other analog work to digital format if a digital version of the work is not available to the institution, or, if a digital version *is* available, it is subject to technological protective measures that prevent it from being used for the 110(2) exemption.[47]

This is only a taste of the TEACH Act. Many universities, as well as library and educational associations, offer very good information about the Act, and also helpful links.[48]

---

47. 17 U.S.C.A § 112(f)(2) (West Supp. 2003).
48. *See, e.g.,* Kenneth D. Crews, *New Copyright Law for Distance Education: The Meaning and Importance of the TEACH Act* (Sept. 30, 2002), *available at* <http://www.ala.org>. See also the National Education Association's website (http://www.nea.org), and that of the Association of Research Libraries (http://www.arl.org).

Slide Collections

Many academic and special libraries maintain collections or archives of slides. Some are purchased, while others were reproduced from photographs or books of photographs. Two questions come to mind. First, may a library create slides from a published source, what is often called copystand photograph? Second, may a library digitize slides already in its collection?

Because photographs are subject to copyright protection, an educator or librarian may create slides from protected photos only with permission of the copyright owner unless the use is a fair use or otherwise allowed under the Copyright Act. An important exception, however, are photographs of works in the public domain, which, according to a 1998 federal court decision, are not copyrightable because they lack originality.[49]

A compilation of photos or images may be copyrighted as a collective work. When this is the case, copying dozens of photos from, say, a coffee-table book of rock 'n' roll posters also may require permission of the entity that has copyright in the compilation. This is true even when the original work is not protected. For example, copying numerous photos from a book that reproduces 19th Century artwork may violate copyright in the collective work, even though both the original paintings and the photographs of those paintings are in the public domain.

To suggest that libraries must destroy their collection of copystand-created slides would be presumptuous. Such collections have been common practice in libraries and archives for decades. One might suggest that such collections—presumably created without complaint by any copyright owners—are legitimate.

Having a slide collection is different from going high-tech and digitizing them, however. This is an unsettled area of law, so for guidance I will rely on the Visual Resources Association's Committee on Intellectual Property Rights, which in 1999 published "Image Collection Guidelines: The Acquisition and Use of Images in Non-Profit Educational Visual Resources Collections."[50] Many colleges and universities have either adopted or adapted the Guidelines to help

---

49. Bridgeman Art Library, Ltd v. Corel Corp., 36 F.Supp.2d 191 (S.D.N.Y. 1999). (Amended from 25 F.Supp.2d 421 (S.D.N.Y. 1998).)
50. The VRA Guidelines are included as an appendix to this book. The Guidelines and other resources from the VRA may be found at <www.vraweb.org>.

them collect and manage their image collections. The Guidelines are included in Appendix M, but here are some highlights:

> Libraries may purchase, license, or otherwise legally acquire and maintain a permanent archives of slides or digital files from museums, galleries, vendors, image providers, and educational or professional organizations, or via onsite photography. Donors should be encouraged to give the library rights for extended use and physical custody of donated photographs.

> Images created by copystand photography and scanning from published materials are subject to the following considerations:

> - ❧ suitable quality images are not readily available at a reasonable cost and in a reasonable time from the above sources
> - ❧ images will not be shared if sharing is prohibited by the terms of the acquisition
> - ❧ images will be used for instructional, scholarly, or other non-profit educational purposes

> Public domain images where neither the underlying work nor the photographic reproduction are copyrighted may be acquired by any means, and have unrestricted use.

> Images should have appropriate attribution.

> Digital materials should be available in the same manner as analog images. Analog images may be used in digital format as follows:

> - ❧ if purchased or licensed, subject to the conditions specified when acquired
> - ❧ gifts and donations are subject to donor restrictions, and
> - ❧ images made by copystand photography may be digitized and used digitally under the same conditions under which they were originally acquired

> Institutions should have someone who overseer who will carry out the above principles and discuss policies with legal counsel. Faculty, staff, and students should follow the institution's policy.

The VRA Guidelines seem reasonable, but some institutions do add or subtract from them. For example, a library may wisely choose

- ❧ to limit to a reasonable amount the number of images taken from a single published source
- ❧ to limit access to digital images to students enrolled in the course
- ❧ not to use if images scanned for a particular course in a subsequent course
- ❧ without first checking for availability,

€ to post these guidelines on the university's website and where the collections are maintained

Many images are available on the internet for free, but a significant commercial source for both images and motion footage is the Corbis Corporation,[51] which acquired the Bettman Archive and its millions of images. Corbis also is a rights clearance agency, and has specific licensing arrangements for educational institutions.

---

51. For more information on Corbis, go to <http://www.corbis.com>.

Chapter Nine
CONCLUSION

ഔരുജ്

Although this book could not provide black-and-white answers to every question you may have about applying copyright law in your workplace, hopefully it gave you a better understanding of U.S. copyright law, and some confidence when confronted with those questions. This is not, of course, the only book that addresses library copyright issues. Over the last few years, several helpful books have been published on this topic, and I have included a brief selective bibliography as an appendix. Furthermore, several websites offer useful information on U.S. copyright law and its interpretation. They too are included as an appendix.

Other appendices include various guidelines mentioned throughout this book, including the *Classroom Guidelines*, the *ALA Model Policy*, the *CONTU Section 108(g)(2) Guidelines*, the *Off-air Recording Guidelines*, and the *CONFU Electronic Reserve Guidelines*. Also included are guidelines that were not cited, such as the Music Library Association's *Guidelines for Educational Uses of Music* and *Statement on Electronic Reserves*, and the American Association of Law Libraries' *Fair Use Guidelines* and *Model Law Firm Copyright Policy*.

Finally, you will find selected provisions of the U.S. Copyright Act. Because Congress continually tinkers with copyright law, make certain that the text you are reading is currently in force.

The last two documents in this book contain fifty questions on copyright issues in libraries, and include my responses to them. Not all of these questions lend themselves to black-and-white answers, and reasonable minds may differ.

The Bottom Line: Use your best judgment when trying to figure out whether a use is, or is not, permitted under our copyright laws. When you have a close call, remember the purpose of copyright as expressed in the Constitution: "To Promote the Progress of Science and the Useful Arts."

Appendix A
SOME USEFUL COPYRIGHT WEBSITES

☜☞

Association of American Publishers (AAP)
<www.publishers.org>

Copyright and Fair Use (Stanford University)
<http://fairuse.stanford.edu>

Copyright and Intellectual Property (Association of Research Libraries)
<www.arl.org>

Copyright Clearance Center
<www.copyright.com>

Copyright, Intellectual Property Rights, and Licensing Issues (U.C. Berkeley) <sunsite.berkeley.edu/copyright.html>

Legal Information Institute Copyright Law Materials (Cornell University)
<www.law.cornell.edu/topics/copyright>

United States Patent and Trademark Office
<www.uspto.gov>

United States Copyright Office
<lcweb.loc.gov/copyright>

United States Government Printing Office, GPO Access
<www.access.gpo.gov>

University of Texas Crash Course in Copyright
<www.utsystem.edu/ogc/intellectualproperty>

World Intellectual Property Organization (WIPO)

Appendix B
COPYRIGHT TEXTS FOR LIBRARIANS: A SELECTIVE BIBLIOGRAPHY

ဆာ၄ဢ

The Library's Legal Answer Book. Mary Minow and Tomas A. Lipinski. ALA, 2003.

The Copyright Handbook: How to Protect and Use Written Works. Stephen Fishman. Nolo Press, 7th ed., 2003.

Patent, Copyright & Trademark. Stephen Elias & Richard Stim. Nolo Press, 6th ed., 2003.

Librarian's Guide to Intellectual Property in the Digital Age. Timothy Lee Wherry. ALA, 2002.

Licensing Digital Content: A Practical Guide for Librarians. Lesley Ellen Harris. ALA, 2002.

Patent, Copyright & Trademark: An Intellectual Property Desk Reference. Stephen Elias and Richard Stim. Nolo Press, 6th ed., 2002.

Copyright in Cyberspace: Questions and Answers for Librarians. Gretchen McCord Hoffmann. Neal-Schuman, 2001.

Copyright Plain & Simple. Cheryl Besenjak. Career Press, 2nd ed. 2001.

Copyright Your Software. Stephen Fishman. Nolo Press, 3rd ed. 2001.

Copyright Essentials for Librarians and Educators. Kenneth D. Crews. ALA, 2000.

The Copyright Guide: A Friendly Guide to Protecting and Profiting from Copyrights. Lee Wilson. Allworth Press, revised ed., 2000.

Getting Permission. Richard Stim. Nolo Press, 2000.

The Public Domain: How to Find & Use Copyright-Free Writings, Music, Art & More. Stephen Fishman. Nolo Press, 2001.

The Copyright Book: A Practical Guide. William S. Strong. MIT Press, 5th ed. 1999.

The Copyright Permission and Libel Handbook. Lloyd Jassin & Steven Schechter. Wiley, 1998.

Copyrights and Trademarks for Media Professionals. Arnold P. Lutzker. Focal Press, 1997.

Copyright: A Guide to Information and Resources. Gary H. Becker. Gary H. Becker, 2nd ed. 1997.

Technology and Copyright Law: A Guidebook for the Library, Research, and Teaching Professions. Arlene Bielefield and Lawrence Cheesman. Neal-Schuman, 1997 and Supp.

Does Your Project Have a Copyright Problem? A Decision-Making Guide for Librarians. Mary Brandt Jensen. McFarland, 1996.

The Copyright Primer for Librarians and Educators. Janis H. Bruwelheide. American Library Association/National Education Association, 2nd ed. 1995.

Document Delivery Services: Issues and Answers. Eleanor Mitchell and Sheila A. Walters. Learned Information, 1995.

Libraries and Copyright: A Guide to Copyright Law in the 1990's. Laura N. Gasaway and Sarah K. Wiant. Special Libraries Association, 1994.

Libraries & Copyright Law. Arlene Bielefield and Lawrence Cheeseman. Neil-Schuman. 1993.

Adoptable Copyright Policy. Charles W. Vlcek. Copyright Information Services (for the Association for Educational Communications and Technology), 1992.

The Library Copyright Guide. Ruth H. Dukelow. Copyright Information Services (for the Association for Educational Communications and Technology), 1992.

Copyright Handbook. James S. Heller and Sarah K. Wiant. Fred B. Rothman & Co. (for the American Association of Law Libraries), 1984.

Appendix C
AGREEMENT ON GUIDELINES FOR CLASSROOM COPYING IN NOT-FOR-PROFIT EDUCATIONAL INSTITUTIONS WITH RESPECT TO BOOKS AND PERIODICALS

ᘓᘐ

The purpose of the following guidelines is to state the minimum and not the maximum standards of educational fair use under Section 106 of H.R. 2223. The parties agree that the conditions determining the extent of permissible copying the educational purpose may change in the future; that certain types of copying permitted under these guidelines may not be permissible in the future; and conversely that in the future other types of copying not permitted under these guidelines may be permissible under revised guidelines.

Moreover, the following statement of guidelines is not intended to limit the types of copying permitted under the standards of fair use under judicial decision and which are stated in Section 107 of the Copyright Revision Bill. There may be instances in which copying which does not fall within the guidelines stated below may nonetheless be permitted under the criteria of fair use.

Guidelines

I. Single Copying for Teachers

A single copy may be made of any of the following by or for a teacher at his or her individual request for his or her scholarly research or use in teaching or preparation to teach a class:

A. A chapter from a book;

B. An article from a periodical or newspaper;

C. A short story, short essay, or short poem, whether or not from a collective work;

D. A chart, graph, diagram, drawing, cartoon or picture from a book, periodical, or newspaper.

II. Multiple Copies for Classroom Use

Multiple copies (not to exceed in any event more than one copy per pupil in a course) may be made by or for the teacher giving the course for classroom use or discussion; provided that:

A. The copying meets the tests of brevity and spontaneity as defined below; and,

B. Meets the cumulative effect test as defined below; and,

C. Each copy includes a notice of copyright.

Definitions

Brevity

(i) Poetry: (a) A complete poem if less than 250 words and if printed on not more than two pages or, (b) from a longer poem, an excerpt of not more than 250 words.

(ii) Prose: (a) Either a complete article, story or essay of less than 2,500 words, or (b) an excerpt from any prose work of not more than 1,000 words or 10% of the work, whichever is less, but in any event a minimum of 500 words.

[Each of the numerical limits stated in "i" and "ii" above may be expanded to permit the completion of an unfinished line of a poem or of an unfinished prose paragraph.]

(iii) Illustration: One chart, graph, diagram, drawing, cartoon or picture per book or per periodical issue.

(iv) "Special" works: Certain works in poetry, prose or in "poetic prose" which often combine language with illustrations and which are intended sometimes for children and at other times for a more general audience fall short of 2,500 works in their entirety. Paragraph "ii" above notwithstanding such "special works" may not be reproduced in their entirety; however, an excerpt comprising not more than two of the published pages of such special work and containing not more than 10% of the works found in the text thereof, may be reproduced.

Spontaneity

(i)   The copying is at the instance and inspiration of the individual teacher.
(ii) The inspiration and decision to use the work and the moment of its use for maximum teaching effectiveness are so close in time that it would be unreasonable to expect a timely reply to a request for permission.

Cumulative Effect

(i)   The copying of the material is for only one course in the school in which the copies are made.
(ii) Not more than one short poem, article, story, essay or two excerpts may be copies from the same author, nor more than three from the sane collective work or periodical volume during one class term.
(iii) There shall not be more than nine instances of such multiple copying for one course during one class term.

[The limitations stated in "ii" and "iii" above shall not apply to current news periodicals and newspapers and current news sections of other periodicals.]

III. Prohibitions as to I and II Above

Notwithstanding any of the above, the following shall be prohibited:

A. Copying shall not be used to create or to replace or substitute for anthologies, compilations or collective works. Such replacement or substitution may occur whether copies of various works or excerpts therefrom are accumulated or reproduced and used separately.
B. There shall be no copying of or from works intended to be "consumable" in the course of study or of teaching. These include workbooks, exercises, standardized tests and test booklets and answer sheets and like consumable material.

C. Copying shall not:
  (a) substitute for the purchase of books, publishers' reprints or periodicals;
  (b) be directed by higher authority;
  (c) be repeated with respect to the same item by the same teacher from term to term.

  D. No charge shall be made to the student beyond the actual cost of the photocopying.

Agreed March 19, 1976.

Ad Hoc Committee on Copyright Law Revision by Sheldon Elliott Steinbach.
Author-publisher Group and Authors League of America by Irwin Karp, Counsel.
Association of American Publishers, Inc. by Alexander C. Hoffman, Chairman, Copyright Committee.

Appendix D
MODEL POLICY CONCERNING COLLEGE AND UNIVERSITY PHOTOCOPYING FOR CLASSROOM, RESEARCH AND LIBRARY RESERVE USE

෨෬

This model policy, another in a series of copyright advisory documents developed by the American Library Association (ALA), is intended for the guidance and use of academic librarians, faculty, administrators, and legal counsel in response to implementation of the rights and responsibilities provisions of Public Law 94-553, General Revision of the Copyright Law, which took effect on January 1, 1978.

Prepared by ALA Legal Counsel Mary Hutchings of the law firm Sidley & Austin, with advise and assistance from the Copyright Sub-committee (ad hoc) of ALA's Legislation Committee, Association of College and Research Libraries (ACRL) Copyright Committee, Association of Research Libraries (ARL) and other academic librarians and copyright attorneys, the model policy outlines "fair use" rights in the academic environment for classroom teaching, research activities and library services. Please note that it does not address other library photocopying which may be permitted under other sections of the Copyright Law, e.g., § 108 (Reproduction by Libraries and Archives).

Too often, members of the academic community have been reluctant or hesitant to exercise their rights of fair use under the law for fear of courting an infringement suit. It is important to understand that in U.S. law, copyright is a limited statutory monopoly and the public's right to use materials must be protected. Safeguards have been written into the legislative history accompanying the new copyright law protecting librarians, teachers, researchers and scholars and guaranteeing their rights of access to information as they carry out their responsibilities for educating or conducting research. It is, therefore, important to heed the advise of a former U.S. Register of Copyrights: "If you don't use fair use, you will lose it!"

I. The Copyright Act and Photocopying

From time to time, the faculty and staff of this University [College] may use photocopied materials to supplement research and teaching. In many cases, photocopying can facilitate the University's [College's] mission; that is, the development and transmission of information. However, the photocopying of copyrighted materials is a right granted under the copyright law's doctrine of "fair use" which must not be abused. This report will explain the University's [College's} policy concerning the photocopying of copyrighted materials by faculty and library staff. Please note that this policy does not address other library photocopying which may be permitted under sections of the copyright law, e.g., 17 U.S.C. § 108.

Copyright is a constitutionally conceived property right which is designed to promote the progress of science and the useful arts by securing for an author the benefits of his or her original work of authorship for a limited time. U.S. Constitution, Art. I, Sec. 8. The Copyright statute, 17 U.S.C. § 101 et seq., implements this policy by balancing the author's interest against the public interest in the dissemination of information affecting areas of universal concern, such as art, science, history and business. The grand design of this delicate balance is to foster the creation and dissemination of intellectual works for the general public.

The Copyright Act defines the rights of a copyright holder and how they may be enforced against an infringer. Included within the Copyright Act is the "fair use" doctrine which allows, under certain conditions, the copying of copyrighted material. While the Act lists general factors under the heading of "fair use" it provides little in the way of specific directions for what constitutes fair use.

The law states:

17 U.S.C. § 107. Limitations on exclusive rights: Fair use

Notwithstanding the provisions of section 106, the fair use of a copyrighted work, including such use by reproduction in copies or phonorecords or by any other means specified by that section, for purposes such as criticism, comment, news reporting, teaching (including multiple copies for classroom use), scholarship, or research, is not an infringement of copyright. In determining whether the use made of a work in any particular case is a fair use the factors to be considered shall include—

(1)   the purpose and character of the use, including whether such use is of a commercial nature or is for nonprofit educational purposes;
(2)   the nature of copyrighted work;

(3)   the amount and substantiality of the portion used in relation to the copyrighted work as a whole; and

(4)   the effect of the use upon the potential market for or value of the copyrighted work.

The purpose of this report is to provide you, the faculty and staff of this University [College}, with an explanation of when the photocopying of copyrighted material in our opinion is permitted under the fair use doctrine. Where possible, common examples of research, classroom, and library reserve photocopying have been included to illustrate what we believe to be the reach and limits of fair use.

Please note that the copyright law applies to all forms of photocopying, whether it is undertaken at a commercial copying center, at the University's [College's] central or departmental copying facilities or at a self-service machine. While you are free to use the services of a commercial establishment, you should be prepared to provide documentation of permission from the publisher (if such permission is necessary under this policy), since many commercial copiers will require such proof.

We hope this report will give you an appreciation of the factors which weight in favor of fair use and those factors which weigh against fair use, but faculty members must determine for themselves which works will be photocopied. This University [College] does not condone a policy of photocopying instead of purchasing copyrighted works where such photocopying would constitute an infringement under the Copyright law, but it does encourage faculty members to exercise good judgment in serving the best interests of students in an efficient manner.

Instructions for securing permission to photocopy copyrighted works when such copying is beyond the limits of fair use appear at the end of this report. It is the policy of this University that the user (faculty, staff or librarian) secure such permission whenever it is legally necessary.

II. Unrestricted Photocopying
A. Uncopyrighted Published Works

Writing published before January 1, 1978 which have never been copyrighted may be photocopied without restriction. Copies of works protected by copyright must bear a copyright notice, which consists of the letter "c" in a circle, or the word "Copyright," or the abbreviation "Copr.", plus the year of first publication, plus the name of the copyright owner. 17 U.S.C. § 401. As to works published before January 1, 1978, in the case of a book, the notice must be placed on the title page or the reverse side of the title page. In the case of a periodical the notice must be placed either on the title page, the first page of text, or in the masthead. A pre-1978 failure to comply with the notice requirements results in the work being injected into the public domain, i.e., unprotected. Copyright notice requirements have been relaxed since 1978, so that the absence of notice on copies of a work published after January 1, 1978 does not necessarily mean the work in the public domain. 17 U.S.C. § 405 (a) and (c). However, you will not be liable for damages for copyright infringement of works published after that date, if, after normal inspection, you photocopy a work on which you cannot find a copyright symbol and you have not received actual notice of the fact the work is copyrighted. 17 U.S.C. § 405(b). However, a copyright owner who found out about your photocopying would have the right to prevent further distribution of the copies if in fact the work were copyrighted and the copies are infringing. 17 U.S.C. § 405(b).

B. Published Works with Expired Copyrights

Writings with expired copyrights may be photocopied without restriction. All copyrights prior to 1906 have expired. 17 U.S.C. § 304(b). Copyrights granted after 1906 may have been renewed; however the writing will probably not contain notice of the renewal. Therefore, it should be assumed all writings dated 1906 or later are covered by a valid copyright, unless information to the contrary is obtained from the owner or the U.S. Copyright Office (see Copyright Office Circular 15t).

Copyright Office Circular R22 explains how to investigate the copyright status of a work. One way is to use the Catalog of Copyright Entries published by the Copyright Office and available in [the University Library] many libraries. Alternatively you may request the Copyright Office to conduct a search of its registration and/or assignment records. The Office charges an hourly fee for this service. You will need to submit as much information as you have concerning the work in which you are interested, such as the title, author, approximate date of publication, the type of work or any available copyright data. The Copyright Office does caution that its searches are not conclusive; for instance, if a work obtained copyright less than 28 years ago, it may be fully protected although there has been no registration or deposit.

C. Unpublished Works

Unpublished works, such as theses and dissertations, may be protected by copyright. If such a work was created before January 1, 1978 and has not been copyrighted or published without copyright notice, the work is protected under the new Act for the life of the author plus fifty years, 17 U.S.C. § 303, but in no case earlier than December 31, 2002. If such a work is published on or before that date, the copyright will not expire before December 31, 2027. Works created after January 1, 1978 and not published enjoy copyright protection for the life of the author plus fifty years. 17 U.S.C. § 302.

D. U.S. Government Publications

All U.S. Government publications with the possible exception of some National Technical Information Service Publications less than five years old may be photocopied without restrictions, except to the extent they contain copyrighted materials from other sources. 17 U.S.C. § 105. U.S. Government publications are documents prepared by an official or employee of the government in an official capacity. 17 U.S.C. § 101. Government publications include the opinions of courts in legal cases, Congressional Reports on proposed bills, testimony offered at Congressional hearings and the works of government employees in their official capacities.

Works prepared by outside authors on contract to the government may or may not be protected by copyright, depending on the specifics of the contract. In the absence of copyright notice on such works, it would be reasonable to assume they are government works in the public domain. It should be noted that state government works may be protected by copyright. See 17 U.S.C. § 105. However, the opinions of state courts are not protected.

III. Permissible Photocopying of Copyrighted Works

The Copyright Act allows anyone to photocopy copyrighted works without securing permission from the copyright owner when the photocopying amounts to a "fair use" of the material. 17 U.S.C. § 107. The guidelines in this report discuss the boundaries for fair use of photocopied material used in research or the classroom or in a library reserve operation. Fair use cannot always be expressed in numbers— either the number of pages copied or the number of copies distributed. Therefore, you should weigh the various factors listed in the Act and judge whether the intended use of photocopied, copyrighted material is within the spirit of the fair use doctrine. Any serious questions concerning whether a particular photocopying constitutes fair use should be directed to University [College] counsel.

A. Research Uses

At the very least, instructors may make a single copy of any of the following for scholarly research or use in teaching or preparing to teach a class:

1. A chapter from a book;
2. An article from a periodical or newspaper;
3. A short story, short essay, or short poem, whether or not from a collective work; and
4. A chart, diagram, graph, drawing, cartoon or picture from a book, periodical, or newspaper.

These examples reflect the most conservative guidelines for fair use. They do not represent inviolate ceilings for the amount of copyrighted material which can be photocopied within the boundaries of fair use. When exceeding these minimum levels, however, you again should consider the four factors listed in Section 107 of the Copyright Act to make sure that any additional photocopying is justified. The following demonstrate situations where increased levels of photocopying would continue to remain within the ambit of fair use:

1. the inability to obtain another copy of the work because it is not available from another library or source cannot be obtained within your time constraints;
2. the intention to photocopy the material only once and not to distribute the material to others;
3. the ability to keep the amount of material photocopied within a reasonable proportion to the entire work (the larger the work, the greater amount of material which may be photocopied).

Most single-copy photocopying for your personal use in research—even when it involves a substantial portion of a work—may well constitute fair use.

B. Classroom Uses

Primary and secondary school educators have, with publishers, developed the following guidelines, which allow a teacher to distribute photocopied material to students in a class without the publisher's prior permission, under the following conditions:

1. the distribution of the same photocopied material does not occur every semester;
2. only one copy is distributed for each student which copy must become the student's property;
3. the material includes a copyright notice on the first page of the portion of material photocopied;

4. the students are not assessed any fee beyond the actual cost of the photocopying.

The educators also agreed that the amount of material distributed should not exceed certain brevity standards. Under those guidelines, a prose work may be reproduced in its entirety if it is less than 2500 words in length. If the work exceeds such length, the excerpt reproduced may not exceed 1000 words, or 10% of the work, whichever is less. In the case of poetry, 250 words is the maximum permitted.

These minimum standards normally would not be realistic in the University setting. Faculty members needing to exceed these limits for college education should not feel hampered by these guidelines, although they should attempt a "selective and sparing" use of photocopied, copyrighted material.

The photocopying practices of an instructor should not have a significant detrimental impact on the market for the copyrighted work. 17 U.S.C. § 107(4). To guard against this effect, you usually should restrict use of an item of photocopied material to one course and you should not repeatedly photocopy excepts from one periodical or author without the permission of the copyright owner.

C. Library Reserve Uses
At the request of a faculty member, a library may photocopy and place on reserve excerpts from copyrighted works in its collection in accordance with guidelines similar to those governing formal classroom distribution for face-to-face teaching discussed above. This University [College] believes that these guidelines apply to the library reserve shelf to the extent it functions as an extension of classroom readings or reflects an individual student's right to photocopy for his personal scholastic use under the doctrine of fair use. In general, librarians may photocopy materials for reserve room use for the convenience of students both in preparing class assignments and in pursuing informal educational activities which higher education requires, such as advanced independent study and research.

If the request calls for only one copy to be placed on reserve, the library may photocopy an entire article, or an entire chapter from a book, or an entire poem. Requests for multiple copies on reserve should meet the following guidelines:

1. the amount of material should be reasonable in relation to the total amount of material assigned for one term of a course taking into account the nature of the course, its subject matter and level, 17 U.S.C. §§ 107(1) and (3);
2. the number of copies should be reasonable in light of the number of students enrolled, the difficulty and timing of assignments, and the number of other courses which may assign the same material, 17 U.S.C. §§ 107(1) and (3);

3.   the material should contain a notice of copyright, see 17 U.S.C. § 401;
4.   the effect of photocopying the material should not be detrimental to the market for the work. (In general, the library should own at least one copy of the work.) 17 U.S.C. § 107(4).

For example, a professor may place on reserve as a supplement to the course textbook a reasonable number of copies of articles from academic journals or chapters from trade books. A reasonable number of copies will in most instances be less than six, but factors such as the length or difficulty of the assignment, the number of enrolled students and the length of time allowed for completion of the assignment may permit more in unusual circumstances.

In addition, a faculty member may also request that multiple copies of photocopied, copyrighted material be placed on the reserve shelf if there is insufficient time to obtain permission from the copyright owner. For example, a professor may place on reserve several photocopies of an entire article from a recent issue of Time magazine or the New York Times in lieu of distributing a copy to each member of the class. If you are in doubt as to whether a particular instance of photocopying is fair use in the reserve reading room, you should waive any fee for such a use.

D. Uses of Photocopied Material Requiring Permission

1.   Repetitive copying: The classroom or reserve use of photocopied materials in multiple courses or successive years will normally require advance permission from the owner of the copyright, 17 U.S.C. § 107(3).
2.   Copying for profit: Faculty should not charge students more than the actual cost of photocopying the material, 17 U.S.C. § 107(1).
3.   Consumable works: The duplication of works that are consumed in the classroom, such as standardized tests, exercises, and workbooks, normally requires permission from the copyright owner, 17 U.S.C. § 107(4).
4.   Creation of anthologies as basic text material for a course: Creation of a collective work or anthology by photocopying a number of copyrighted articles and excerpts to be purchased and used together as the basic text for a course will in most instances require the permission of the copyrighted owners. Such photocopying of a book and thus less likely to be deemed fair use, 17 U.S.C. § 107(4).

E. How to Obtain Permission

When a use of photocopied material requires that you request permission, you should communicate complete and accurate information to the copyright owner. The American Association of Publishers suggests that the following information be included in a permission request letter in order to expedite the process:

1. Title, author and/or editor, and edition of materials to be duplicated.
2. Exact material to be used, giving amount, page numbers, chapters and, if possible, a photocopy of the material.
3. Number of copies to be made.
4. Use to be made of duplicated materials.
5. Form of distribution (classroom, newsletter, etc.).
6. Whether or not the material is to be sold.
7. Type of reprint (ditto, photography, offset, typeset).

The request should be sent, together with a self-addressed return envelope, to the permissions department of the publisher in question. If the address of the publisher does not appear at the front of the material, it may be readily obtained in a publication entitled The Literary Marketplace, published by the R. R. Bowker Company and available in all libraries.

The process of granting permission requires time for the publisher to check the status of the copyright and to evaluate the nature of the request. It is advisable, therefore, to allow enough lead time to obtain permission before the materials are needed. In some instances, the publisher may assess a fee for the permission. It is not inappropriate to pass this fee on to the student who receive copies of the photocopied material.

The Copyright Clearance Center also has the right to grant permission and collect fees for photocopying rights for certain publications. Libraries may copy from any journal which is registered with the CCC and report the copying beyond fair use to CCC and pay the set fee. A list of publications for which the CCC handles fees and permissions is available from CCC, 310 Madison Avenue, New York, N.Y. 10017.

Appendix E
FINAL REPORT OF THE NATIONAL COMMISSION ON NEW TECHNOLOGICAL USES OF COPYRIGHTED WORKS, JULY 31, 1978

ℬꙅ

CONTU Guidelines on Photocopying under Interlibrary Loan Arrangements

The CONTU guidelines were developed to assist librarians and copyright proprietors in understanding the amount of photocopying for use in interlibrary loan arrangements permitted under the copyright law. In the spring of 1976 there was realistic expectation that a new copyright law, under consideration for nearly twenty years, would be enacted during that session of Congress. It had become apparent that the House subcommittee was giving serious consideration to modifying the language concerning "systematic reproduction" by libraries in Section 108(g)(2) of the Senate-passed bill to permit photocopying under interlibrary arrangements, unless such arrangements resulted in the borrowing libraries obtaining "such aggregate quantities as to substitute for a subscription to or purchase of" copyrighted works.

The Commission discussed this proposed amendment to the Senate bill at its meeting on April 2, 1976. Pursuant to a request made at that meeting by the Register of Copyrights, serving in her ex officio role, the Commission agreed that it might aid the House and Senate subcommittees by offering its good offices in bringing the principal parties together to see whether agreement could be reached on a definition of "such aggregate quantities." This offer was accepted by the House and Senate subcommittees and the interested parties, and much of the summer of 1976 was spent by the Commission in working with the parties to secure agreement on "guidelines" interpreting what was to become the proviso in Section 108(g)(2) relating to "systematic reproduction" by libraries. The pertinent parts of that section, with the proviso added by the House emphasized, follow.

> The rights of reproduction and distribution under this section extend to the isolated and unrelated reproduction or distribution of a single copy or phonorecord of the same material on separate occasions, but do not extend to cases where the library or archives, or its employee . . .

> (2) engages in the systematic reproduction or distribution of single or multiple copies or phonorecords of material described in subsection (d): Provided, That nothing in this clause prevents a library or archives from participating in interlibrary arrangements that do not have, as their purpose of effect, that the library or archives receiving such copies or phonorecords for distribution does so in such aggregate quantities as to substitute for a subscription to or purchase of such work.

Before enactment of the new copyright law, the principal library, publisher, and author organizations agreed to the following detailed guidelines defining what "aggregate quantities" would constitute the "systematic reproduction" that would exceed the statutory limitations on a library's photocopying activities.

Photocopying-Interlibrary Arrangements

Introduction
Subsection 108(g)(2) of the bill deals, among other things, with limits on interlibrary arrangements for photocopying. It prohibits systematic photocopying of copyrighted materials but permits interlibrary arrangements "that do not have, as their purpose or effect, that the library or archives receiving such copies or phonorecords for distribution does so in such aggregate quantities as to substitute for a subscription to or purchase of such work."

The National Commission on New Technological Uses of Copyrighted Works offered its good offices to the House and Senate subcommittees in bringing the interested parties together to see if agreement could be reached on what a realistic definition would be of "such aggregate quantities." The Commission consulted with the parties and suggested the interpretation which follows, on which there has been substantial agreement by the principal library, publisher, and author organizations. The Commission considers the guidelines which follow to be a workable and fair interpretation of the intent of the proviso portion of subsection 108(g)(2).

These guidelines are intended to provide guidance in the application of section 108 to the most frequently encountered interlibrary case: a library's obtaining from another library, in lieu of interlibrary loan, copies of articles from relatively recent issues of periodicals—those published within five years prior to the date of the request. The guidelines do not specify what aggregate quantity of copies of an article or articles published in a periodical, the issue date of which is more than five years prior to the date when the request for the copy thereof is made, constitutes a substitute for a subscription to such periodical. The meaning of the proviso to subsection 108(g)(2) in such case is left to future interpretation.

The point has been made that the present practice on interlibrary loans and use of photocopies in lieu of loans may be supplemented or even largely replaced by a system in which one or more agencies or institutions, public or private, exist for the specific purpose of providing a central source for photocopies. Of course, these guidelines would not apply to such a situation.

Guidelines for the Proviso of Subsection 108(g)(2)

1. As used in the proviso of subsection 108(g)(2), the words "such aggregate quantities as to substitute for a subscription to or purchase of such work" shall mean:

   (a) with respect to any given periodical (as opposed to any given issue of a periodical), filled requests of a library or archives (a "requesting entity") within any calendar year for a total of six or more copies of an article or articles published in such periodical within five years prior to the date of the request. These guidelines specifically shall not apply, directly or indirectly, to any request of a requesting entity for a copy or copies of an article or articles published in any issue of a periodical, the publication date of which is more than five years prior to the date when the request is made. These guidelines do not define the meaning, with respect to such a request, of ". . . such aggregate quantities as to substitute for a subscription to [such periodical]."

   (b) With respect to any other material described in subsection 108(d), including fiction and poetry), filled requests of a requesting entity within any calendar year for a total of six or more copies or phonorecords of or from any given work (including a collective work) during the entire period when such material shall be protected by copyright.

2. In the event that a requesting entity:

(a) shall have in force or shall have entered an order for a sub-
     scription to a periodical, or

(b) has within its collection, or shall have entered an order for, a
     copy of phonorecord of any other copyrighted work, materials
     from either category of which it desires to obtain by copy
     from another library or archives (the "supplying entity"),
     because the material to be copied is not reasonably available
     for use by the requesting entity itself, then the fulfillment of
     such request shall be treated as though the requesting entity
     made such copy from its own collection. A library or archives
     may request a copy or phonorecord from a supplying entity
     only under those circumstances where the requesting entity
     would have been able, under the other provisos of section
     108, to supply such copy from materials in its own collection.

3. No request for a copy or phonorecord of any materials to which
   these guidelines apply may be fulfilled by the supplying entity
   unless such request is accompanied by a representation by the
   requesting entity that the request was made in conformity with
   these guidelines.

4. The requesting entity shall maintain records of all requests made
   by it for copies or phonorecords of any materials to which these
   guidelines apply and shall maintain records of the fulfillment of
   such requests, which records shall be retained until the end of the
   third complete calendar year after the end of the calendar year in
   which the respective request shall have been made.

5. As part of the review provided for in subsection 108(i), these
   guidelines shall be reviewed not later than five years from the
   effective date of this bill.

These guidelines were accepted by the Conference Committee and
were incorporated into its report on the new act. During the ensuing
twenty months, both library and publisher organizations have
reported considerable progress toward adapting their practices to
conform with the CONTU guidelines.

The guidelines specifically leave the status of periodical articles
more than five years old to future determination. Moreover, institutions set up for the specific purpose of supplying photocopies of
copyrighted material are excluded from coverage of the guidelines.

Appendix F
GUIDELINES FOR OFF-AIR RECORDINGS OF BROADCAST PROGRAMMING FOR EDUCATIONAL PURPOSES

ഇരുഭ

In March 1979, Congressman Robert Kastenmeier, chairman of the House Subcommittee on Courts, Civil Liberties, and Administration of Justice, appointed a Negotiating Committee consisting of representatives of education organizations, copyright proprietors, and creative guilds and unions. The following guidelines reflect the Negotiating Committee's consensus as to the application of "fair use" to the recording, retention, and use of television broadcast programs for educational purposes. They specify periods of retention and use of such off-air recordings in classrooms and similar places devoted to instruction and for homebound instruction. The purpose of establishing these guidelines is to provide standards for both owners and users of copyrighted television programs.

1. The guidelines were developed to apply only to off-air recording by nonprofit educational institutions.
2. A broadcast program may be recorded off-air simultaneously with broadcast transmission (including simultaneous cable retransmission) and retained by a nonprofit educational institution for a period not to exceed the first forty-five (45) consecutive calendar days after date of recording. Upon conclusion of such retention period, all off-air recordings must be erased or destroyed immediately. "Broadcast programs" are television programs transmitted by television stations for reception by the general public without charge.
3. Off-air recordings may be used once by individual teachers in the course of relevant teaching activities, and repeated once

only when instructional reinforcement is necessary, in classrooms and similar places devoted to instruction within a single building, cluster or campus, as well as in the homes of students receiving formalized home instruction, during the first ten (10) consecutive school days in the forty-five (45) day calendar day retention period. "School days" are school session days—not counting weekends, holidays, vacations, examination periods, and other scheduled interruptions—within the forty-five (45) calendar day retention period.

4. Off-air recordings may be made only at the request of and used by individual teachers, and may not be regularly recorded in anticipation of requests. No broadcast program may be recorded off-air more than once at the request of the same teacher, regardless of the number of times the program may be broadcast.

5. A limited number of copies may be reproduced from each off-air recording to meet the legitimate needs of teachers under these guidelines. Each such additional copy shall be subject to all provisions governing the original recording.

Appendix G
FAIR-USE GUIDELINES FOR ELECTRONIC RESERVE SYSTEMS (CONFU) REVISED MARCH 5, 1996

ぞつひ

Author's note: These guidelines were developed during the CONFU process. For a full explanation of their status, see CONFU: The Conference on Fair Use (available at the U.S. Patent and Trademark Office website: <www.uspto.gov>). The Electronic Reserve Systems Guidelines did not garner consensus support from the conferees.

Introduction
Many college, university, and school libraries have established reserve operations for readings and other materials that support the instructional requirements of specific courses. Some educational institutions are now providing electronic reserve systems that allow storage of electronic versions of materials that students may retrieve on a computer screen, and from which they may print a copy for their personal study. When materials are included as a matter of fair use, electronic reserve systems should constitute an ad hoc or supplemental source of information for students, beyond a textbook or other materials. If included with permission from the copyright owner, however, the scope and range of materials is potentially unlimited, depending upon the permission granted. Although fair use is determined on a case-by-case basis, the following guidelines identify an understanding of fair use for the reproduction, distribution, display, and performance of materials in the context of creating and using an electronic reserve system.

Making materials accessible through electronic reserve systems raises significant copyright issues. Electronic reserve operations include the making of a digital version of text, the distribution and display of that version at workstations, and downloading and printing of copies. The complexities of the electronic environment, and the growing potential for implicating copyright infringements, raise the need for a fresh understanding of fair use. These guidelines are not intended to burden the facilitation of reserves unduly, but instead offer a workable path that educators and librarians may follow in order to exercise a meaningful application of fair use, while also acknowledging and respecting the interests of copyright owners.

These guidelines focus generally on the traditional domain of reserve rooms, particularly copies of journal articles and book chapters, and their accompanying graphics. Nevertheless, they are not meant to apply exclusively to textual materials and may be instructive for the fair use of other media. The guidelines also focus on the use of the complete article or the entire book chapter. Using only brief excerpts from such works would most likely also be fair use, possibly without all of the restrictions or conditions set forth in these guidelines. Operators of reserve systems should also provide safeguards for the integrity of the text and the author's reputation, including verification that the text is correctly scanned.

The guidelines address only those materials protected by copyright and for which the institution has not obtained permission before including them in an electronic reserve system. The limitations and conditions set forth in these guidelines need not apply to materials in the public domain—such as works of the U.S. government or works on which copyright has expired—or to works for which the institution has obtained permission for inclusion in the electronic reserve system. License agreements may govern the uses of some materials. Persons responsible for electronic reserve systems should refer to applicable license terms for guidance. If an instructor arranges for students to acquire a work by some means that includes permission from the copyright owner, the instructor should not include that same work on an electronic reserve system as a matter of fair use.

These guidelines are the outgrowth of negotiations among diverse parties attending the Conference on Fair Use ("CONFU") meetings sponsored by the Information Infrastructure Task Force's Working Group on Intellectual Property Rights. While endorsements of any guidelines by all conference participants is unlikely, these guidelines have been endorsed by the organizations whose names appear at the end. These guidelines are in furtherance of the Working Group's objective of encouraging negotiated guidelines of fair use.

This introduction is an integral part of these guidelines and should be included with the guidelines wherever they may be reprinted or adopted by a library, academic institution, or other organization or association. No copyright protection of these guidelines is claimed by any person or entity, and anyone is free to reproduce and distribute this document without permission.

A. Scope of Material

1. In accordance with fair use (Section 107 of the U.S. Copyright Act), electronic reserve systems may include copyrighted materials at the request of a course instructor.

2. Electronic reserve systems may include short items (such as an article from a journal, a chapter from a book or conference proceedings, or a poem from a collected work) or excerpts from longer items. "Longer items" may include articles, chapters, poems, and other works that are of such length as to constitute a substantial portion of a book, journal, or other work of which they may be a part. "Short items" may include articles, chapters, poems, and other works of a customary length and structure as to be a small part of a book, journal, or other work, even if that work may be marketed individually.

3. Electronic reserve systems should not include any material unless the instructor, the library, or another unit of the educational institution possesses a lawfully obtained copy.

4. The total amount of material included in electronic reserve systems for a specific course as a matter of fair use should be a small proportion of the total assigned reading for a particular course.

B. Notices and Attributions

1. On a preliminary or introductory screen, electronic reserve systems should display a notice, consistent with the notice described in Section 108(f)(1) of the Copyright Act. The notice should include additional language cautioning against further electronic distribution of the digital work

2. If a notice of copyright appears on the copy of a work that is included in an electronic reserve system, the following statement shall appear at some place where users will likely see it in connection with access to the particular work: "The work from which this copy is made includes this notice: [restate the elements of the statutory copyright notice: e.g., Copyright 1996, XXX Corp.]"

3. Materials included in electronic reserve systems should include appropriate citations or attributions to their sources.

C. Access and Use

1. Electronic reserve systems should be structured to limit access to students registered in the course for which the items have been placed on reserve, and to instructors and staff responsible for the course or the electronic system.

2. The appropriate methods for limiting access will depend on available technology. Solely to suggest and not to prescribe options for implementation, possible methods for limiting access may include one or more of the following or other appropriate methods:

   (a) individual password controls or verification of a student's registration status; or
   (b) password system for each class; or
   (c) retrieval of works by course number or instructor name, but not by author or title of the work; or
   (d) access limited to workstations that are ordinarily used by, or are accessible to, only enrolled students or appropriate staff or faculty.

3. Students should not be charged specifically or directly for access to electronic reserve systems.

D. Storage and Reuse

1. Permission from the copyright holder is required if the item is to be reused in a subsequent academic term for the same course offered by the same instructor, or if the item is a standard assigned or optional reading for an individual course taught in multiple sections by many instructors.

2. Material may be retained in electronic form while permission is being sought or until the next academic term in which the material might be used, but in no event for more than three calendar years, including the year in which the materials are last used.

3. Short-term access to materials included on electronic reserve systems in previous academic terms may be provided to students who have not completed the course.

Appendix H
GUIDELINES FOR EDUCATIONAL USES OF MUSIC

ઇଠଓଃ

The following guidelines were developed and approved in April 1976 by the Music Publishers' Association of the United States, Inc., the National Music Publishers' Association, Inc., the Music Teachers National Association, the Music Educators National Conference, the National Association of Schools of Music, and the Ad Hoc Committee on Copyright Law Revision.

Guidelines for Educational Uses of Music
The purpose of the following guidelines is to state the minimum and not the maximum standards of educational fair use under Section 107 of HR 2223. The parties agree that the conditions determining the extent of permissible copying for educational purposes may change in the future; that certain types of copying permitted under these guidelines may not be permissible in the future, and conversely that in the future other types of copying not permitted under these guidelines may be permissible under revised guidelines.

Moreover, the following statement of guidelines is not intended to limit the types of copying permitted under the standards of fair use under judicial decision and which are stated in Section 107 of the Copyright Revision Bill. There may be instances in which copying which does not fall within the guidelines stated below may nonetheless be permitted under the criteria of fair use.

A. Permissible Uses
1. Emergency copying to replace purchased copies which for any reason are not available for an imminent performance provided

purchased replacement copies shall be substituted in due course.

2. For academic purposes other than performance, single or multiple copies of excerpts of works may be made, provided that the excerpts do not comprise a part of the whole which would constitute a performable unit such as a section, movement or aria, but in no case more than 10 percent of the whole work. The number of copies shall not exceed one copy per pupil.

3. Printed copies which have been purchased may be edited or simplified provided that the fundamental character of the work is not distorted or the lyrics, if any, altered or lyrics added if none exist.

4. A single copy of recordings of performances by students may be made or evaluation or rehearsal purposes and may be retained by the educational institution or individual teacher.

5. A single copy of a sound recording (such as a tape, disc, or cassette) of copyrighted music may be made from sound recordings owned by an educational institution or an individual teacher for the purpose of constructing aural exercises or examinations and may be retained by the educational institution or individual teacher. (This pertains only to the copyright of the music itself and not to any copyright which may exist in the sound recording.)

B. Prohibitions

1. Copying to create or replace or substitute for anthologies, compilations or collective works.

2. Copying of or from works intended to be "consumable" in the course of study or of teaching such as workbooks, exercises, standardized tests and answer sheets and like material.

3. Copying for the purpose of performance, except as in A(1) above.

4. Copying for the purpose of substituting for the purchase of music, except as in A(1) and A(2) above.

5. Copying without inclusion of the copyright notice which appears on the printed copy.

Appendix I
Music Library Association Statement on the Digital Transmission of Electronic Reserves[1]

ഌരു

Music educators cannot effectively teach the structure of a musical work without providing aural access to the complete work. Attempting to comprehend an entire musical composition through excerpts, or even sections, is no more effective than attempting to comprehend a novel, architectural plan, poem, or painting in the same manner. At best, only a sense of style is conveyed, not compositional structure. Additionally, educators who teach the history, culture, theory, composition, or performance of music require the flexibility to select the compositions they teach based on educational relevance and instructional objectives. Recognition of the appropriateness of providing such flexibility in instruction is expressed within Section 110 of the copyright law, which states:

> Notwithstanding the provisions of section 106, the following are not infringements of copyright:
>
> (1) performance or display of a work by instructors or pupils in the course of face-to-face teaching activities of a nonprofit educational institution, in a classroom or similar place devoted to instruction, unless, in the case of a motion picture or other audiovisual work, the performance, or the display of individual images, is given by means of a copy that was not lawfully made under this title, and

---

1. Source: Music Library Association webpage, at <http://www.musiclibraryassoc.org>.

that the person responsible for the performance knew or had reason to believe was not lawfully made; . . . .

The American Library Association's "Model Policy Concerning College and University Photocopying for Classroom, Research and Library Reserve Use" (C&RL News (April 1982): 127–131), as drafted by Mary Hutchins, states the view that the library reserve room may be considered an extension of the classroom. The Music Library Association fully supports this view as well as the consequent view that students enrolled in a class have the educational right to aurally access its assigned musical works both in the classroom and through class reserves. The MLA also believes that the dubbing or digital copying of musical works for class reserves falls within the spirit of the fair use provision of the copyright law.

In light of the above, the Music Library Association supports the creation and transmission of digital audio file copies of copyrighted recordings of musical works for course reserves purposes, under the following conditions:

ᔥ Access to such digital copies must be through library-controlled equipment and campus-restricted networks.

ᔥ Access to digital copies from outside of the campus should be limited to individuals who have been authenticated: namely, students enrolled either in a course or in formal independent study with an instructor in the institution.

ᔥ Digital copies should be made only of works that are being taught in the course or study.

ᔥ Digital copies may be made of whole movements or whole works.

ᔥ Either the institution or the course instructor should own the original that is used to make the digital file. The Library should make a good faith effort to purchase a commercially available copy of anything that is provided by the instructor.

ᔥ The library should remove access to the files at the completion of the course.

ᔥ The library may store course files for future re-use. This includes the digital copy made from an instructor's original if the library has made a good faith effort to purchase its own copy commercially.

Appendix J
REQUESTING PERMISSION: SAMPLE LETTER TO COPYRIGHT OWNER/PUBLISHER

ഇൽരു

[Date]

[Name and Address]

Dear _____ :

I am writing to request permission to use [name of article/chapter from book/illustration . . .] for use in classes I teach at _____ during the 2003/04 academic year and in future semesters.

[If a Book]	[If an Article]
Title:	Title:
Author:	Author:
Chapter:	Volume Number and Pages:
Copyright Date:	Copyright Date:
ISBN #	ISSN #

The materials will be distributed to students enrolled in my classes, or made available through the library's reserve operations or electronically. If the materials are placed on reserve, we will make no more than five copies. If the materials are made available electronically, they will be distributed only to students enrolled in the class on a secure website, and we will implement control procedures that restrict further distribution.

I greatly appreciate your supporting my students and their coursework. I hope you will agree to this non-profit academic use of your materials by returning this letter, with your signature, in the self-addressed envelope that I have enclosed for your convenience. Alternatively, you may e-mail your permission to me at [   ].

Again, many thanks,

Name:_____
Title:_____
School Name/ Address:_____
Phone Number/Fax Number/E-mail address: _____

Permission to Use the Materials Listed Above is Granted

Name:_____
Title:_____
Date:_____

Appendix K
AMERICAN ASSOCIATION OF LAW LIBRARIES GUIDELINES ON THE FAIR USE OF COPYRIGHTED WORKS BY LAW LIBRARIES

ಐ(ಐಲ

May 1997, Revised January 2001
Approved by the Copyright Committee, January 2001.[1]

1. Introduction

1.1. Preamble

The Copyright Act[2] sets out the rights of copyright ownership,[3] as well as the limits to those exclusive rights.[4] Two of the most important limits for law libraries are fair use (Section 107 of the Copyright Act) and the library exemption (Section 108 of the Copyright Act). The purpose of these Guidelines is to provide guidance to law librarians on copying by the library and by users under fair use and the library exemption, rather than by authorization from the copyright owners.

---

1. The American Association of Law Libraries encourages the free reproduction and distribution of the AALL Guidelines on the Fair Use of Copyrighted Works by Law Libraries without permission. Because digital technology is in a dynamic phase, there may come a time when it is necessary to revise the Guidelines. All institutions should review their own policies to ensure compliance with all applicable laws.
2. Title 17 of the United States Code.
3. 17 U.S.C. § 106.
4. 17 U.S.C. §§ 107–122.

These Guidelines describe conditions under which fair use and the library exemption should generally apply. A particular use that exceeds these Guidelines may or may not be a fair use, but the more one exceeds the Guidelines, the greater the risk that fair use does not apply. The American Association of Law Libraries believes that operation within these Guidelines provides a safe harbor, although only the courts can determine authoritatively whether a particular use is a fair use.

The limitations and conditions set forth in these Guidelines do not apply to works in the public domain for which there are no restrictions (such as facts, U.S. government works, or works in which copyright has expired), or to works for which the institution has obtained permission for the particular use. License agreements or contracts may govern the uses of some works, in particular, electronic information products; users should refer to the applicable license or contract terms for guidance on the use of those works.

These Guidelines represent the American Association of Law Libraries' collective understanding of fair use in law libraries. This Preamble is an integral part of these Guidelines and should be included whenever the Guidelines are reprinted or adopted by libraries or their parent organizations and institutions.

1.2. Background and Intent

The AALL Electronic Fair Use Committee was appointed in 1994 to develop Guidelines on the fair use of legal materials by U.S. law libraries. The AALL 2000–2001 Copyright Committee felt it important to update the 1997 Guidelines due to subsequent federal legislation and case law.

These Guidelines represent recommendations for "best practices" in all types of law libraries. Because of differences in types of institutions and different uses made of copyrighted works, and because certain exemptions apply only to nonprofit educational institutions, some Guidelines relate only to one type of library. Government libraries, such as court, county and agency libraries, and bar association and other membership libraries, are nonprofit libraries and generally fall somewhere between non-profit law school and for-profit law firm libraries in these Guidelines.

These Guidelines cover the reproduction, distribution, transmission, and display of copyrighted works, or substantial portions thereof, whether published in print or available in digital format. Further, the copying may be analog (i.e., photocopying or microform) or electronic (i.e., scanning or transmission). The Guidelines assume that the library's "original" copy is a legal copy.

1.3. Fair Use (Section 107)

Fair use is a legal principle that limits the exclusive rights[5] of copyright owners. There is no simple test to determine what is fair use. Section 107 of the Copyright Act[6] lists four factors that must be considered to determine whether a use is a "fair use;" other factors may also be considered based on the particular facts of a given case.[7] Section 107 states:

> Notwithstanding the provisions of sections 106 and 106A, the fair use of a copyrighted work, including such use by reproduction in copies or phonorecords or by any other means specified by that section, for purposes such as criticism, comment, news reporting, teaching (including multiple copies for classroom use), scholarship, or research, is not an infringement of copyright. In determining whether the use made of a work in any particular case is a fair use the factors to be considered shall include—
>
> the purpose and character of the use, including whether such use is of a commercial nature or is for nonprofit educational purposes;
>
> the nature of the copyrighted work;
>
> the amount and substantiality of the portion used in relation to the copyrighted work as a whole; and
>
> the effect of the use upon the potential market for or value of the copyrighted work.

The fact that a work is unpublished shall not itself bar a finding of fair use if such finding is made upon consideration of all the above factors.[8]

1.4. The Library Exemption (Section 108)

Much of the copying covered by these Guidelines is permitted under § 108 of the Copyright Act.[9] The exemptions provided in § 108 are available to all types of libraries that meet the requirements of § 108(a). To qualify for the § 108 exemptions, copying must not be for direct or indirect commercial advantage, each copy reproduced must include the notice of copyright that appears on the original work or a legend if no such notice appears on the work (see 1.4.1 for additional detail), and the collection must be open to the public or available to researchers doing research in a specialized field. A library that makes its collection available to others by interlibrary loan or otherwise meets the "open and available" requirement.[10]

---

5. *See* 17 U.S.C. § 106.
6. The Copyright Act of 1976, as amended, is codified at 17 U.S.C. §§ 101 et seq.
7. Campbell v. Acuff-Rose Music, Inc., 510 U.S. 569 (1994).
8. 17 U.S.C. § 107.
9. 17 U.S.C. §§ 109, 110, and 117 may also be relevant to these Guidelines.
10. H.R. REP. NO. 1476, 94th Cong., 2d Sess. (1976), *reprinted in* OMNIBUS COPYRIGHT REVISION LEGISLATION 75 (1977).

Section 108(d) provides that a library which meets the § 108(a) requirements may, at the request of a user, reproduce one copy of an article from a periodical issue or other contribution to a collective work either from material the library owns or from material owned by another library. The copy must become the property of the user. The library must post the warning prescribed in 37 C.F.R. § 201.14 at the place where the orders are placed, and must include it on the order form.[11] Further, the library should have no notice that the user will use the copy for other than fair use purposes.

Under § 108(d), libraries that qualify for the Library Exemption may provide a single copy to an external user upon request from that user. (See 2.1 below.) The copy provided may be either a photocopy or an electronic copy. Consistent with § 108(a)(1), the library may charge a reasonable fee for making the copy as long as the charge does not exceed reasonable cost recovery.

1.4.1. Notice of Copyright Under Section 108

A notice of copyright should appear on each print and electronic copy reproduced.

Under § 108, copies should include the notice of copyright that appears on the copy being reproduced. Absent such notice, the copy should include a legend such as "This work may be protected by copyright; further reproduction and distribution in violation of United States copyright law is prohibited."[12]

2. Reproducing Single Copies within the Firm, School, Court, or Other Institutions

---

11. Notice Warning Concerning Copyright Restrictions

    The copyright law of the United States (title 17, United States Code) governs the making of photocopies or other reproductions of copyrighted material.

    Under certain conditions specified in the law, libraries and archives are authorized to furnish a photocopy or other reproduction. One of these specific conditions is that the photocopy or reproduction is not to be "used for any purpose other than private study, scholarship, or research." If a user makes a request for, or later uses, a photocopy or reproduction for purposes in excess of "fair use," that user may be liable for copyright infringement.

    This institution reserves the right to refuse to accept a copying order if, in its judgment, fulfillment of the order would involve violation of copyright law.

    37 C.F.R. § 201.14(b).

12. The Digital Millennium Copyright Act amended Section 108(a)(3) to require that a library copy include the notice of copyright that appears on the work. It is not clear from the language of the statute or the legislative history whether this requirement applies to copying the copyright notice in front matter of the volume when copying independently authored articles from a journal or compilation.

2.1. Copying from the Library's Own Collection

Fair Use: Purposes for copying from the library's collection include teaching, scholarship, or research, such as preparation in teaching, background research for drafting a court opinion, a client letter, a brief or a memorandum of law, and writing an article or book. Attorneys may offer reproductions of court opinions, statutes, articles, and sections of treatises into evidence in court proceedings. This also includes reproducing and distributing copies as required for administrative proceedings.

Library Exemption

A library which meets the § 108(a) requirements may, at the request of a user, reproduce one copy of an article from a periodical issue or other contribution to a collective work either from material the library owns or from material owned by another library.[13] The copy must become the property of the user; it may not be added to the library's collection. The library must post the warning prescribed by the Copyright Office at the place where the orders are placed, and must include it on the order form.[14] Further, the library should have no notice that the user will use the copy for other than fair use purposes.

For-Profit Library Copying for External Users

Libraries in the for-profit sector may provide a single copy of an article, a chapter, or a portion of another copyrighted work to clients to support work done for the client. The copy provided may be either a photocopy or an electronic copy, provided it includes the appropriate notice (see 1.4.1 above).

For-Profit Library Copying for Internal Users

Law firm and other law libraries in the for-profit sector should be aware that the *Texaco* decision[15] may apply to them. The AALL Model Law Firm Copyright Policy cautions against copying and distributing articles for later (rather than current) use and creating personal libraries. Libraries are also cautioned against systematically routing journals with knowledge or reason to believe that recipients will copy the articles for later (rather than current) use and creating personal libraries. Libraries may copy tables of contents, but should not solicit requests for copies of articles that would constitute systematic copying.[16]

---

13. 17 U.S.C. § 108(d).
14. *See supra* note 11.
15. American Geophysical Union v. Texaco, 60 F.3d 913 (2d Cir. 1994).
16. AALL MODEL LAW FIRM COPYRIGHT POLICY, *available at* <http://www.aallnet.org>.

2.1.1. Printed Copies of Printed Works
To satisfy a user's request, a library may make a photocopy or other printed copy of a printed work such as an article, a chapter or portions of other copyrighted works.

2.1.2. Electronic Copies of Printed Works
To satisfy a user's request, a library may scan an article from a periodical issue, a chapter, or portions of other copyrighted works and provide an electronic copy to the user in lieu of a photocopy. Because the copy must become the property of the user, the library may not retain the scanned image. A copy may be faxed or otherwise transmitted electronically to the user, but the library should destroy any temporary copy made incidental to the transmission. In other words, an incidental copy made to facilitate transmission is a fair use, as long as that copy is not retained.

2.1.3. Printed Copies of Digital Works
Unless prohibited or otherwise restricted by the terms of a valid license agreement, a library may print a copy of an article, a chapter, or portions of other copyrighted works at the request of a user.

2.1.4. Electronic Copies of Digital Works
Unless prohibited or otherwise restricted by the terms of a valid license agreement, a library may download a copy of an article, a chapter, or portions of other copyrighted works at the request of a user and forward it electronically to the user.

2.2. Obtaining Copies from Another Library

2.2.1 Interlibrary Loan Copies
A library may request single copies of articles, book chapters, or portions of other copyrighted works from the collection of another library to satisfy user requests as described above. The receiving library may deliver the copy to the user in print or electronic format. Neither the borrowing nor lending library may retain the print or digital image. Libraries may request print or electronic copies of works through interlibrary loan, but borrowing libraries of all types should be aware of the CONTU suggestion of five.[17] The more a library exceeds the suggestion of five, the less likely it is that the interlibrary loan request is fair use.

---

17. The suggestion of five permits libraries to copy five articles from the most recent five years of a single title without paying a royalty. All copying of articles more than five years old is considered permissible without paying a royalty. Records are maintained by the requesting entity. H.R. REP. NO. 1733, 94th Cong., 2d Sess. (1976), *reprinted in* OMNIBUS COPYRIGHT REVISION LEGISLATION 72–74 (1977).

2.2.2. Access to Digital Works by External Users[18]
Terms of a valid license agreement may prohibit access to or reproduction of digital works for external users, including interlibrary loan, or may limit the external constituencies to which a law library may supply either print or electronic copies of digital works. If the license agreement is silent on providing copies to external users, then the library may make either printed or digital copies for external users.

3. Multiple Copying of Copyrighted Works

3.1. Multiple Copying in General
Multiple copying is limited under the Copyright Act and under these Guidelines. Section 108 of the Act (the Library Exemption) is restricted to single copies. There are, however, instances in which multiple copying might be considered fair use under § 107.

3.1.1. Academic Law Libraries
Under the Classroom Guidelines,[19] nonprofit educational institutions may, under certain circumstances, make multiple copies of articles, book chapters, and portions of other copyrighted works for classroom use. The Classroom Guidelines restrict use to one term, and also impose tests such as brevity, spontaneity and cumulative effects. Scholars, librarians, and publishers agree that uses within the terms of the Classroom Guidelines are fair.

The Classroom Guidelines were designed to cover uses in primary and secondary schools. In higher education, including nonprofit law school-sponsored continuing legal education programs, however, fair use should encompass copying beyond that which is permitted in the Classroom Guidelines. The word limitations in the Classroom Guidelines are especially problematic for legal education due to the length of most copyrightable legal documents and scholarship.

Academic libraries may make a limited number of copies of articles, chapters, and portions of other copyrighted works for library reserve collections as an extension of the classroom. The ALA Model Policy suggests that no more than six copies be made for reserve for any one class.[20] The copies may be print or electronic. In the case of electronic copies, access should be limited to no more than six simultaneous users. For electronic reserves, the institution should take reasonable steps to ensure copies are only accessible to enrolled students.

---

18. For example, secondary users not affiliated with the institution.
19. H.R. REP. NO. 1476, 94th Cong., 2d Sess. (1976), *reprinted in* OMNIBUS COPYRIGHT REVISION LEGISLATION 68–70 (1977).
20. Model Policy Concerning College and University Photocopying for Classroom, Research and Library Reserve Use, American Library Association, Washington Office, Washington, DC (Mar. 1982).

3.1.2. Other Law Libraries

Multiple simultaneous copying generally is not permitted under the library exemption. There may be instances, however, where such copying would be permitted under fair use. The library should apply the four fair use factors to determine whether making the copies qualifies for the fair use exemption.

3.2. Preservation

A library may make three copies of either a published or unpublished work for preservation purposes under specified conditions.[21] Such copies may be in analog or digital formats, but digital copies may not be used outside the premises of the library nor sent to other libraries.

3.2.1. Obsolete Devices

A library may make three copies of a published work when the format in which the work is stored has become obsolete. A format is obsolete if the equipment or device necessary to perceive the work is no longer manufactured or not reasonably available in the commercial marketplace.[22]

3.2.2. Unpublished Works

A library that has a copy of an unpublished work in its collection may make a copy of that work for deposit in another library that qualifies for the Library Exemption [see 1.4 above]. Such copies may only be in analog format.

3.3. Copying Newsletters

Libraries generally may reproduce only small portions of copyrighted newsletters. All types of libraries should avoid multiple copying of newsletters or routing newsletters if they have knowledge or reason to believe that recipients will reproduce the newsletter or articles therein for a later use or create personal libraries.

4. Copying Database Search Results

4.1. Signed License Agreements

Most libraries sign license agreements to obtain access to legal and other databases. Because libraries must comply with the terms of a valid license agreement, they should review the terms of all licenses closely.

4.2. Redistribution of Results—
Single Copy to a User

---

21. 17 U.S.C. §§ 108(b)–(c).
22. 17 U.S.C. § 108(c).

Distribution of database search results to a single user clearly is permitted under fair use unless prohibited by a valid license agreement. This includes providing a copy of search results to any library patron, including a faculty member, student, judge, or law firm client. Public domain information is not subject to any of these limitations.

4.3. Redistribution of Results—Multiple Users

Absent a license agreement that restricts redistribution of non-public domain research results, redistribution to multiple users may be permitted. Libraries should seek permission for multiple distributions of research results, whether by print or via electronic means, if that use exceeds these Guidelines.

– –

In July, 1994, AALL President Carol Billings appointed the Special Committee to Advance the Fair Use of Electronic Information Resources in Law Libraries and by Law Librarians. Dubbed the "Electronic Fair Use Committee," its charge was to develop policies/guidelines relating to the fair use of electronic information resources in law libraries and by law librarians with specific reference to networking, downloading, retransmission, re-use and combining information and to any other relevant issues.

The Electronic Fair Use Committee, chaired by Laura N. Gasaway, held hearings to determine what AALL members believed to be fair use in the electronic environment. The original Guidelines, which were adopted by the AALL Executive Board in July, 1997, represented this effort.

The AALL Copyright Committee has continuing responsibility for these Guidelines, as well as others relating to intellectual property. The 2000–01 Copyright Committee revised the original Guidelines to reflect changes in the law since 1997.

Members of AALL's 2000–01 Copyright Committee:

James Heller, Chair
Wesley Cochran
Charles Cronin
Joanne Dugan
Carol Ebbinghouse
Jonathan Franklin
Susan Lewis-Somers
David Mao

Appendix L
AMERICAN ASSOCIATION OF LAW LIBRARIES MODEL LAW FIRM COPYRIGHT POLICY

࿋ࣿ࿋

October, 1996, Revised January, 2001
Approved by the Copyright Committee, January 2001

Introductory Statement: Reproducing copyrighted materials is governed by the Copyright Act of 1976, subsequent legislation, and interpretive case law. AALL reaffirms the application of the fair use provision (17 U.S.C. § 107) and the library exemption (17 U.S.C. § 108) in the law firm environment. This Policy is intended solely for the consideration of law firm libraries as suggested procedures in complying with copyright law. Firmwide implementation should be done with the input and advice of firm management.

Firm Statement: [FIRM] does not condone the unauthorized reproduction of copyrighted materials, in any format. Unauthorized reproduction includes copying done beyond that which is permitted under the Copyright Act, if it is done without permission and/or payment of royalties.

Responsibility Statement: Compliance with the Copyright Act is the individual responsibility of every employee, including partners, associates, paralegals, other staff members, and independent contractors working at or for the firm.

Sources of Copies: Under this Policy, sources of copies should be the lawfully obtained original copyrighted work, whether found in the library, obtained through inter-library loan from a lending library, or retrieved from an online service or document delivery service that receives permission from or pays royalties to the copyright owner.

Definitions:
1. **Copy:** For purposes of this Policy, a copy is either (1) a photoreproduction of text or images via a copier; (2) transmission or downloading of text or images from a computer, or (3) any other replication of text or images by way of electronic means, or other form of transcription.

2. **Reproduction Equipment**: Reproduction equipment includes photocopiers, printers, scanners, facsimile machines, microform reader/printers, networked workstations and other electronic transmission devices. It is not intended that copyright notices be posted on individual computer workstations throughout the firm.

3. **Reproduction Centers**: Reproduction centers include areas of the firm staffed by personnel, either employed by the firm or by a third party, who have the primary responsibility for attending to copiers and other reproduction equipment. It should be noted that reproduction centers that are staffed by third party vendors may not be able to take advantage of the Section 108 library exemption to the same extent as reproduction centers staffed by firm employees.

Signage: Notice on Equipment: The firm should post the following signs on all reproduction equipment: "THE MAKING OF A COPY MAY BE SUBJECT TO THE UNITED STATES COPYRIGHT LAW (Title 17 United States Code)." Alternatively, the firm may elect to use the following notice recommended by the American Library Association—"THE COPYRIGHT LAW OF THE UNITED STATES (Title 17 U.S. Code) GOVERNS THE MAKING OF PHOTOCOPIES OR OTHER REPRODUCTIONS OF COPYRIGHTED MATERIAL. THE PERSON USING THIS EQUIPMENT IS LIABLE FOR ANY INFRINGEMENT."

Signage: Notice on Copies: The notice of copyright that appears on the original work should be reproduced and affixed to the copy. If no such notice appears on the original work, the printed copy should include the following notice stamped on or affixed to the first page of every copyrighted item reproduced by the library or reproduction center: "THIS MATERIAL IS SUBJECT TO THE UNITED STATES COPYRIGHT LAW; FURTHER REPRODUCTION IN VIOLATION OF THAT LAW IS PROHIBITED."

Signage: Notice Where Orders Are Placed and on Request Form: The Library or reproduction center should display the following sign where copying orders are placed, and should include this notice on the actual copying request form:

NOTICE
WARNING CONCERNING COPYRIGHT RESTRICTIONS

The copyright law of the United States (Title 17, United States Code) governs the making of photocopies or other reproduction of copyrighted material.

Under certain conditions specified in the law, libraries and archives are authorized to furnish a photocopy or other reproduction. One of these specified conditions is that the photocopy or reproduction is not to be "used for any purpose other than private study, scholarship or research." If a user makes a request for, or later uses, a photocopy or reproduction for purposes in excess of "fair use", that user may be liable for copyright infringement.

This institution reserves the right to refuse to accept a copying order if, in its judgment, fulfillment of the order would involve violation of copyright law.

Routing and Library Reproduction: The Library may route originals and/or copies of tables of contents. When the length of the routing list becomes excessive, the firm should purchase additional copies of a copyrighted work. Libraries are cautioned against systematically routing journals with knowledge or reason to believe that recipients will reproduce the articles for later (rather than current) use and to create personal libraries.

The library or reproduction center may make one copy of an article in response to a specific request from an employee or partner for individual scholarship, research or educational use. Recipients are cautioned against systematic reproduction of articles for later (rather than current) use and creating personal libraries. Although in most instances making subsequent copies from the original copy requires permission, circumstances may exist—such as making a single copy for one client or co-counsel, or for submission to a court—where the copying may be a fair use.

The Library or reproduction center should not, nor should individuals, make multiple copies of articles, or cover-to-cover copies of newsletters, periodical issues or volumes. This practice should be observed for both standard library materials and materials obtained from online services. NOTE: Because of the typically short length of newsletters, the library or reproduction center, as a general rule, may reproduce only small portions of newsletters subject to copyright protection. Libraries may reproduce tables of contents, but should not solicit requests for copies of articles that would constitute systematic reproduction.

Interlibrary Lending/Document Delivery: The library typically may borrow or lend only lawfully obtained original copies of copyrighted materials, or the original copyrighted work.

> **Lending:** In response to requests from other libraries, the library may make one copy of an article so long as the requester attests, and the library reasonably believes, that the request complies with the Copyright Act or the CONTU guidelines.

> **Borrowing:** In requesting materials from other libraries, the library may request a single copy of an article or brief excerpts from a book, so long as the request complies with the Copyright Act or the CONTU guidelines. (CONTU suggests that a library subscribe to a journal title if it requests photocopies of articles published in the periodical within five years prior to the date of the request more than five times within a given year).

Computer Programs: According to Section 117 of the Copyright Act, the firm may make one archival copy of software it has purchased, and may also adapt purchased software so that it can be used on firm equipment. Firm personnel should not load any unauthorized copy of any computer program, or portion thereof, onto any computer, file server, or other magnetic or electronic media storage device belonging to the firm. License agreements should be strictly followed with regard to the use of all authorized copies of software programs. The general rule for software use in law firms is that each copy is for a single computer. A site license should be considered for multiple copies on multiple computers, or for access by multiple simultaneous users.

Permissions and Royalties: This Policy expresses minimum standards of fair use. Circumstances may exist where copying beyond this Policy is permitted under the Copyright Act. However, reproducing materials beyond that which is permitted by this Policy generally will require permission, and, when necessary, payment of royalties. Royalties may be made directly to the copyright owner or its agent.

Questions/For More Information: Please direct any copyright concerns to [Librarian and/or Intellectual Property Attorney].

Review and Implementation: Firm management should review the copyright law—particularly 17 U.S.C. § 106–109—as well as firmwide copying and other copyright related activities before implementing a copyright policy. At a minimum level, this should include a review of Copyright Office Circular R21: Reproduction of Copyrighted Words by Educators and Librarians. Other recommended resources are; Stephen Fishman, *The Copyright Handbook: How to Protect and Use Written Works* (Nolo Press, 2000); William S. Strong, *The Copyright Book: A Practical Guide* (MIT Press, 1999); and Arlene Bielefield, *Technology and Copyright Law* (Neal-Schuman 1997).

Management should review carefully all firmwide online database, CD-ROM and software contracts.

- -

1. Title 17 of the United States Code includes the Copyright Act of 1976 and subsequent legislation.
2. For an expanded discussion of what constitutes fair use, see the AALL Guidelines on the Fair Use of Copyrighted Works by Law Libraries (revised, January 2001) [hereinafter AALL Fair Use Guidelines].
3. See Nimmer on Copyright § 13.05[D][2] (2000).
4. For additional examples of what constitutes fair use, see AALL Fair Use Guidelines.
5. National Commission on New Technological Uses of Copyrighted Works (CONTU) (1976).
6. For an expanded discussion of what constitutes fair use, see AALL Fair Use Guidelines.

Members of AALL's 2000–01 Copyright Committee:
James Heller, Chair
Wesley Cochran
Charles Cronin
Joanne Dugan
Carol Ebbinghouse
Jonathan Franklin
Susan Lewis-Somers
David Mao

Appendix M
VISUAL RESOURCES ASSOCIATION IMAGE COLLECTION GUIDELINES: THE ACQUISITION AND USE OF IMAGES IN NON-PROFIT EDUCATIONAL VISUAL RESOURCES COLLECTIONS

ಬುಡಗ

As published by the VRA Committee on Intellectual Property Rights

Many educational disciplines are dependent upon the use of illustrative images for teaching purposes. Visual resources collections which support those disciplines strive to assemble the best resources in terms of technical quality, fidelity to the underlying work, accuracy of basic identifying information, and flexibility of access and utilization. The development and use of these resources should be guided by the following principles in regard to acquisition, attribution, display and responsibility.

The acquisition and use of image resources, as with any intellectual property, is governed by legal conditions, as well as by practical, technical, and scholarly considerations. Intellectual property law, including the concept of Copyright, attempts to balance the sometimes competing interests of those who produce or provide such resources, and those who use them. It is the intent of this Guide to enable the visual resources professional to acquire image resources for educational, non-profit use in a manner that respects the rights and concerns of providers, while acknowledging public domain rights and educational exemptions such as Fair Use.

Although these guidelines have been reviewed by legal counsel, the content represents the consensus of visual resources curators and does not constitute a legal document. For further guidance on acquisition, attribution, display, and responsibility, individual visual resources curators should consult the legal counsel of their respective educational institutions.

A. ACQUISITION
Acquisition of visual resources falls into several categories: purchase and license, donation, and copystand photography.

1. Purchase, license, or otherwise legally acquire, the following in developing permanent archives of images:

a) slides or digital files from museums, galleries or other such institutions
b) slides or digital files from vendors and image providers
c) original on-site photography produced for sale by professional or highly skilled photographers.
d) slides or digital files distributed on a free-use basis through recognized educational or professional institutions, organizations and consortia.

2. Gifts and donations are considered legitimate forms of acquisition, even though they may be subject to restrictions or requirements by the donors. It is recommended that donors of original photographic images in whatever form be encouraged to grant in writing to the recipient institution discretionary rights over extended use, as well as physical custody, of the photographic materials.

3. Images created by copystand photography and scanning from published materials for inclusion in the permanent archive are subject to the following considerations:

a) images of suitable quality are not readily available at a reasonable cost and in a reasonable time from any of the options listed above
b) images will not be shared between or among other educational institutions if such use is prohibited by the terms of their acquisition.
c) images will be used for comment, criticism, review, analysis, discussion, or other similar purpose associated with instruction or scholarship
d) images will be used for purposes that are both nonprofit and educational.

If these conditions can be met, it is likely that making images and digital files from published materials will be within "fair use" as outlined in the Copyright Act of 1976.

Uses outside the understood parameters described above, such as use on an unrestricted website or in print publications, including scholarly publications, are not covered in this document. Such uses to be considered fair must be judged independently and individually, using the four-factor analysis described in Section 107 of the Copyright Act of 1976. The four factors to be considered in determining if a use is a fair use are: (1) purpose and character of the use; (2) nature of the copyrighted work; (3) amount and substantiality of the material used; and (4) the effect on the market.

4. Public Domain images (those in which neither the underlying work of art documented nor the photographic reproduction itself is subject to copyright) may be safely acquired by any appropriate means, including copystand photography or scanning. Use of such images is unrestricted. (**see VRA Copy Photography Computator)

B. ATTRIBUTION

To the extent that such information is available, it is recommended that all images acquired for the permanent archive of an educational institution should be identified with the following:

1) source of image
2) year of acquisition
3) in the case of a purchased or licensed image, the provider's inventory or identifying number or code.

C. DISPLAY

While the traditional means of display for such image archives have been through projection, or otherwise viewing the physical surrogate (photograph, slide, video, film), the introduction of new technologies, specifically the digital environment of the Internet and the World Wide Web has expanded the display options. There is little in the way of legal precedent, code, or case law which addresses the issues particular to educational image archives. However, it seems reasonable to expect that digital materials should be available to the same user group that the analog collection serves, for the same purposes.

Analog materials acquired as outlined above may be used in digital format as follows:

1) Images purchased or licensed are subject to the conditions specified at the time of purchase or according to license agreement. 2) Gifts and donations are subject to restrictions made at the time of contribution. In addition, a gift of images purchased by the donor may be subject to the conditions of the original purchase.

3) Images made by copystand photography may be digitized and used digitally according to the same criteria under which they were originally acquired for analog use.

D. RESPONSIBILITY

The educational institution holding such an archive should have a designated overseer who is responsible for carrying out the principles outlined above. A budget sufficient to make purchases described above should be allocated. Information on source data should be available to the collection users.

Under the law, liability may be held by both the institution and the individual; however, individual liability may depend on the institution's policies. Usually, although not always, individuals who adhere to institutional policies will be indemnified by their institutions against all the costs they may suffer if they are sued. Following institutional policy is a good way for individuals to stay within the protections of a good-faith fair use defense. It is recommended that the designated overseer discuss institutional policies with the institution's legal counsel.

Appendix N
SELECTED PROVISIONS FROM THE U.S. COPYRIGHT ACT (TITLE 17, UNITED STATES CODE)

ഇരുഗ

§ 101. Definitions

Except as otherwise provided in this title, as used in this title, the terms below and their variant forms mean the following.

"Audiovisual works" are works that consist of a series of related images which are intrinsically intended to be shown by the use of machines or devices such as projectors, viewers, or electronic equipment, together with accompanying sounds, if any, regardless of the nature of the material objects, such as films or tapes, in which the works are embodied.

The "Berne Convention" is the Convention for the Protection of Literary and Artistic Works, signed at Berne, Switzerland, on September 9, 1886, and all acts, protocols, and revisions thereto.

A "collective work" is a work, such as a periodical issue, anthology, or encyclopedia, in which a number of contributions, constituting separate and independent works in themselves, are assembled into a collective whole.

A "compilation" is a work formed by the collection and assembling of preexisting materials or of data that are selected, coordinated, or arranged in such a way that the resulting work as a whole constitutes an original work of authorship. The term "compilation" includes collective works.

"Copies" are material objects, other than phonorecords, in which a work is fixed by any method now known or later developed, and from which the work can be perceived, reproduced, or otherwise communicated, either directly or with the aid of a machine or device. The term "copies" includes the material object, other than a phonorecord, in which the work is first fixed.

"Copyright owner," with respect to any one of the exclusive rights comprised in a copyright, refers to the owner of that particular right.

A "derivative work" is a work based upon one or more preexisting works, such as a translation, musical arrangement, dramatization, fictionalization, motion picture version, sound recording, art reproduction, abridgment, condensation, or any other form in which a work may be recast, transformed, or adapted. A work consisting of editorial revisions, annotations, elaborations, or other modifications which, as a whole, represent an original work of authorship, is a "derivative work."

A "digital transmission" is a transmission in whole or in part in a digital or other non-analog format.

To "display" a work means to show a copy of it, either directly or by means of a film, slide, television image, or any other device or process or, in the case of a motion picture or other audiovisual work, to show individual images nonsequentially.

A work is "fixed" in a tangible medium of expression when its embodiment in a copy or phonorecord, by or under the authority of the author, is sufficiently permanent or stable to permit it to be perceived, reproduced, or otherwise communicated for a period of more than transitory duration. A work consisting of sounds, images, or both, that are being transmitted, is "fixed" for purposes of this title if a fixation of the work is being made simultaneously with its transmission.

An "international agreement" is—
    (1) the Universal Copyright Convention;
    (2) the Geneva Phonograms Convention;
    (3) the Berne Convention;
    (4) the WTO Agreement;
    (5) [Caution . . .]
    (7) any other copyright treaty to which the United States is a party.

To "perform" a work means to recite, render, play, dance, or act it, either directly or by means of any device or process or, in the case of a motion picture or other audiovisual work, to show its images in any sequence or to make the sounds accompanying it audible.

"Publication" is the distribution of copies or phonorecords of a work to the public by sale or other transfer of ownership, or by rental, lease, or lending. The offering to distribute copies or phonorecords to a group of persons for purposes of further distribution, public performance, or public display, constitutes publication. A public performance or display of a work does not of itself constitute publication.

To perform or display a work "publicly" means—

(1)   to perform or display it at a place open to the public or at any place where a substantial number of persons outside of a normal circle of a family and its social acquaintances is gathered; or

(2)   to transmit or otherwise communicate a performance or display of the work to a place specified by clause (1) or to the public, by means of any device or process, whether the members of the public capable of receiving the performance or display receive it in the same place or in separate places and at the same time or at different times.

A "transfer of copyright ownership" is an assignment, mortgage, exclusive license, or any other conveyance, alienation, or hypothecation of a copyright or of any of the exclusive rights comprised in a copyright, whether or not it is limited in time or place of effect, but not including a nonexclusive license.

To "transmit" a performance or display is to communicate it by any device or process whereby images or sounds are received beyond the place from which they are sent. A "work of the United States Government" is a work prepared by an officer or employee of the United States Government as part of that person's official duties.

A "work made for hire" is—

(1)   a work prepared by an employee within the scope of his or her employment; or

(2)   a work specially ordered or commissioned for use as a contribution to a collective work, as a part of a motion picture or other audiovisual work, as a translation, as a supplementary work, as a compilation, as an instructional text, as a test, as answer material for a test, or as an atlas, if the parties expressly agree in a written instrument signed by them that the work shall be considered a work made for hire. . . .

§ 102. Subject Matter of Copyright: In General

(a) Copyright protection subsists, in accordance with this title, in original works of authorship fixed in any tangible medium of expression, now known or later developed, from which they can be perceived, reproduced, or otherwise communicated, either directly or with the aid of a machine or device. Works of authorship include the following categories:

    (1)   literary works;
    (2)   musical works, including any accompanying words;
    (3)   dramatic works, including any accompanying music;
    (4)   pantomimes and choreographic works;
    (5)   pictorial, graphic, and sculptural works;
    (6)   motion pictures and other audiovisual works;
    (7)   sound recordings; and
    (8)   architectural works.

(b) In no case does copyright protection for an original work of authorship extend to any idea, procedure, process, system, method of operation, concept, principle, or discovery, regardless of the form in which it is described, explained, illustrated, or embodied in such work.

§ 103. Subject Matter of Copyright: Compilations and Derivative Works

(a) The subject matter of copyright . . . includes compilations and derivative works, but protection for a work employing preexisting material in which copyright subsists does not extend to any part of the work in which such material has been used unlawfully.

(b) The copyright in a compilation or derivative work extends only to the material contributed by the author of such work, as distinguished from the preexisting material . . . and does not imply any exclusive right in the preexisting material. The copyright in such work is independent of, and does not affect or enlarge the scope, duration, ownership, or subsistence of, any copyright protection in the preexisting material.

§ 104. Subject Matter of Copyright: National Origin

(a) Unpublished works. The works specified by sections 102 and 103, while unpublished, are subject to protection under this title without regard to the nationality or domicile of the author.

(b) Published works. The works specified by sections 102 and 103, when published, are subject to protection under this title if—

(1)   on the date of first publication, one or more of the authors is a national or domiciliary of the United States, or is a national, domiciliary, or sovereign authority of a treaty party, or is a stateless person, wherever that person may be domiciled; or

(2)   the work is first published in the United States or in a foreign nation that, on the date of first publication, is a treaty party; or . . .

(5)   the work is first published by the United Nations or any of its specialized agencies, or by the Organization of American States; or

(6)   the work comes within the scope of a Presidential proclamation. . . .

(c)   Effect of Berne Convention. No right or interest in a work eligible for protection under this title may be claimed by virtue of, or in reliance upon, the provisions of the Berne Convention, or the adherence of the United States thereto. Any rights in a work eligible for protection under this title that derive from this title, other Federal or State statutes, or the common law, shall not be expanded or reduced by virtue of, or in reliance upon, the provisions of the Berne Convention, or the adherence of the United States thereto. . . .

§ 105. Subject Matter of Copyright: United States Government Works

Copyright protection under this title is not available for any work of the United States Government, but the United States Government is not precluded from receiving and holding copyrights transferred to it by assignment, bequest, or otherwise.

§ 106. Exclusive Rights in Copyrighted Works

Subject to sections 107 through 120, the owner of a copyright under this title has the exclusive rights to do and to authorize any of the following:

(1)   to reproduce the copyrighted work in copies or phonorecords;

(2)   to prepare derivative works based upon the copyrighted work;

(3)   to distribute copies or phonorecords of the copyrighted work to the public by sale or other transfer of ownership, or by rental, lease, or lending;

(4)   in the case of literary, musical, dramatic, and choreographic works, pantomimes, and motion pictures and other audio-visual works, to perform the copyrighted work publicly;

(5)   in the case of literary, musical, dramatic, and choreographic works, pantomimes, and and pictorial, graphic, or sculptural works, including the individual images of a motion picture or

other audiovisual work, to display the copyrighted work publicly; and

(6)   in the case of sound recordings, to perform the copyrighted work publicly by means of a digital audio transmission.

§ 107. Limitations on Exclusive Rights: Fair Use

Notwithstanding the provisions of sections 106 and 106A, the fair use of a copyrighted work, including such use by reproduction in copies or phonorecords or by any other means specified by that section, for purposes such as criticism, comment, news reporting, teaching (including multiple copies for classroom use), scholarship, or research, is not an infringement of copyright. In determining whether the use made of a work in any particular case is a fair use the factors to be considered shall include—

(1)   the purpose and character of the use, including whether such use is of a commercial nature or is for nonprofit educational purposes;
(2)   the nature of the copyrighted work;
(3)   the amount and substantiality of the portion used in relation to the copyrighted work as a whole; and
(4)   the effect of the use upon the potential market for or value of the copyrighted work.

The fact that a work is unpublished shall not itself bar a finding of fair use if such finding is made upon consideration of all the above factors.

§ 108. Limitations on Exclusive Rights: Reproduction by Libraries and Archives

(a)   Except as otherwise provided in this title and notwithstanding the provisions of section 106, it is not an infringement of copyright for a library or archives, or any of its employees acting within the scope of their employment, to reproduce no more than one copy or phonorecord of a work, except as provided in subsections (b) and (c), or to distribute such copy or phonorecord, under the conditions specified by this section, if—

(1)   the reproduction or distribution is made without any purpose of direct or indirect commercial advantage;
(2)   the collections of the library or archives are (i) open to the public, or (ii) available not only to researchers affiliated with the library or archives or with the institution of which it is a part, but also to other persons doing research in a specialized field; and
(3)   the reproduction or distribution of the work includes a notice of copyright that appears on the copy or phonorecord that is

reproduced under the provisions of this section, or includes a legend stating that the work may be protected by copyright if no such notice can be found on the copy or phonorecord that is reproduced under the provisions of this section.

(b) The rights of reproduction and distribution under this section apply to three copies or phonorecords of an unpublished work duplicated solely for purposes of preservation and security or for deposit for research use in another library or archives of the type described by clause (2) of subsection (a), if—

(1) the copy or phonorecord reproduced is currently in the collections of the library or archives; and

(2) any such copy or phonorecord that is reproduced in digital format is not otherwise distributed in that format and is not made available to the public in that format outside the premises of the library or archives.

(c) The right of reproduction under this section applies to three copies or phonorecords of a published work duplicated solely for the purpose of replacement of a copy or phonorecord that is damaged, deteriorating, lost, or stolen, or if the existing format in which the work is stored has become obsolete, if—

(1) the library or archives has, after a reasonable effort, determined that an unused replacement cannot be obtained at a fair price; and

(2) any such copy or phonorecord that is reproduced in digital format is not made available to the public in that format outside the premises of the library or archives in lawful possession of such copy.

For purposes of this subsection, a format shall be considered obsolete if the machine or device necessary to render perceptible a work stored in that format is no longer manufactured or is no longer reasonably available in the commercial marketplace.

(d) The rights of reproduction and distribution under this section apply to a copy, made from the collection of a library or archives where the user makes his or her request or from that of another library or archives, of no more than one article or other contribution to a copyrighted collection or periodical issue, or to a copy or phonorecord of a small part of any other copyrighted work, if—

(1) the copy or phonorecord becomes the property of the user, and the library or archives has had no notice that the copy or phonorecord would be used for any purpose other than private study, scholarship, or research; and

(2) the library or archives displays prominently, at the place where orders are accepted, and includes on its order form, a warning of copyright in accordance with requirements that

the Register of Copyrights in accordance with requirements that the Register of Copyrights shall prescribe by regulation.

(e) The rights of reproduction and distribution under this section apply to the entire work, or to a substantial part of it, made from the collection of a library or archives where the user makes his or her request or from that of another library or archives, if the library or archives has first determined, on the basis of a reasonable investigation, that a copy or phonorecord of the copyrighted work cannot be obtained at a fair price, if—

(1)   the copy or phonorecord becomes the property of the user, and the library or archives has had no notice that the copy or phonorecord would be used for any purpose other than private study, scholarship, or research; and

(2)   the library or archives displays prominently, at the place where orders are accepted, and includes on its order form, a warning of copyright in accordance with requirements that the Register of Copyrights shall prescribe by regulation.

(f) Nothing in this section—

(1)   shall be construed to impose liability for copyright infringement upon a library or archives or its employees for the unsupervised use of reproducing equipment located on its premises: *Provided*, That such equipment displays a notice that the making of a copy may be subject to the copyright law;

(2)   excuses a person who uses such reproducing equipment or who requests a copy or phonorecord under subsection (d) from liability for copyright infringement for any such act, or for any later use of such copy or phonorecord, if it exceeds fair use as provided by section 107;

(3)   shall be construed to limit the reproduction and distribution by lending of a limited number of copies and excerpts by a library or archives of an audiovisual news program, subject to clauses (1), (2), and (3) of subsection (a); or

(4)   in any way affects the right of fair use as provided by section 107, or any contractual obligations assumed at any time by the library or archives when it obtained a copy or phonorecord of a work in its collections.

(g) The rights of reproduction and distribution under this section extend to the isolated and unrelated reproduction or distribution of a single copy or phonorecord of the same material on separate occasions, but do not extend to cases where the library or archives, or its employee—

(1)   is aware or has substantial reason to believe that it is engaging in the related or concerted reproduction or distribution of multiple copies or phonorecords of the same material, whether made on one occasion or over a period of time, and whe-

ther intended for aggregate use by one or more individuals or for separate use by the individual members of a group; or

(2)   engages in the systematic reproduction or distribution of single or multiple copies or phonorecords of material described in subsection (d): *Provided,* That nothing in this clause prevents a library or archives from participating in interlibrary arrangements that do not have, as their purpose or effect, that the library or archives receiving such copies or phonorecords for distribution does so in such aggregate quantities as to substitute for a subscription to or purchase of such work.

(h) (1)   For purposes of this section, during the last 20 years of any term of copyright of a published work, a library or archives, including a nonprofit educational institution that functions as such, may reproduce, distribute, display, or perform in facsimile or digital form a copy or phonorecord of such work, or portions thereof, for purposes of preservation, scholarship, or research, if such library or archives has first determined, on the basis of a reasonable investigation, that none of the conditions set forth in subparagraphs (A), (B), and (C) of paragraph (2) apply.

(2)   No reproduction, distribution, display, or performance is authorized under this subsection if—

(A)   the work is subject to normal commercial exploitation;

(B)   a copy or phonorecord of the work can be obtained at a reasonable price; or

(C)   the copyright owner or its agent provides notice pursuant to regulations promulgated by the Register of Copyrights that either of the conditions set forth in subparagraphs (A) and (B) applies.

(3)   The exemption provided in this subsection does not apply to any subsequent uses by users other than such library or archives.

(i) The rights of reproduction and distribution under this section do not apply to a musical work, a pictorial, graphic or sculptural work, or a motion picture or other audiovisual work other than an audiovisual work dealing with news, except that no such limitation shall apply with respect to rights granted by subsections (b) and (c), or with respect to pictorial or graphic works published as illustrations, diagrams, or similar adjuncts to works of which copies are reproduced or distributed in accordance with subsections (d) and (e).

§ 109. Limitations on Exclusive Rights: Effect of Transfer of Particular Copy or Phonorecord

(a) Notwithstanding the provisions of section 106(3), the owner of a particular copy or phonorecord lawfully made under this title, or any person authorized by such owner, is entitled, without the authority of the copyright owner, to sell or otherwise dispose of the possession of that copy or phonorecord. Notwithstanding the preceding sentence, copies or phonorecords of works subject to restored copyright under section 104A that are manufactured before the date of restoration of copyright or, with respect to reliance parties, before publication or service of notice under section 104A(e), may be sold or otherwise disposed of without the authorization of the owner of the restored copyright for purposes of direct or indirect commercial advantage only during the 12-month period beginning on—

(1) the date of the publication in the Federal Register of the notice of intent filed with the Copyright Office under section 104A(d)(2)(A), or

(2) the date of the receipt of actual notice served under section 104A(d)(2)(B),whichever occurs first.

(B)(1)

(A) Notwithstanding the provisions of subsection (a), unless authorized by the owners of copyright in the sound recording or the owner of copyright in a computer program (including any tape, disk, or other medium embodying such program), and in the case of a sound recording in the musical works embodied therein, neither the owner of a particular phonorecord nor any person in possession of a particular copy of a computer program (including any tape, disk, or other medium embodying such program), may, for the purposes of direct or indirect commercial advantage, dispose of, or authorize the disposal of, the possession of that phonorecord or computer program (including any tape, disk, or other medium embodying such program) by rental, lease, or lending, or by any other act or practice in the nature of rental, lease, or lending. Nothing in the preceding sentence shall apply to the rental, lease, or lending of a phonorecord for nonprofit purposes by a nonprofit library or nonprofit educational institution. The transfer of possession of a lawfully made copy of a computer program by a nonprofit educational institution to another nonprofit educational institution or to faculty, staff, and students does not constitute rental, lease, or lending for direct or indirect commercial purposes under this subsection.

(B) This subsection does not apply to—

(i) a computer program which is embodied in a machine or product and which cannot be copied during the ordinary operation or use of the machine or product; or

(ii) a computer program embodied in or used in conjunction with a limited purpose computer that is designed for playing video games and may be designed for other purposes.

(C) Nothing in this subsection affects any provision of chapter 9 of this title [17 U.S.C.S. §§ 901 et seq.].

(2)(A) Nothing in this subsection shall apply to the lending of a computer program for nonprofit purposes by a nonprofit library, if each copy of a computer program which is lent by such library has affixed to the packaging containing the program a warning of copyright in accordance with requirements that the Register of Copyrights shall prescribe by regulation. . . .

(4) Any person who distributes a phonorecord or a copy of a computer program (including any tape, disk, or other medium embodying such program) in violation of paragraph (1) is an infringer of copyright under section 501 of this title and is subject to the remedies set forth in sections 502, 503, 504, 505, and 509. Such violation shall not be a criminal offense under section 506 or cause such person to be subject to the criminal penalties set forth in section 2319 of title 18.

(c) Notwithstanding the provisions of section 106(5), the owner of a particular copy lawfully made under this title, or any person authorized by such owner, is entitled, without the authority of the copyright owner, to display that copy publicly, either directly or by the projection of no more than one image at a time, to viewers present at the place where the copy is located.

(d) The privileges prescribed by subsections (a) and (c) do not, unless authorized by the copyright owner, extend to any person who has acquired possession of the copy or phonorecord from the copyright owner, by rental, lease, loan, or otherwise, without acquiring ownership of it.

(e) . . . .

§ 110. Limitations on Exclusive Rights: Exemption of Certain Performances and Displays

Notwithstanding the provisions of section 106, the following are not infringements of copyright:

(1) performance or display of a work by instructors or pupils in the course of face-to-face teaching activities of a nonprofit educational institution, in a classroom or similar place devoted to instruction, unless, in the case of a motion picture or other audiovisual work, the performance, or the display of individual

images, is given by means of a copy that was not lawfully made under this title, and that the person responsible for the performance knew or had reason to believe was not lawfully made;

(2) except with respect to a work produced or marketed primarily for performance or display as part of mediated instructional activities transmitted via digital networks, or a performance or display that is given by means of a copy or phonorecord that is not lawfully made and acquired under this title, and the transmitting government body or accredited nonprofit educational institution knew or had reason to believe was not lawfully made and acquired, the performance of a nondramatic literary or musical work or reasonable and limited portions of any other work, or display of a work in an amount comparable to that which is typically displayed in the course of a live classroom session, by or in the course of a transmission, if—

(A) the performance or display is made by, at the direction of, or under the actual supervision of an instructor as an integral part of a class session offered as a regular part of the systematic mediated instructional activities of a governmental body or an accredited nonprofit educational institution;

(B) the performance or display is directly related and of material assistance to the teaching content of the transmission;

(C) the transmission is made solely for, and, to the extent technologically feasible, the reception of such transmission is limited to—
  (i) students officially enrolled in the course for which the transmission is made; or
  (ii) officers or employees of governmental bodies as a part of their official duties or employment; and

(D) the transmitting body or institution—
  (i) institutes policies regarding copyright, provides informational materials to faculty, students, and relevant staff members that accurately describe, and promote compliance with, the laws of the United States relating to copyright, and provides notice to students that materials used in connection with the course may be subject to copyright protection; and
  (ii) in the case of digital transmissions—
    (I) applies technological measures that reasonably prevent—
      (aa) retention of the work in accessible form by recipients of the transmission from the transmitting body or institution for longer than the class session; and
      (bb) unauthorized further dissemination of the work in accessible form by such recipients to others; and
    (II) does not engage in conduct that could reasonably be expected to interfere with technological measures used by

copyright owners to prevent such retention or unauthorized further dissemination;. . . .

§ 117. Limitation on Exclusive Rights: Computer Programs

(a) . . . it is not an infringement for the owner of a copy of a computer program to make or authorize the making of another copy or adaptation of that computer program provided:

(1) that such a new copy or adaptation is created as an essential step in the utilization of the computer program in conjunction with a machine and that it is used in no other manner, or

(2) that such new copy or adaptation is for archival purposes only and that all archival copies are destroyed in the event that continued possession of the computer program should cease to be rightful.

(b) . . . Any exact copies prepared in accordance with the provisions of this section may be leased, sold, or otherwise transferred, along with the copy from which such copies were prepared, only as part of the lease, sale, or other transfer of all rights in the program. Adaptations so prepared may be transferred only with the authorization of the copyright owner.

(c) . . . it is not an infringement for the owner or lessee of a machine to make or authorize the making of a copy of a computer program if such copy is made solely by virtue of the activation of a machine that lawfully contains an authorized copy of the computer program, for purposes only of maintenance or repair of that machine, if—

(1) such new copy is used in no other manner and is destroyed immediately after the maintenance or repair is completed; and

(2) with respect to any computer program or part thereof that is not necessary for that machine to be activated, such program or part thereof is not accessed or used other than to make such new copy by virtue of the activation of the machine.

(d) Definitions. For purposes of this section—

(1) the "maintenance" of a machine is the servicing of the machine in order to make it work in accordance with its original specifications and any changes to those specifications authorized for that machine; and

(2) the "repair" of a machine is the restoring of the machine to the state of working in accordance with its original specifications and any changes to those specifications authorized for that machine.

§ 302. Duration of Copyright: Works Created on or after January 1, 1978

(a) In general. Copyright in a work created on or after January 1, 1978, subsists from its creation and, except as provided by the following subsections, endures for a term consisting of the life of the author and 70 years after the author's death.

(b) Joint works. In the case of a joint work prepared by two or more authors who did not work for hire, the copyright endures for a term consisting of the life of the last surviving author and 70 years after such last surviving author's death.

(c) Anonymous works, pseudonymous works, and works made for hire. In the case of an anonymous work, a pseudonymous work, or a work made for hire, the copyright endures for a term of 95 years from the year of its first publication, or a term of 120 years from the year of its creation, whichever expires first. If, before the end of such term, the identity of one or more of the authors of an anonymous or pseudonymous work is revealed in the records of a registration made for that work under subsections (a) or (d) of section 408, or in the records provided by this subsection, the copyright in the work endures for the term specified by subsection (a) or (b), based on the life of the author or authors whose identity has been revealed. Any person having an interest in the copyright in an anonymous or pseudonymous work may at any time record, in records to be maintained by the Copyright Office for that purpose, a statement identifying one or more authors of the work; the statement shall also identify the person filing it, the nature of that person's interest, the source of the information recorded, and the particular work affected, and shall comply in form and content with requirements that the Register of Copyrights shall prescribe by regulation.

. . . .

§ 504. Remedies for Infringement: Damages and Profits

(a) In General. Except as otherwise provided by this title, an infringer of copyright is liable for either—

    (1) the copyright owner's actual damages and any additional profits of the infringer, as provided by subsection (b); or

    (2) statutory damages, as provided by subsection (c).

(b) Actual Damages and Profits. The copyright owner is entitled to recover the actual damages suffered by him or her as a result of the infringement, and any profits of the infringer that are attributable to the infringement and are not taken into account in computing the actual damages. In establishing the infringer's profits, the copyright owner is required to present proof only of the infringer's gross revenue, and the infringer is required to prove his or her deductible expenses and the elements of profit attributable to factors other than the copyrighted work.

(c) Statutory Damages

   (1) Except as provided by clause (2) of this subsection, the copyright owner may elect, at any time before final judgment is rendered, to recover, instead of actual damages and profits, an award of statutory damages for all infringements involved in the action, with respect to any one work, for which any one infringer is liable individually, or for which any two or more infringers are liable jointly and severally, in a sum of not less than $750 or more than $30,000 as the court considers just. For the purposes of this subsection, all the parts of a compilation or derivative work constitute one work.

   (2) In a case where the copyright owner sustains the burden of proving, and the court finds, that infringement was committed willfully, the court in its discretion may increase the award of statutory damages to a sum of not more than $150,000. In a case where the infringer sustains the burden of proving, and the court finds, that such infringer was not aware and had no reason to believe that his or her acts constituted an infringement of copyright, the court in its discretion may reduce the award of statutory damages to a sum of not less than $200. The court shall remit statutory damages in any case where an infringer believed and had reasonable grounds for believing that his or her use of the copyrighted work was a fair use under section 107, if the infringer was: (i) an employee or agent of a nonprofit educational institution, library, or archives acting within the scope of his or her employment who, or such institution, library, or archives itself, which infringed by reproducing the work in copies or phonorecords; or (ii) a public broadcasting entity which or a person who, as a regular part of the nonprofit activities of a public broadcasting entity (as defined in subsection (g) of section 118) infringed by performing a published nondramatic literary work or by reproducing a transmission program embodying a performance of such a work.

(d) Additional Damages in Certain Cases. In any case in which the court finds that a defendant proprietor of an establishment who claims as a defense that its activities were exempt under section 110(5) did not have reasonable grounds to believe that its use of a copyrighted work was exempt under such section, the plaintiff shall be entitled to, in addition to any award of damages under this section, an additional award of two times the amount of the license fee that the proprietor of the establishment concerned should have paid the plaintiff for such use during the preceding period of up to three years.

§ 512: Limitations on Liability Relating to Material Online

(a) Transitory Digital Network Communications.—A service provider shall not be liable for monetary relief, or, except as provided in subsection (j), for injunctive or other equitable relief, for infringement of copyright by reason of the provider's transmitting, routing, or providing connections for, material through a system or network controlled or operated by or for the service provider, or by reason of the intermediate and transient storage of that material in the course of such transmitting, routing, or providing connections, if—

  (1) the transmission of the material was initiated by or at the direction of a person other than the service provider;
  (2) the transmission, routing, provision of connections, or storage is carried out through an automatic technical process without selection of the material by the service provider;
  (3) the service provider does not select the recipients of the material except as an automatic response to the request of another person;
  (4) no copy of the material made by the service provider in the course of such intermediate or transient storage is maintained on the system or network in a manner ordinarily accessible to anyone other than anticipated recipients, and no such copy is maintained on the system or network in a manner ordinarily accessible to such anticipated recipients for a longer period than is reasonably necessary for the transmission, routing, or provision of connections; and
  (5) the material is transmitted through the system or network without modification of its content.

(b) System Caching

  (1) Limitation on liability. A service provider shall not be liable for monetary relief, or, except as provided in subsection (j), for injunctive or other equitable relief, for infringement of copyright by reason of the intermediate and temporary storage of material on a system or network controlled or operated by or for the service provider in a case in which—

    (A) the material is made available online by a person other than the service provider;
    (B) the material is transmitted from the person described in subparagraph (A) through the system or network to a person other than the person described in subparagraph (A) at the direction of that other person; and
    (C) the storage is carried out through an automatic technical process for the purpose of making the material available to users of the system or network who, after

the material is transmitted as described in subparagraph (B), request access to the material from the person described in subparagraph (A), if the conditions set forth in paragraph (2) are met.

(2) Conditions. The conditions referred to in paragraph (1) are that—

(A) the material described in paragraph (1) is transmitted to the subsequent users described in paragraph (1)(C) without modification to its content from the manner in which the material was transmitted from the person described in paragraph (1)(A);

(B) the service provider described in paragraph (1) complies with rules concerning the refreshing, reloading, or other updating of the material when specified by the person making the material available online in accordance with a generally accepted industry standard data communications protocol for the system or network through which that person makes the material available, except that this subparagraph applies only if those rules are not used by the person described in paragraph (1)(A) to prevent or unreasonably impair the intermediate storage to which this subsection applies;

(C) the service provider does not interfere with the ability of technology associated with the material to return to the person described in paragraph (1)(A) the information that would have been available to that person if the material had been obtained by the subsequent users described in paragraph (1)(C) directly from that person, except that this subparagraph applies only if that technology—

(i) does not significantly interfere with the performance of the provider's system or network or with the intermediate storage of the material;

(ii) is consistent with generally accepted industry standard communications protocols; and

(iii) does not extract information from the provider's system or network other than the information that would have been available to the person described in paragraph (1)(A) if the subsequent users had gained access to the material directly from that person;

(D) if the person described in paragraph (1)(A) has in effect a condition that a person must meet prior to having access to the material, such as a condition based on payment of a fee or provision of a password or other information, the service provider permits access to the stored material in significant part only to users of its system or network that have met those conditions and only in accordance with those conditions; and

(E) if the person described in paragraph (1)(A) makes that material available online without the authorization of the copyright owner of the material, the service provider responds expeditiously to remove, or disable access to, the material that is claimed to be infringing upon notification of claimed infringement as described in subsection (c)(3), except that this subparagraph applies only if—

(i) the material has previously been removed from the originating site or access to it has been disabled, or a court has ordered that the material be removed from the originating site or that access to the material on the originating site be disabled; and

(ii) the party giving the notification includes in the notification a statement confirming that the material has been removed from the originating site or access to it has been disabled or that a court has ordered that the material be removed from the originating site or that access to the material on the originating site be disabled.

(c) Information Residing on Systems or Networks At Direction of Users—

(1) In general. A service provider shall not be liable for monetary relief, or, except as provided in subsection (j), for injunctive or other equitable relief, for infringement of copyright by reason of the storage at the direction of a user of material that resides on a system or network controlled or operated by or for the service provider, if the service provider—

(A) (i) does not have actual knowledge that the material or an activity using the material on the system or network is infringing;

(ii) in the absence of such actual knowledge, is not aware of facts or circumstances from which infringing activity is apparent; or

(iii) upon obtaining such knowledge or awareness, acts expeditiously to remove, or disable access to, the material;

(B) does not receive a financial benefit directly attributable to the infringing activity, in a case in which the service provider has the right and ability to control such activity; and

    (C)   upon notification of claimed infringement as described in paragraph (3), responds expeditiously to remove, or disable access to, the material that is claimed to be infringing or to be the subject of infringing activity.

(2) Designated agent. The limitations on liability established in this subsection apply to a service provider only if the service provider has designated an agent to receive notifications of claimed infringement described in paragraph (3), by making available through its service, including on its website in a location accessible to the public, and by providing to the Copyright Office, substantially the following information:

    (A)   the name, address, phone number, and electronic mail address of the agent.
    (B)   other contact information which the Register of Copyrights may deem appropriate.

The Register of Copyrights shall maintain a current directory of agents available to the public for inspection, including through the Internet, in both electronic and hard copy formats, and may require payment of a fee by service providers to cover the costs of maintaining the directory.

(3) Elements of notification—

    (A)   To be effective under this subsection, a notification of claimed infringement must be a written communication provided to the designated agent of a service provider that includes substantially the following.

        (i)   A physical or electronic signature of a person authorized to act on behalf of the owner of an exclusive right that is allegedly infringed.
        (ii)   Identification of the copyrighted work claimed to have been infringed, or, if multiple copyrighted works at a single online site are covered by a single notification, a representative list of such works at that site.
        (iii)   Identification of the material that is claimed to be infringing or to be the subject of infringing activity and that is to be removed or access to which is to be disabled, and information reasonably sufficient to permit the service provider to locate the material.
        (iv)   Information reasonably sufficient to permit the service provider to contact the complaining party, such as an address, telephone number, and, if available, an electronic mail address at which the complaining party may be contacted.

    (v) A statement that the complaining party has a good faith belief that use of the material in the manner complained of is not authorized by the copyright owner, its agent, or the law.

    (vi) A statement that the information in the notification is accurate, and under penalty of perjury, that the complaining party is authorized to act on behalf of the owner of an exclusive right that is allegedly infringed."

(B) (i) Subject to clause (ii), a notification from a copyright owner or from a person authorized to act on behalf of the copyright owner that fails to comply substantially with the provisions of subparagraph (A) shall not be considered under paragraph (1)(A) in determining whether a service provider has actual knowledge or is aware of facts or circumstances from which infringing activity is apparent.

    (ii) In a case in which the notification that is provided to the service provider's designated agent fails to comply substantially with all the provisions of subparagraph (A) but substantially complies with clauses (ii), (iii), and (iv) of subparagraph (A), clause (i) of this subparagraph applies only if the service provider promptly attempts to contact the person making the notification or takes other reasonable steps to assist in the receipt of notification that substantially complies with all the provisions of subparagraph (A).

(d) Information Location Tools. A service provider shall not be liable for monetary relief, or, except as provided in subsection (j), for injunctive or other equitable relief, for infringement of copyright by reason of the provider referring or linking users to an online location containing infringing material or infringing activity, by using information location tools, including a directory, index, reference, pointer, or hypertext link, if the service provider—

(1) (A) does not have actual knowledge that the material or activity is infringing;

    (B) in the absence of such actual knowledge, is not aware of facts or circumstances from which infringing activity is apparent; or

    (C) upon obtaining such knowledge or awareness, acts expeditiously to remove, or disable access to, the material;

(2) does not receive a financial benefit directly attributable to the infringing activity, in a case in which the service provider has the right and ability to control such activity; and

(3) upon notification of claimed infringement as described in subsection (c)(3), responds expeditiously to remove, or dis-

able access to, the material that is claimed to be infringing or to be the subject of infringing activity, except that, for purposes of this paragraph, the information described in subsection (c)(3)(A)(iii) shall be identification of the reference or link, to material or activity claimed to be infringing, that is to be removed or access to which is to be disabled, and information reasonably sufficient to permit the service provider to locate that reference or link.

(e) Limitation on liability of nonprofit educational institutions—

(1) When a public or other nonprofit institution of higher education is a service provider, and when a faculty member or graduate student who is an employee of such institution is performing a teaching or research function, for the purposes of subsections (a) and (b) such faculty member or graduate student shall be considered to be a person other than the institution, and for the purposes of subsections (c) and (d) such faculty member's or graduate student's knowledge or awareness of his or her infringing activities shall not be attributed to the institution, if—

(A) such faculty member's or graduate student's infringing activities do not involve the provision of online access to instructional materials that are or were required or recommended, within the preceding 3-year period, for a course taught at the institution by such faculty member or graduate student;

(B) the institution has not, within the preceding 3-year period, received more than two notifications described in subsection (c)(3) of claimed infringement by such faculty member or graduate student, and such notifications of claimed infringement were not actionable under subsection (f); and

(C) the institution provides to all users of its system or network informational materials that accurately describe, and promote compliance with, the laws of the United States relating to copyright.

(2) Injunctions.—For the purposes of this subsection, the limitations on injunctive relief contained in subsections (j)(2) and (j)(3), but not those in (j)(1), shall apply.

(f) Misrepresentations. Any person who knowingly materially misrepresents under this section—

(1) that material or activity is infringing, or

(2) that material or activity was removed or disabled by mistake or misidentification, shall be liable for any damages, including costs and attorneys' fees, incurred by the alleged infringer, by any copyright owner or copyright owner's authorized licensee,

or by a service provider, who is injured by such misrepresentation, as the result of the service provider relying upon such misrepresentation in removing or disabling access to the material or activity claimed to be infringing, or in replacing the removed material or ceasing to disable access to it. . . .

(k) Definitions—

   (1) Service provider—

      (A) As used in subsection (a), the term 'service provider' means an entity offering the transmission, routing, or providing of connections for digital online communications, between or among points specified by a user, of material of the user's choosing, without modification to the content of the material as sent or received.

      (B) As used in this section, other than subsection (a), the term 'service provider' means a provider of online services or network access, or the operator of facilities therefor, and includes an entity described in subparagraph (A). . . .

Appendix O
COPYRIGHT QUESTIONS FOR LIBRARIANS

ಐ೧೦ನ

React to the following situations by indicating whether you think the activity is permissible, problematic, or possibly infringing.

1. Someone has razor-bladed thirty pages from a book. The librarian requests photocopies of these pages from a nearby library.

2. A faculty member/corporate researcher asks the librarian to copy for her an article from the *New England Journal of Medicine* for information on Prozac.

3. A professor/lawyer asks the library to copy for her four articles from a five-article symposium issue.

4. A law school dean asks the library to make ten copies of an article from a journal to distribute to new professors at a training session.

5. A professor asks the library to make five copies of an article for reserve for use by students in his class.

6. A professor asks the library to make five copies of an article for reserve for use by students. The journal includes a notice that it is registered with Copyright Clearance Center (CCC) and that those who copy articles must pay a royalty fee of $2.00 per article.

7. The librarian is asked to make five photocopies of a weekly news-letter each week, one for each faculty member.

8. A sixteen-page weekly newsletter to which the library subscribes includes a one-page table of contents. The library routinely makes copies of the table of contents page for several interested teachers/corporate researchers.

9. The library routes the weekly *Current Contents* to five faculty members.

235

10.   The library routes copies of the weekly *Current Contents* to five faculty. The routing list includes a message that the library will photocopy for the recipient of the list any article(s) circled.

11.   A faculty member/corporate researcher is working on a short-term project. She asks the librarian to photocopy for her any articles on that topic that come to the librarian's attention.

12.   A private publisher reprints a 80-page non-copyrighted report prepared originally by the Department of Health and Human Services. The publisher charges $40.00 for the report, which is unavailable from either HHS or the U.S. Government Printing Office. The library purchases a copy from the publisher. Two faculty members/corporate researchers ask you to make copies for them.

13.   You borrow from another library a 1950 governmental report now produced on microfiche by a commercial publisher. The lending library tells you that you may add the fiche to your collection.

14.   Rather than add the fiche, you make a print copy and add it to your collection.

15.   A library system has a main library and two branches. All three libraries subscribe to a specific journal. Due to budget cuts, the subscriptions for the branches are canceled. Users at the branches are told that the main library will copy articles from the journal for them on demand, and have a courier deliver them to the branch.

16.   After receiving a copy of an out-of-print volume from a document delivery service, the library anticipates future demand for the title. The library makes a copy of the work for its collection.

17.   After a long search the library obtains a copy of an obscure journal article for a user. The library makes another copy, gives one to the requestor, and keeps one for its collection.

18.   Through interlibrary loan, last year the library requested copies of seven articles published in the *Journal of Reproductive Rights* during the last five years. The year before, the library requested eight articles published during the last five years.

19.   Each year the library destroys the prior year's document delivery borrowing records.

20.   The library receives a request from another library to copy three articles totaling 120 pages of text from a 200-page journal issue. The ILL form includes an attestation that request complies with the Copyright Act or CONTU Guidelines.

21.   The library receives a request from a for-profit document delivery company for a copy of a journal article.

22.   Several faculty members determine that no textbook adequately meets their needs. Each professor contributes materials they have

read—copies of articles and book chapters. Copies are made, compiled and sold to students at the bookstore.

23. The library decides to implement a fee-based service for outside users. The library plans to charge $7.00 for each document copied (an article, for example), plus $0.25 cents per page copied.

24. The library prepares a copyright policy that attempts to define the rights and responsibilities of its staff. A staff member violates the policy.

25. The librarian in a corporation decides to build an in-house database for its employees and inputs a copyrighted work onto the database that anyone may access, at anytime.

26. The librarian completes a DIALOG search and retains a copy for future searches, which she will give to future patrons when appropriate.

27. The librarian downloads the results of a DIALOG search, reformats the results, and prepares a bibliography for use by several faculty/corporate researchers.

28. The librarian purchases one copy of an audio cassette. She makes a copy of the tape for circulation, and holds onto the original as a "master."

29. The central public library purchases one copy of a videotape and duplicates copies for its branches.

30. A staff member videotaped a PBS series and offers to donate the tapes to the library.

31. A faculty member wants to show a film to her class. The library rents the film from a video store. The video contains a "For Home Use Only" warning label.

32. The library wants to convert several of its 3/4" U-Matic videos to 1/2" VHS or DVD format so that they can be shown using the library's video equipment.

33. The library leases an interactive, multi-media video that includes a prohibition against lending it outside the library. Another library asks to borrow the video.

34. A professor asks the library to produce slides of the majority of photographs in a book to show to her class. She wants the library to retain the slides.

35. The library downloads a copyrighted document and forwards it electronically to a faculty member/corporate researcher.

36. The library downloads a copyrighted work to a network. Only one faculty member/corporate researcher in the institution can access the document at one time.

37. The library downloads a document to a network. All faculty/researchers can access the document simultaneously.

38. A professor downloads a document for students in her class. Only one student can access the document at a time.

39. A professor downloads a document for students in her class. Each student in the class can access the document simultaneously.

40. The library purchases QUATTRO for use by the director's administrative assistant. The head of accounting asks to borrow a copy of the software to install it on her computer.

41. A librarian decides to do some work at home. She copies a spreadsheet program from her office computer to a disk and takes it home and installs it on her computer.

42. The same librarian gets an upgrade to the spreadsheet program she uses at work. She copies the old program and installs it on her home computer.

43. A university library circulates some of its software programs to its patrons. A student makes a copy of the program.

44. The university library is asked by another library to lend it a software program.

45. The university library obtains a single-user license for a CD-ROM and makes it available on the campus network.

46. After determining that it cannot find a replacement copy, the library makes a digital copy of a deteriorating published work. Another library asks for a digital copy of the work.

47. The library wants to preserve an unpublished manuscript by making a digital copy of it. Subsequently, another library asks the library for a copy of it.

48. The library wants to scan a photo from someone's webpage to illustrate its own webpage.

49. The library needs to view a Web product to decide whether it wants to purchase it. The product has a protection system that prevents access to non-subscribers, but the technology guru knows how to circumvent it.

50. The institution subscribes to Blackboard.com and Bigchalk, software platforms for course management systems. Professors use these packages for course syllabi, digital content, electronic communications, and links to digital information. Eventually several professors decide to disengage from Blackboard and Bigchalk, but want to use the structure, graphics, and other features from Blackboard and Bigchalk in their own homegrown electronic courseware.

Bonus Question: Which Marx Brothers film is not mentioned in this book?

Appendix P
COPYRIGHT QUESTIONS—
WITH ANSWERS[1]

ຄວຸ

1. Someone has razor-bladed thirty pages from a book. The librarian requests photocopies of these pages from a nearby library.

   O.K. if you meet the requirements of § 108(c).

2. A faculty member/corporate researcher asks the librarian to copy for her an article from the *New England Journal of Medicine* for information on Prozac.

   O.K. Notwithstanding the *Texaco* decision, even in the for-profit sector this non-systematic activity appears to be permissible either as a fair use or under § 108(d).

3. A professor/ lawyer asks the library to copy for her four articles from a five-article symposium issue.

   No, unless §108(e) applies: if a new or used copy is unavailable at a fair price.

4. A law school dean asks the library to make ten copies of an article from a journal to distribute to new professors at a training session.

   Iffy. The safe approach would be to get permission. However, this probably is a fair use if the request is made on short notice.

---

1. Note: Remember that copyright is not black and white, and the questions do not necessarily have straightforward answers. That you disagree with some of these answers does not make you a bad person.

5. A professor asks the library to make five copies of an article for reserve use by students in his class.

   O.K. if the number is reasonable in light of the number of students in the class.

6. A professor asks the library to make five copies of an article for reserve use by students. The journal includes a notice that it is registered with Copyright Clearance Center (CCC) and that those who copy articles must pay a royalty fee of $2.00 per article.

   Same answer as above. The CCC notice is irrelevant. Royalties need not be paid if the use is permitted under the Act.

7. The librarian is asked to make five photocopies of a weekly newsletter each week, one for each faculty member.

   Never.

8. A sixteen-page weekly newsletter to which the library subscribes includes a one-page table of contents. The library routinely makes copies of the table of contents page for several interested teachers/corporate researchers.

   This probably is O.K., but newsletters can be troublesome. Do not encourage the recipients to ask the library to copy newsletter articles.

9. The library routes the weekly *Current Contents* to ten department heads.

   It is O.K. to route issues so long as they are not being copied a la *Texaco*.

10. The library routes copies of the weekly *Current Contents* to five faculty members. The routing list includes a message that the library will photocopy for the recipient of the list any article(s) circled.

    This becomes more problematic when the libraries solicit copies due to the § 108(g)(1) and (g)(2) provisos. Although it may be O.K. in colleges and universities, it definitely is questionable in the for-profit sector.

11. A faculty member/corporate researcher is working on a short-term project. She asks the librarian to photocopy for her any articles on that topic that come to the librarian's attention.

    This is probably O.K. in a non-profit environment, but the extensiveness of the copying may determine whether you violate the § 108(g)(1) and (2) provisos, especially if many copies come from the same journal title. This is very

problematic in the private sector. A better approach: Call
their attention to the articles first. Reactive is better than
proactive.

12.   A private publisher reprints a eighty-page non-copyrighted report
       prepared originally by the Department of Health and Human
       Services. The publisher charges $40.00 for the report, which is
       unavailable from either HHS or the U.S. Government Printing
       Office. The library purchases a copy from the publisher, and
       several lawyers/professors ask you to make copies for them.

       This seems O.K. if the publisher does not add any original
       material. The U.S. government work is in the public domain.

13.   You borrow from another library a 1950 governmental report now
       produced on microfiche by a commercial publisher. The lending
       library tells you that you may add the fiche to your collection.

       Same answer as above.

14.   Rather than add the fiche, you make a print copy and add it to
       your collection.

       Same answer.

15.   A library system has a main library and two branches. All three
       libraries subscribe to a specific journal. Due to budget cuts, the
       subscriptions for the branches are canceled. Users at the branches
       are told that the main library will copy articles from the journal
       for them on demand, and have a courier deliver them to the
       branch.

       Whether the copying is systematic will depend on amount of
       copying. Copying between libraries in the same system are
       not exempt from the CONTU guidelines.

16.   After receiving a copy of an out-of-print volume from a document
       delivery service, the library anticipates future demand for the title.
       The library makes a copy of the work for its collection.

       No; not a replacement copy under § 108(c).

17.   After a long search the library obtains a copy of an obscure journal
       article for a user. The library makes another copy, gives one to the
       user, and keeps one for its collection.

       No. Section 108 requires that the copy be given to the user.
       It may not be added to the library's collection.

18.   Through interlibrary loan last year the library requested copies of
       seven articles published in the *Journal of Reproductive Rights* dur-

ing the last five years. During the prior year, the library requested eight articles that were published during the last five years.

Remember the CONTU guidelines. The "Rule of 5" is not a "rule," but rather a suggestion of sorts, and going a few copies beyond the "5" does not bother me. Other factors could be whether this is a short-term project (perhaps the research is being done under a grant) or if it is ongoing.

19. Each year the library destroys the prior year's document delivery borrowing records.

No. CONTU says three years. This part is not a "suggestion," but rather a rule.

20. The library receives a request from another library to copy three articles totaling 120 pages of text from a 200-page journal issue. The ILL form includes an attestation that request complies with the Copyright Act or CONTU Guidelines.

Maybe. Some libraries have internal policies that limit copying to no more than a certain percentage of a journal issue. Personally, I would not honor this request unless the library specifically attested that the request was being made under § 108(c).

21. The library receives a request from a for-profit document delivery company for a copy of a journal article.

I suggest "no."

22. Several faculty members determine that no textbook adequately meets their needs. Each professor contributes materials they have read—copies of articles and book chapters. Copies are made, compiled and sold to students at the bookstore.

No. The Classroom Guidelines and the ALA Model Policy both say "no" to coursepacks. So did the courts in the *Kinko's* and *MDS* cases.

23. The library decides to implement a fee-based service for outside users. The library plans to charge $7.00 for each document copied (e.g., an article or a case) plus $0.25 cents per page copied.

This is O.K. if it covers the cost of copying. You cannot profit.

24. The library prepares a copyright policy that attempts to define the rights and responsibilities of its staff. A staff member violates the policy.

The person who copies could be personally liable. The library and its parent institution might be vicariously liable if it does not enforce its policy.

25. The librarian in a corporation decides to build an in-house database for employees, and inputs a copyrighted work onto the database.

    No, unless it will use the full text only temporarily to create a different work (such as an abstract) that is not considered a derivative work.

26. The librarian completes a DIALOG search and retains a copy for future searches, which she will give to future patrons when appropriate.

    Iffy. You certainly may retain the search query. Check your contract.

27. The librarian downloads the results of a DIALOG search, reformats the results, and prepares a bibliography for use by several faculty/corporate researchers.

    This is O.K. in any setting.

28. The librarian purchases one copy of an audio cassette. She makes a copy of the tape for circulation, and holds onto the original as a "master."

    No.

29. The central library purchases one copy of a videotape and duplicates copies for its branches.

    No.

30. A staff member videotaped a PBS series and offers to donate the tapes to the library.

    No.

31. A faculty member wants to show a film to her class. The library rents the film from a video store. The video contains a "For Home Use Only" warning label.

    O.K. The use is allowed under § 110(1), and the warning label does not constitute a contract.

32. The library wants to convert several of its 3/4" U-Matic videos to
     1/2" VHS or a DVD format so that they can be shown using the
     library's video equipment.

     First, see if you can buy the work in VHS or as a DVD. If you
     cannot buy an unused replacement at a fair price, § 108(c)
     permits making a copy if the format in which the work is
     stored has become obsolete. A format is "obsolete" if the
     machine necessary to make the work perceptible is no longer
     manufactured or not reasonably available in the
     marketplace.

33. The library leases an interactive, multi-media video that includes
     a prohibition against lending it outside the library. Another library
     asks to borrow the video.

     No. This is a lease rather than a sale, and the library does
     not own the copy. The § 109 "first sale doctrine" does not
     apply. If the library owned the work, the answer is yes.

34. A professor asks the library to produce slides of the majority of
     photographs in a book to show to her class. She wants the library
     to retain the slides for future use.

     No and No.

35. The library downloads a copyrighted document and forwards it
     electronically to a faculty member/corporate researcher.

     O.K. For the most part the library can do digitally what it
     can do in print. The library should not retain a copy on a
     computer or the network. If the digital copy was made
     pursuant to § 108(b) (an unpublished work duplicated for
     preservation or security), the library may not transmit the
     digital version.

36. The library downloads a copyrighted work to a network. Only one
     faculty member/corporate researcher in the institution can access
     the document at one time.

     I think the answer is no.

37. The library downloads a document to a network. All faculty/
     researchers can access the document simultaneously.

     No.

38. A professor downloads a document for students in her class. Only
     one student can access the document at a time.

     This is probably O.K., but some would argue that it is not. If
     the library is involved, this should be O.K. if you use an
     electronic reserve system that limits access to students in the

class and prohibits further distribution. If possible, the professor could link to the document rather than download it.

39. A professor downloads a document for students in her class. Each student in the class can access the document simultaneously.

    This is a closer call. I think it is a little excessive, and would limit access to only a few students at one time.

40. The library purchases QUATTRO for use by the director's administrative assistant. The head of accounting asks to borrow a copy of the software to install it on her computer.

    No, unless the license permits this (which it probably does not).

41. A librarian decides to do some work at home. She copies a spreadsheet program from her office computer to a disk and takes it home and installs it on her computer.

    No, unless the single-user licenses permits the licensee to install and use the program both in her office and her home.

42. The same librarian gets an upgrade to the spreadsheet program she uses at work. She copies the old program and installs it on her home computer.

    The license may describe this as a "functional upgrade" and prohibit transfer of the older version to another machine. Functional upgrades are less expensive than acquiring a new copy, and the license may restrict or prohibit transfer of the old version. Absent a license that says no, this seems fine to me.

43. A university library circulates some of its software programs to its patrons. A student makes a copy of the program.

    Section 109(b)(2) permits a non-profit library to lend software to patrons as long as there is no direct or indirect commercial advantage. The exemption permits "transfer of possession" and "lending" of programs by schools and libraries for users, but not unauthorized copying by patrons. The library is not responsible for the student's actions unless contributory infringement or vicarious liability is established.

44. The university library is asked by another library to lend it a software program.

    Section 109(b)(2) permits this if the library affixes on the disk or its container the required warning label.

45. The university library obtains a single-user license for a CD-ROM and makes it available on the campus network.

     The single-user license would certainly prohibit this.

46. After determining that it cannot find a replacement copy, the library makes a digital copy of a deteriorating published work. Another library asks for a digital copy of the work.

     No. Section 108(c)(2), as amended by the DMCA, provides that the digital copy cannot be made available to public outside library premises. You may make a paper copy and send it to the requesting library.

47. The library wants to preserve an unpublished manuscript by making a digital copy of it. Subsequently, another library asks the library for a copy of it.

     Section 108(b) permits up to three digital copies, but the digital copy cannot be made available outside the "owning" library's premises.

48. The library wants to scan a photo from someone's webpage to illustrate its own webpage.

     Section 102 protects pictorial and graphic works. Photos and images are protected if they meet the "original work of authorship fixed in a tangible medium of expression" test. Because the owner has the right to copy, prepare, and distribute his or her work publicly, you must have permission. Ask for permission.

49. The library needs to view a Web-based product to decide whether it wants to purchase it. The product has a protection system that prevents access to non-subscribers, but the technology guru knows how to circumvent it.

     Libraries are exempted from the anti-circumvention provisions to evaluate a work prior to purchase. Typically vendors will let you look at their products for a couple of weeks, and will give you passwords to do so. Do not waste your time trying to override the technology; just ask the vendor.

50. The institution subscribes to Blackboard.com and Bigchalk, software platforms for course management systems. Professors use these packages for course syllabi, digital content, electronic communications, and links to digital information. Eventually several professors decide to disengage from Blackboard and Bigchalk, but want to use the structure, graphics, and other features from Blackboard and Bigchalk in their own homegrown electronic courseware.

The license controls. You can find the Blackboard and Bigchalk licenses on their respective websites. You will see that the answer is no.

Bonus Question: Which Marx Brothers film is not mentioned in this book?

Answer: Their last film, *Love Happy*, which came out in 1950. Actually, the correct answer is "none of them." With this answer, every released Marx Brothers movie has been mentioned in this book. (The 1921 self-produced short film, *Humor Risk*, was never released.)

TABLE OF CASES

ಱಉಅ

INDEX

८ාСЗ